MICHAEL MORITZ

AUSLÄNDER

One family's story of escape and exile

Profile Books

First published in Great Britain in 2026 by
PROFILE BOOKS LTD
29 Cloth Fair
London EC1A 7JQ

www.profilebooks.com

Copyright © Michael Moritz, 2026

3 5 7 9 10 8 6 4 2

Original design by Philip Lewis

Printed and bound in Great Britain by
CPI Group (UK) Ltd, Croydon CR0 4YY

The moral right of the author has been asserted.

All rights reserved. Without limiting the rights under copyright reserved above, no part of this publication may be reproduced, stored or introduced into a retrieval system, or transmitted, in any form or by any means (electronic, mechanical, photocopying, recording or otherwise), without the prior written permission of both the copyright owner and the publisher of this book.

A CIP catalogue record for this book is available from the British Library.

Our product safety representative in the EU is BGC Sustainability & Compliance, 7 avenue du Général Leclerc, Paris, 75014, France https://baldwinglobalconsulting.com

ISBN 978 1 80522 834 9
eISBN 978 1 80522 880 6

For Harriet, Jake and Will,
who opened my eyes

CONTENTS

Simplified Moritz Family Tree	10
Expiration Date	13
It Can Happen	17
The Empty Piazza	24
The Secret Jew	32
Ludwig, as in Alfred	45
Below the Surface	59
Jones the Jew	70
Labor Omnia Vincit	77
You Want It Darker	83
Counting Swastikas	93
Lives in Photographs	96
Non-Aryan Members	106
Intellectual Debris	120
The Swimming Bath	135
A Postcard from Dachau	144
The Wretched Refuse	154

The Lost Generation	175
A Leg of Goat	183
The Municipal Slaughterhouse	191
A Ninety-Minute Meeting	198
No Sitting on Trams	202
A Crime Without a Name	219
Any Jews Here?	223
Enemy Aliens	229
There Is No More Joy	238
Pass Freely	249
Do Not Make Yourself Conspicuous	262
The Best German-English	271
Passover Reunion	283
The Sins of the Past	288
Ausländer	297
Thank You	315

Simplified Moritz Family Tree

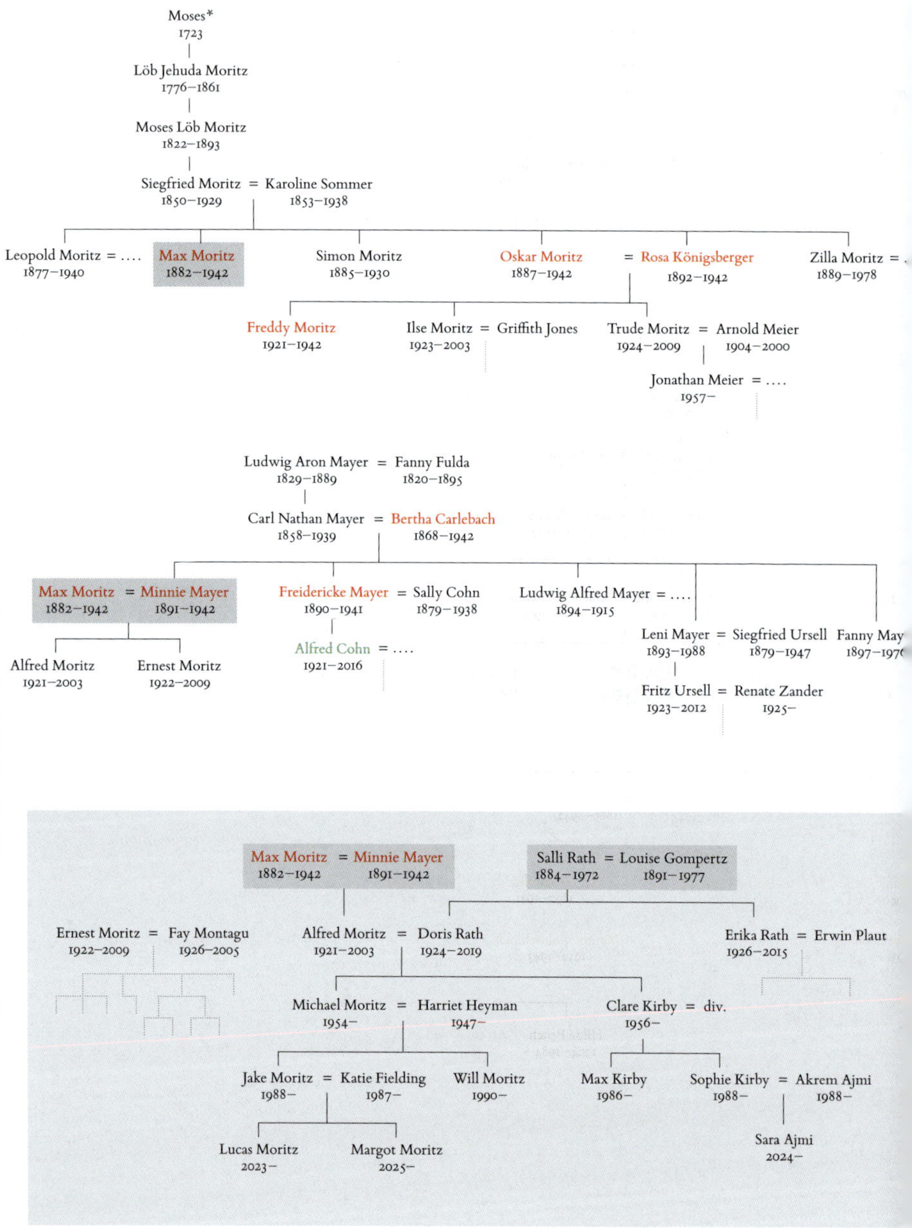

Moses*
1723
|
Löb Jehuda Moritz
1776–1861
|
Moses Löb Moritz
1822–1893
|
Siegfried Moritz = Karoline Sommer
1850–1929   1853–1938

Leopold Moritz = ...   Max Moritz   Simon Moritz   Oskar Moritz = Rosa Königsberger   Zilla Moritz = ...
1877–1940   1882–1942   1885–1930   1887–1942   1892–1942   1889–1978

                                        Freddy Moritz   Ilse Moritz = Griffith Jones   Trude Moritz = Arnold Meier
                                        1921–1942   1923–2003   1924–2009   1904–2000

                                                                                            Jonathan Meier = ...
                                                                                            1957–

Ludwig Aron Mayer = Fanny Fulda
1829–1889   1820–1895
|
Carl Nathan Mayer = Bertha Carlebach
1858–1939   1868–1942

Max Moritz = Minnie Mayer   Friedericke Mayer = Sally Cohn   Ludwig Alfred Mayer = ...
1882–1942   1891–1942   1890–1941   1879–1938   1894–1915

Alfred Moritz   Ernest Moritz   Alfred Cohn = ...   Leni Mayer = Siegfried Ursell   Fanny May
1921–2003   1922–2009   1921–2016   1893–1988   1879–1947   1897–1970

                                                                        Fritz Ursell = Renate Zander
                                                                        1923–2012   1925–

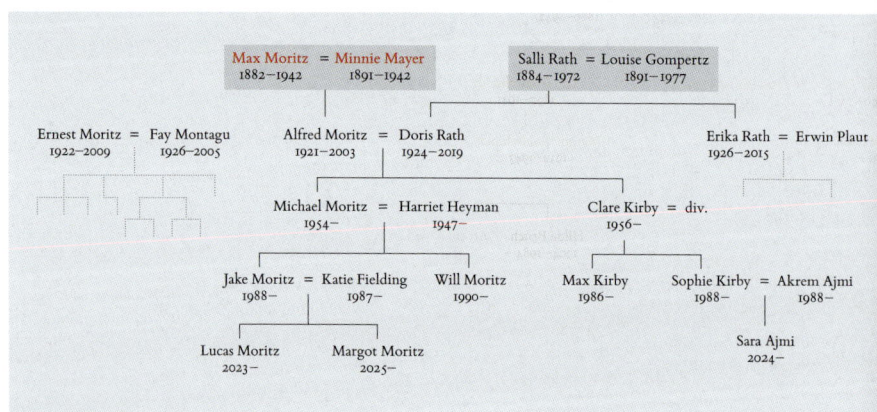

Max Moritz = Minnie Mayer   Salli Rath = Louise Gompertz
1882–1942   1891–1942   1884–1972   1891–1977

Ernest Moritz = Fay Montagu   Alfred Moritz = Doris Rath   Erika Rath = Erwin Plaut
1922–2009   1926–2005   1921–2003   1924–2019   1926–2015

                              Michael Moritz = Harriet Heyman   Clare Kirby = div.
                              1954–   1947–   1956–

                        Jake Moritz = Katie Fielding   Will Moritz   Max Kirby   Sophie Kirby = Akrem Ajmi
                        1988–   1987–   1990–   1986–   1988–   1988–

                              Lucas Moritz   Margot Moritz   Sara Ajmi
                              2023–   2025–   2024–

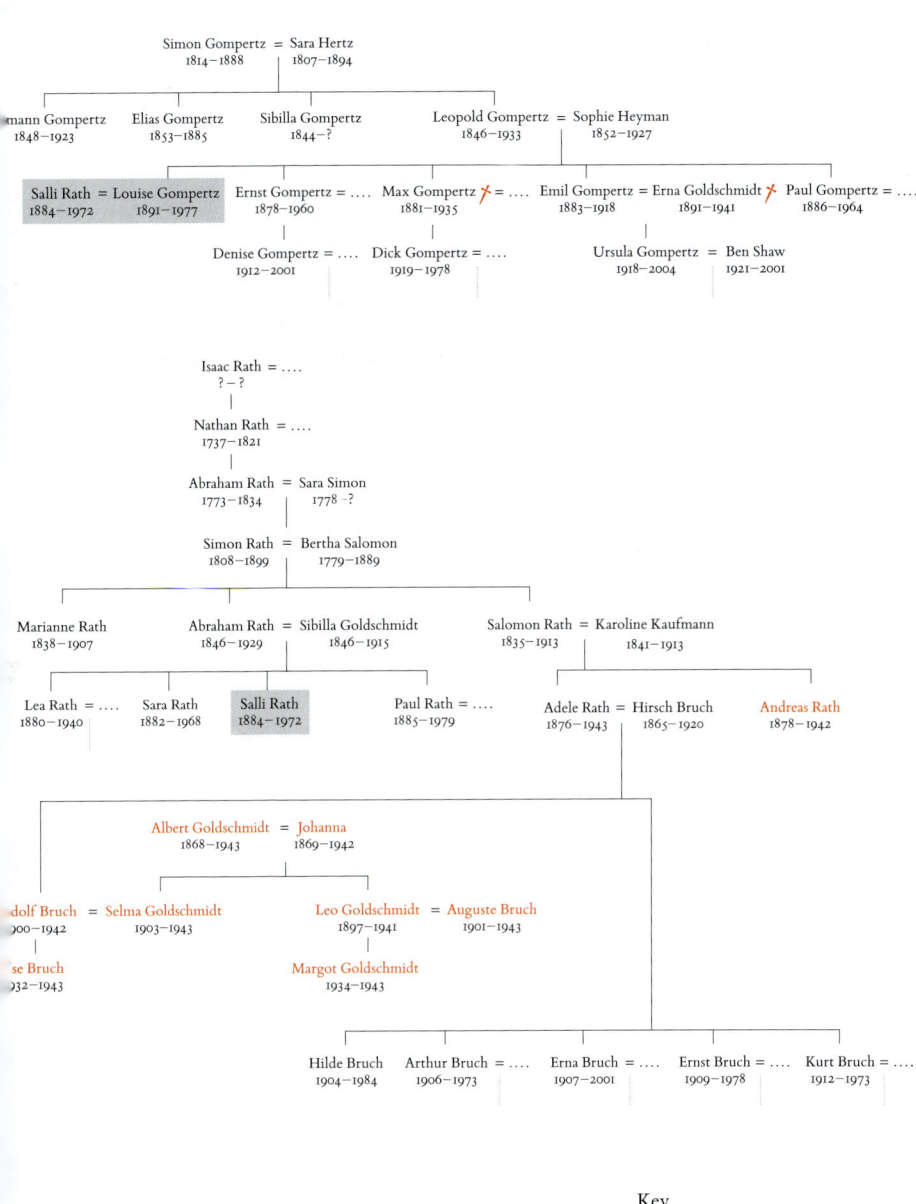

EXPIRATION DATE

I DISCOVERED MY ILLNESS by chance in 2006. I was conducting an interview in a conference room at Sequoia Capital, in a low-slung office park near the northern California coastal range, when I was overcome by giddiness and slithered unconscious beneath the table. The paramedics were summoned and, before I knew it, I was hooked to a twelve-point cardiograph, had plastic oxygen lines inserted in my nose and a saline drip in my arm, and was wheeled into the parking lot on a gurney towards a fire engine and ambulance. My diary notes say, 'All very theatrical.'

After months of testing, my doctors discovered a genetic abnormality that produces a rare form of blood cancer. When I was shown the microscopic images of my blood, I thought that the abstract, pale-magenta pattern formed by my red blood cells would make for a good wallpaper design. I later learned that the propensity of the body to produce an abnormal number of red blood cells struck men more than women, and those with Jewish ancestors originating in Central and Eastern Europe are at higher risk. It turned out that the crackpot theory of the murderous Nazis was correct – I did have special blood – or, more accurately, I shared an errant gene with a small population of others, many of them Jewish. There was no escaping my heritage. It coursed through me.

I began treatment in 2007 and, five years later, after the drug regimen had been gradually increased, I posed a question to my kindly haematologist. I told him there were only two answers – one had three letters, the other two. And then I asked, 'Will I be alive when I am seventy?' He gave the answer with two letters and, based on that bleak outlook, I relinquished the leadership of Sequoia Capital.

Some months later, my wife, Harriet, and I flew to Minnesota to meet the doctor generally acknowledged to be the man most capable of predicting the course of the pale-magenta patterns. He was a charming, irreverent, bespectacled immigrant from Ethiopia with a forehead the colour of weathered ebony. He went to Tel Aviv once or twice a year to see patients from all over Israel, where he was treated like the Messiah. He had no patience with accepted doctrine and even less for pharmaceutical companies peddling expensive remedies that only addressed the symptoms of the cancer but had no effect on the underlying disease. He asked me to predict my own life expectancy, by showing me a bell curve and asking me to put my finger on the spot that belonged to me. I was stumped. The doctor's eyes danced with mischievous triumph. He observed the obvious: despite the data, nobody can predict their expiry date.

The verdicts from Minnesota and San Francisco were the same: I am a genuine, card-carrying member of an ethnic minority. I even have the scientific proof. According to the analysis of my genetic profile by 23andMe, I am not Welsh (the country of my birth), not British (even though I carry a British passport) and not American (even though I moved to the United States in 1976 and have been a citizen for almost thirty years). I am 100 per cent an Ashkenazi Jew (a minority whose roots are in Central and Eastern Europe) although I haven't belonged to a synagogue since I left my hometown almost fifty years ago.

I am a man with an ethnicity that is sometimes convenient for others to recognise and, more frequently, for people to ignore. Either way, it's an ethnicity of which I have grown increasingly aware as the years pass, and which has seen me become better versed in our tendency towards tribalism. This is a reflection, not a lament or complaint. I do not consider myself a victim, just different. I'm an Ashkenazi Jew. It's the condition I was born with – an inheritance, a state of being. Not an exercise in self-pity. Antisemitism is a condition of humanity, as it has been for thousands of years. Over the centuries, for many religions and countries, Jews have always been the source of all evil. And for many, the only good Jew is a dead Jew. So be it. I have long accepted that nothing about this will change but rather to make the most of the good fortune that has come my way.

Whenever I am involved in a discussion of the suitable composition of a corporate board, which, for any California public company with six or more directors, must include at least three women and at least three people who come from an 'under-represented community', I have a private chuckle. In California, 'under-represented community' means, according to the filing requirements, anyone who identifies as Black, African American, Hispanic, Latino, Asian, Pacific Islander, Native American, Native Hawaiian, Native Alaskan or gay, lesbian, bisexual or transgender. I always wonder how my colleagues would react if I declared myself a member of an ethnic minority. I'm sure they pigeonhole me as male and white and privileged, especially since I still speak with an English accent.

Ever since I received my medical diagnosis, I have always assumed there is nothing pre-ordained about the year in which I will be three score years and ten. This was underlined, well after my diagnosis, when I heard from the wife of a long-time friend, informing me that he did not have 'gallons of time left'. I had known this man for over thirty years. In his prime, he had built and run a chain of radio stations but now, in his seventies, he was barely eating and slept for much of the morning. He and I used to have lunch every month and, after catching up on old friends and fresh gossip, the conversation would inevitably turn towards another shared topic – the rare form of cancer which, years ago, we had discovered was killing him more rapidly than it was killing me. As my friend became sicker and thinner, and eventually died, and as my haematologist's expiration date drew nearer, I kept drifting towards the beginning.

IT CAN HAPPEN

MY PARENTS WERE ASHKENAZI JEWS and refugees from Nazi Germany. They made their home in Cardiff, Wales, which is where I was born, nine years after the end of World War II and weeks after rationing ended. All my grandparents were born in Germany – my father's side in Bavaria, my mother's in the Rhineland. They were born soon after the end of the Franco-Prussian War, which resulted in German dominance of Europe until World War I. Before them, my family's lineage goes back – until the trail runs cold in the late seventeenth century – to a small area of Germany, northeast of Frankfurt. When our younger son was a child, he once enquired, given our casual regard for ritual observances, whether we were 'full-on Jews'. The answer was, and is, emphatically, 'yes'. To the best of my knowledge, none of my direct ancestors were ever married to someone other than an Ashkenazi Jew. And today I am married to an Ashkenazi Jew.

As the centuries have unfurled, the DNA spawned by my ethnicity increased the odds of Ashkenazim falling prey to my form of blood cancer – as was revealed by recent studies of body fragments from Jews slaughtered in pogroms in fourteenth-century Erfurt, Germany, and some twelfth-century Jews of Norwich, England. (The former were buried, the latter were tossed down a well.) The studies of the extracted DNA showed that the victims had come from different regions and were more genetically distinct than today's population of Ashkenazim. Nonetheless, those skeletons carried many of the same disease-causing gene mutations that afflict Ashkenazim today. However, as the Ashkenazi population has become more concentrated, there is less chance of escaping the errant behaviour of the more concentrated genetic structure.

Occasionally I receive reminders that, because of my ethnicity, others are eager to hasten my demise. Sometimes the evidence appears in the form of antisemitic leaflets deposited on our doormat in San Francisco. These pamphlets, on occasion weighed down by a Ziplock bag filled with white rice, have been peppered with claims that the Jews caused Covid-19 and control the Food and Drug Administration (FDA) and the pharmaceutical industry. But for the most part, they contain the age-old accusations: that I am a member of a global conspiracy; that I murdered Jesus; that I am a Zionist, a usurer; that I use the blood of Christian children when I bake bread; that I control the world order; that I manipulate currencies, the media and movies; that I am sub-human, part of a cosmopolitan elite, a greedy globalist, a communist, a capitalist. And, moreover, these messages sometimes state that the Nazi gas chambers never existed.

It's hard to keep the shadows of Nazi Germany that reach our porch from creeping into our lives – particularly when 55 per cent of all religiously motivated hate crimes committed in America, and 78 per cent of those perpetrated in the country's twenty-one largest cities, are aimed at the 2.4 per cent of the population that is Jewish.

Every time jealousy, resentment and anger are stoked by inflammatory speech, I wonder whether anyone in America who is not a white Christian feels safe. Minorities and immigrants can never rest easily where rabble-rousers, portraying themselves as victims or martyrs, can incite the poorly educated who feel displaced and disenfranchised and are all too willing to believe empty conspiracy theories. It's odd to feel like an outsider when everyone considers you an insider. But that's how I feel eighty years after the Shoah.

It's one thing to smile when a Hasidic Jew, who has uncovered our address in San Francisco and is eager for us to join his sect, stands on our porch with a bag of doughnuts asking why we do not have a mezuzah on our doorpost. It's harder to dismiss the ugly leaflets left on our doorstep as the work of demented, lone rangers – even though I doubt they are part of any well-organised movement.

My fears have grown during the dark age of Trump. I had long known the man was a con, bully, racist and failed entrepreneur with authoritarian instincts but was shaken when others, many of whom I knew well, saw him as a force of reason and, as he began his first campaign, raised money on his behalf. Even after the depths of Trump's depravity became common knowledge and later he became the first American president to be found guilty of criminal actions, these people still clung to his coat-tails. Did they think he would eventually do their bidding? Or were they just spineless? As the shadows of Trump lengthened, the refrain I had heard from my parents while growing up in Wales rang ever more loudly:

> If it did happen, it can happen.
> If it did happen, it will happen.
> If it did happen somewhere, it can happen here.

My alarm grew during the years after 2017, when hundreds of white supremacists in Charlottesville, Virginia, some carrying burning torches, had chanted, 'Jews will not replaces us! You will not replace us!' and Trump, then the occupant of the White House, refused to condemn them. It became impossible to dismiss this as just a rally 'inflamed by the mid-summer heat', as some claimed, when, in the two years that followed, there were mass shootings in synagogues in Pittsburgh and San Diego, leaving twelve people dead. It's painful to look at videos of flags unfurled by a group of thugs over the railings of a bridge crossing Los Angeles's 405 freeway bearing antisemitic messages, or when Kanye West and other celebrities spread antisemitic sentiments to their tens of millions of social media followers.

After Trump unleashed his 'Stop the Steal' campaign following the 2020 election, which culminated in the riots on Capitol Hill, my anxieties soared. I kept comparing Trump's reaction with that of Richard Nixon, who would have delivered the inaugural address on 20 January 1961 had 12,000 votes distributed among five states fallen his way. Shrugging off claims by Republicans of vote-rigging in Illinois, Nixon, who lost the popular count by 112,000 votes (compared to Trump's 7 million), announced that the election of his bitter rival, John F. Kennedy, could not be 'a more striking and eloquent example of the stability of our constitutional system and of the proud tradition of the American people of developing, respecting, and honoring institutions of self-government'. The gulf between the behaviour of the only man forced to resign in disgrace from the presidency and the only man to claim victory in a presidential election he had lost, made me believe that an age of darkness was possible in the US.

More alarming still was the way that this man's lunacy has infected much of America and eroded the nation's moral authority. Why did people shrug when they heard him use words like 'vermin' to describe some Americans, and why would any political party choose to support a candidate who talked about people 'poisoning the blood of our country' and subscribed to puerile genetic theories? It was hard to fathom why tens of millions followed a man without a moral compass, who had been deemed a criminal by the courts while facing countless other charges, who had pardoned soldiers convicted of killing unarmed civilians and prisoners, whose platform of lawlessness rested on a centralisation of coercive power, who promised mass, forced deportations, who vowed that schools would only teach a 'patriotic curriculum', who announced that 'I am your warrior. I am your justice. I am your retribution' and who, in Philip Roth's biting phrase, 'spoke in jerkish', would eventually do what he said?

And then came the first Saturday of October 2023 – October 7 – and the Hamas attack on Israel after which my tribal instincts were aroused and, for the first time, I became emotionally connected with Israel's fate even though the country has often fallen far short of the idealism of its original advocates. I have always found soulmates among the Israelis who work in technology, media and culture and, without whom, Israel would not have an economy or future. But I have never felt kinship with the odious Israeli settlers and their vile political representatives spewing poisonous sentiments, wreathed in the same religious zealotry as the ugliest of the ayatollahs, and for whom all Palestinians, much of whose land has been plundered, are second-class citizens, unworthy of due process and ripe for elimination; or the Orthodox Jews living the life of eighteenth-century villagers who make up about 20 per cent of Israel's population and subsist as wards of the state. For me, the attack on October 7 showed that little had changed since the days – not so long ago – when most of my ancestors had been murdered. A pogrom had occurred in the one place that was supposed to be safe for Jews. And the vow 'Never Again' rang hollower than ever. For Israelis, and for Jews of a certain vintage, October 7 has gruesome analogies with 9 November 1938, Kristallnacht, when 200 synagogues across Germany were burned to the ground.

October 7 was just the latest expression of hatred for a people who make up less than 0.2 per cent of the people on earth. The Hamas attack on the Jews along the Israeli-Gaza border was a continuation of the pogroms stretching back over 1,000 years. The methods of the men who broke through the fences or landed by paraglider on October 7 had plenty of precedents – houses torched, Jews being burned alive, organs cut from living souls, foetuses carved from the wombs of pregnant women, hostages being beaten by crowds of civilians. To someone who grew up amid the memories and shadows of World War II it all sounded familiar.

At home in San Francisco, all the sewage stirred up by Trump on the right was overshadowed by the reaction to October 7. Crowds carried signs reading 'From the river to the sea' (even though some young people thought the river in question was the Euphrates or the Nile) closed the freeways. The windows of an ice cream shop, owned by a Jewish woman, were smashed and spray-painted with a hate message. The then mayor of the city had the courage to call out protestors who, at a Board of Supervisors hearing, greeted a statement read by a Jew with family members who were killed by Hamas, by grunting like pigs, forming devil horns with their hands, and screaming for him to kill himself. The mayor, a Black woman, also said, 'What if we replaced "Jewish" with "Black" or "gay" or "Asian"? Would anyone speak up? I hope we would. I hope we will now.' But few did. In the classrooms and lecture halls of schools and universities in the San Francisco Bay Area and elsewhere in the US, Jewish students were ostracised as thousands of students pitched tents on college campuses and questioned Israel's right to exist. For me, the spread of conspiracy theories and the silences of the masses seemed like the harbingers of mob rule and the collapse of democracy – the darkest fear of any Jew. I began to have a keener sense for why relatives of mine in the Germany of the 1930s, confronted with a nation moving against them, chose suicide over life.

THE EMPTY PIAZZA

WHEN, DURING THE FIRST SUMMER of the pandemic, Harriet and I visited Venice, the past seemed more present than usual. The cruise ships had vanished. Most restaurants and many shops were closed. The hotels had few guests. The tourist sites were empty. The Venice we encountered, after spending ten days in quarantine in Croatia, felt as it must have seemed to visitors in the 1900s – a mysterious, layered assemblage of beauty where foreign visitors measured in the dozens not thousands. measured in the dozens not thousands.. But there was a big difference, an invisible emptiness. There was no longer a Jewish community. It had been annihilated during World War II.

For five consecutive mornings, I rose before dawn, had an espresso, hitched my oil-painting kit onto my shoulder and went to seek a water taxi. On each of these mornings, the boat puttered along the quiet canals – besides which a few Venetians were walking their small dogs or having their first cigarette of the day – until it reached the Ponte de Gheto Novo and I clambered out. I set up my easel in a spot that I knew would stay in the shade until mid-morning. It was in a corner of the Campo de Gheto Novo, the piazza that was once the heart of the area. The only people around were four young men and women who staffed the police post – an octagonal, green wood and glass kiosk. Every so often they would emerge to stretch their

Entrance to Auschwitz

legs or have a smoke. I painted several scenes from the same spot, none of which I felt were good enough to frame. However, after I brought them home to San Francisco I kept returning to one.

It was a view past the police post towards an alley of buildings that gradually narrowed. As I looked at the painting, I kept wondering whether this was the path that the more than 200 Jews of Venice had been forced along at the start of their final journey.

I have come to associate my half-baked effort with a painting I have in my office in our home in San Francisco. I purchased the painting, the first I ever bought, when I was fifteen, from a small art gallery in Cardiff, and gave it to my parents for their wedding anniversary in 1970. It was made by Roger Cecil, a reclusive Welsh artist with a distinctive style never properly appreciated, and depicts coal miners at the end of a shift, bent into a cold wind, walking from an opening in a wall beneath the colliery winding wheel. My parents hung this painting at the top of their staircase, where it stayed until after my mother died. When I bought the picture, I doubt it made me think of what I see in it today: the railway tracks leading to the entrance of Auschwitz.

As the pandemic spread, I found it easier to escape the present by getting lost in the past. When the shutters closed on life, it no longer seemed important to rush from place to place. I realised I had not spent as many consecutive nights in the same bed since I was a child. I only dressed in a suit and tie once – to attend the funeral on the west coast of Ireland of one of my closest friends, wearing the green-and-white socks she had given me in the year before her death that were emblazoned with the message, 'This meeting is bullshit'. Without hours frittered away at business dinners and conferences, I began to lose myself in movies, books, websites and memories as I was drawn to the story of our small family – one chronicle lodged among the millions of sagas of families torn to shreds by the most murderous whirlwind of the twentieth century.

After my mother died, weeks before the start of the pandemic, my sister, Clare, sorted through the papers and photographs that had been left behind in our parents' home in Wales. Eventually, five large boxes arrived at my home in San Francisco, which contained the entire heritage of what we knew about our shattered family.

These boxes were like receiving packages, letters and postcards mailed from the past – an introduction to the lives of those gone before; scenes that barely disturbed the surface of my mind. A moment, and they were gone – dissolving into each other. It was what lay beneath the surface that began to preoccupy me: the memories, the feelings and the interpretations of the first twenty years of my life, as well as the intimate personal moments that have shaped everything that has happened to me in the subsequent decades. It was like assembling my emotional DNA from the written correspondence, legal documents, passports, travel permits, calling cards, poems, post office books, insurance stamps, mortgage deeds, lockets of hair, school reports, tickets, baggage tags, wedding announcements and death certificates.

The decades merge. The sensations of fifty years ago begin to seem sharper than those of yesterday. Places, countries, homes, people all appear in the same dream. It's where identity – or maybe, personal identity – forms; the place where life, dreams, memories and experiences blur.

It was these memories that were etched the deepest – no more removable than the scored lines in a printer's plate.

Perhaps the edges soften with age, perhaps they dull – like a plate used too often for prints – but they are always present and unyielding. I began to write, and as I did so, I became increasingly conscious of the therapeutic benefit associated with committing painful memories and thoughts to paper. I was trying to find the answers to the thousands of questions I had never asked – the questions about sensations and feelings.

During the early stages of my rummaging, I watched *They Shall Not Grow Old*, Peter Jackson's movie about World War I, in which he juxtaposed the horror and camaraderie of war by enhancing 100-year-old footage with colorisation techniques and accented voices. The flanks of horses turned brown and their hocks white, the soldiers' helmets green, their coats khaki, and dark reeds marked the glistening pools of mud in verdant, rutted fields. I felt too that my family history was coming alive and these people – so many of whom had been slaughtered – were no longer black and white, and silent.

A photo editor flipping through the images that were the remnants of several generations of my family – pasted into half a dozen albums or stuffed into cigar and chocolate boxes as well as a wooden one, engraved with an iron cross and the dates '1914' and '1916' – would have digitised them, tweaking the exposure, contrast and tone of these black-and-white images. Instead, I was trying to breathe real life into these photographs, to open once again the individual experiences of these people from the past – my past – using a modest collection of family snaps no larger than what, these days, someone might take on their smartphone during a short weekend break. I had known a few of these people when I was a boy, but the rest were unfamiliar and dead – mostly long dead. They had been exterminated.

★

During the pandemic, when the present collapsed against the past and events telescoped into each other, I felt like part of the world but not truly of it. Harriet and I shuttled between our home in San Francisco and a coastal spot north of San Francisco. We led a life of isolated seclusion, fully aware of our good fortune compared to the billions who were living in cramped surrounds, had lost their incomes, or had expired on ventilators in overcrowded hospitals. We also spent time in Borgo Pignano, a Tuscan estate we bought in dilapidated condition in 1999 (and now is a thriving boutique hotel which friends and family often visit) partly because I was determined not to repeat the mistake of others by waiting until I was in the foothills of old age to fulfil a long-awaited dream. The last thing I wanted to be was a stranger in another foreign place.

For the first time in my life, I began noticing the minute changes of every day – especially on the California coast where the diurnal habits of local birds and animals telegraph the passage of every hour. After the world slowed, I tuned my dial to the passage of time. My compass was pointed east towards Europe. The vapour trails and distant noise of the transcontinental aeroplanes making their final sweep into San Francisco had disappeared. On my bicycle rides along the empty roads of the Point Reyes Peninsula, I became aware for the first time of lambing season and the pupping rituals of elephant seals. In the late afternoons, I witnessed the conventions of scrub jays, starlings, sparrows, swallows and robins conducting their animated exchanges. As the hours passed, the wild turkeys would tuck themselves into their beds in the branches; frogs rasped like a crew of men working with saws; coyotes yipped from afar; our dog barked at the shadows beyond the windows; an owl hooted. In the early-morning hours, the cows greeted the motor of the all-terrain vehicle carrying the alfalfa for their morning feed, and the woodpeckers resumed their insistent drilling on the wooden corners of the house as the sun rose.

I began to understand how artists could paint dozens of versions of a familiar sight – Constable in East Bergholt, Van Gogh in Arles, Monet in Giverny, Morandi and Giacometti in their studios, Hockney in Yorkshire and Normandy, Auerbach in London. It was about intense observation, a preoccupation with a pursuit, and personal interpretation – a dot, a line, a mark; an impression of scenes, objects, figures which, by the time they rendered them on canvas or in wax, contained their own emotions. Their paintings are often explorations of the passage of time. As spring blossoms and leaves become flowers and fruit, turn brown and fall to the ground leaving bare branches, their paintings speak of birth and hope and life and death.

I was sifting through papers, archives and photos which, the more I contemplated them, seemed like my private version of a haystack, lily pond, vase of sunflowers or row of bottles on a shelf. These meditative backdrops – and the extra hours in the day afforded by the work patterns of the pandemic – were sufficient to see me embark on a journey to understand why my parents became who they were and why, in turn, I became who I am. Where does one person end and the next begin?

THE SECRET JEW

MY FATHER, ALFRED, AND MY MOTHER, DORIS, met after World War II, in England, having both escaped as children from the Nazis in the 1930s. My father was born in 1921 in Munich in Bavaria, Hitler's original stronghold in southern Germany. My mother was born in 1924 as Doris Rath in Kempen, a small town surrounded by the pastures of the Rhineland – an area to the east of the Netherlands, Belgium and Luxembourg that was much disputed territory between the world wars. In the early 1950s, my parents moved to Cardiff in Wales, where they lived until the end of their lives.

Whenever someone called my mother or father a 'survivor', they would recoil and reject the label. In their minds they were not survivors. Rather, they were British citizens who had once been refugees. For them, 'survivor' was a title reserved for people like one of their friends in Cardiff, who had given birth to her daughter on a coal wagon while being moved from Auschwitz to Mauthausen in April 1945. A 'survivor' was my second cousin, Alfred Cohn, who had been sent to Auschwitz and who, at the end of the war, walked across much of Europe before eventually reaching what was then Palestine. A 'survivor' was my four-foot, seven-inch-tall great-aunt Sara, who had spent the war in hiding in Holland. They were the true survivors. My parents thought of themselves as one-time escapees. Then they thought of themselves as British. My mother often insisted that she was just 'ordinary'. But nobody is ordinary. Later, I came to realise that, more than anything, I was the son of refugees, and both blessed and marked for being so.

Today, I react the way in which my parents responded to 'survivor' whenever I hear the words 'we got out' – a phrase often used by public stock traders to explain how they sold shares before the fortunes of a company deteriorated. I always find it jarring – not because of its callous nature – but because it's the phrase I heard so often in my childhood. Then, 'we got out' meant only one thing. It meant having a visa, packing a suitcase, boarding a train, travelling by sea and reaching a place where life would be possible.

The more I delved into my parents' past, the more I had a sense that I was exploring the sources of inherited despair – conveyed unwittingly from one generation to another. These are the transmissions that underlie the lifelong struggle all of us wage in the battle to become ourselves, as we try to sort out what we want to banish from the past and what we want to save, and how we prevent infecting those we love with the consequences of our own heritage. How do we interpret and digest the attitudes, tribal instincts, reactions and responses we witnessed as children? How do we react to moments of joy and sadness, to a yearning for adventure, to instability, to a shortage of money? Where does it all come from? All roads point home. But where is home?

The painter R. B. Kitaj had fought the same battle (his mother being Jewish). I was always drawn, without at first knowing its name, to one of his more arresting works, which he painted in the 1970s when he was at the height of his fame. It shows a man sitting on a plump sofa, concentrating on a telephone call. He wears red shorts, a rumpled, white unbuttoned shirt with rolled-up sleeves and a black tie. He is holding the receiver in his right hand and his little finger is adorned with a large signet ring. The outline of the legs could have been drawn by Egon Schiele – such is the confidence and firmness of the lines. The painting radiates a louche wanderlust. As a young man, Kitaj had run away to sea, which is why, at least to me, the window behind the figure has always spoken of a porthole and an ocean.

Born in Ohio, Kitaj had adopted London as his hometown, where his first wife, Elsi, committed suicide and from which he fled after harsh reviews of an exhibition at the Tate and the sudden death of his second wife, Sandra. A black-and-white photograph of Kitaj with his friend, the painter Frank Auerbach, taken after Sandra's funeral, is one of the purest expressions of grief that I know. From time to time, before his own suicide in Los Angeles in 2007, I received commentaries written by Kitaj, neatly penned in red biro on sheets from a yellow writing pad. One observation he made was, 'Jews and what happens to them fascinate me more than Judaism does; well, more than the God of the Jews; the phenomenal history of antisemitism tantalises me far more than a faith I never knew.' Unlike Kitaj, I had been reared in the faith, but as an adult, like the artist, it has been the history of the Jews – particularly that of the past 150 years – that has had me in its grasp. It cannot be an accident that the painting by Kitaj is named 'The Secret Jew' because, for many decades, I too kept my religion invisible.

★

During the time the pandemic brought the world to a stop, I kept drawing parallels between another plague – the ugliness of the political battle in the US, which seemed like a nation at war with itself, and the darkness that had enveloped Europe some ninety years earlier. Despite the vast differences, there were parallels particularly as social media became an amplified form of what radio had been in the thirties – a new tool that could be hijacked for malevolent purposes. The cries emanating from the presidential campaign of 2016, and that have continued ever since, were identical to many employed in Germany between the two world wars: 'the lying press'; the denunciation of anarchists, socialists, minorities, immigrants and the physically impaired; the denigration of the courts, of skilled civil servants and devoted diplomats; the undermining of science; the coded mantra of 'Law and Order'. It seemed so familiar, right down to that torchlit parade in Charlottesville, Virginia, with white supremacists chanting 'Jews will not replace us!' All I could hear was the refrain I had heard as a young boy whenever my parents sensed disturbing political trends:

> If it did happen, it can happen.
> If it did happen, it will happen.
> If it did happen somewhere, it can happen here.
> It will happen here.

As the present closed in, I became transfixed by all the yesterdays.

Two memories swirl through my mind whenever I think about my father and mother. One of warmth, one of fear. One comes from southern Germany, which was where my father spent his childhood, the other from northern Germany, where my mother lived until she was fourteen. Both memories are from the early 1960s.

I thought of the first when, during the time that mass graves were being dug all over the world, masks were in short supply and vaccines but a hope, Harriet and I took evening walks. One twilight, when I happened to pick a date for the completion of the first draft of this book, we were strolling under a cornflower-blue spring sky on California pastureland near the edge of the Pacific Ocean when we encountered a herd of cows beside a high wire fence with their heads turned longingly towards the scent of the freshly cut grass on our side of the barrier. We gathered the grass and tossed the damp clumps over the fence.

Suddenly, I am a boy, it is early morning, and I am making my way between tents and campers pitched and parked on neat plots in a campsite near a lake in the Bavarian Alps, heading towards the communal facilities, with my wash kit tucked under my arm. In the brightly lit bathroom, lined up at rows of basins backed by mirrors, are men, mainly German, some completely naked, others wearing shorts or robes, slapping water on their faces, slathering shaving cream onto their cheeks, dabbing cuts made by their razors, brushing their teeth, combing their hair and snorting, coughing, spitting and farting.

On the afternoon we had arrived at the campsite, my father had parked the well-worn Commer camper van, in which we went on three- or four-week holidays for several years (since my father, as a university professor, and my mother, as a schoolteacher, were both entitled to long summer breaks), near the office at the entrance. There, friends of the owners sat smoking cigarettes, drinking coffee, reading newspapers, playing cards, gossiping and, whenever the door swung open, falling silent to inspect the visitors. My father had presented his British passport but spoke in German, and the woman behind the counter had looked at him, perplexed, as if nobody from Britain could possibly bear our last name or speak German as fluently. '*Herr Moritz?*' she had asked but did not, as she recovered her composure, blurt out the question she seemed to want to pose, '*Juden?*'

We had visited this same village, Bühl-am-Alpsee, in previous years because it was home to Anna Volk, the nanny who had cared for my father and his brother, Ernest, in Munich during the 1920s and early 1930s. Then, when my sister and I were smaller, instead of sleeping in a camper van, we had all stayed with Anna. She lived in the same house which, when she and her husband Sepp dug into all their savings and, aided by friends, built it in the early 1930s was one of only a handful of homes lining a quiet country road some 95 miles southwest of Munich. Sepp (who died before I got to know him) was a stocky man who drove shunting locomotives in the nearby railway yard, for what was named – during the Third Reich – the Deutsche Reichsbahn. The pair supplemented their income by taking holidaymakers into their house, with its steep eaves and balconies, and a view over two Alpine lakes. This house, with which my father and his brother associated their happiest summers, became an emotional refuge for both of them after World War II.

Both Anna and Sepp came to assume mythical importance in our family for the way that they had quietly stood their ground while the Nazis spread their evil. I have sometimes thought about writing a novel based on the people I knew who lived in their house. It would be a tale of light and dark, softness and savagery.

After Sepp died, Anna rented out the downstairs apartment and when I knew her, she was in her late sixties, always wore an apron at home, spoke softly, said little and chewed her cheeks and lips to cushion the discomfort of her false teeth. Her face was creased and her hair, by then grey, was tied in the same tight bun she had worn since youth. When she had guests, Anna slept on the narrow divan in the kitchen which, during the day, lined with cushions, served as seating for her dining table. This table, always covered by a floral oilcloth, was like a chart table on a boat – the centre of all activity. It was where she prepared and later served her meals, read the newspaper, entertained friends, played cards and wrote letters.

An iron range stood in the corner of the kitchen, and a pile of neatly chopped wood lay near the door. The stove was the first thing that Anna attended to every morning – raking out the ashes, prying open the lids on which pots rested and making a fresh fire which, fed and nurtured, would burn until after dinner was made. Today I often think of her while I am washing dishes or pans after dinner because my mother frequently remarked that Anna had the cleanest sink of anyone she knew.

It was in this room, warmed by the wood-fired range, that I suspect my father found a connection to the world and future he had lost, and it was there I suspect that he was happiest. It was there too that as a little boy I slept a few feet above the downstairs apartment in which Stumpfnagel, the one-legged Nazi tax collector, lived with his illegitimate daughter, Marianne, and her husband, Franz, and whose party uniform, with its swastika armband, still hung in his wardrobe. It was this retired tax inspector who, in the afternoons, sat on the stoop in his wheelchair watching the passing traffic and trying to catch my father's eye whenever we entered the house while – grimly fascinating to me – massaging the bandaged stump of his amputated leg.

Often, while day-dreaming, I am walking towards Anna's house, with its raked roof and wooden shutters, the garden of which backed onto steep Alpine pastures and pine-covered hills. In my head, my father and I are frozen in time heading towards it, forever carrying the breakfast we had bought at the little store at the foot of the hill, where the ladies behind the counter wore stiffly starched white jackets, and which smelled of butter and cheese. My father is carrying a bag of hard rolls, and I am holding him by one hand and, in the other, toting a milk churn with a half-litre of fresh milk. At the top of the hill, we cross a road and walk past the gas station, which is operated by a man my father had known as a boy and whose own father, I knew, had been a diehard Nazi. Then we reach safety – Anna's house. The cool morning air is scented with the tang of cow manure and the smell of fresh hay.

My father first visited this house almost a hundred years ago. After World War II it became the place that – with Anna – still had a trace of home about it, and perhaps I thought of the place my father deemed home as mine too, irrespective of the fact that it was not, for either of us. Today it continues to exert a strange pull for me. I often visit, although I have not actually been there for more than sixty years. My trips take place late at night and are made possible by the miracles that are Google Earth and Google Street View. Anna's house is still there, although some nearby newly built houses mean that, were she still alive, she could no longer walk past the chicken coop and step directly into the fields where the cows graze. Now, she and her guests would have to take a small detour before they can start their hike up the small mountain covered in trees – many of which were there when I was a boy, and when my father was a boy, and when my grandparents first visited.

I understand the pull this home exerts on me. But I'm aware that perhaps it is less the sense of the place itself and more the

Minnie, Ernest, Alfred and Max Moritz with
Anna Volk behind, Bühl-am-Alpsee, 1930s

idea of a time. I can still hear the creak of the staircase, smell the floor polish and feel the smoothness of the oilcloth on the table. And I can still see the two balconies that have welcomed three generations named Moritz. I know, from this, that there is an idea called home.

That morning walk with my father, which probably took no longer than thirty minutes and makes me pine for the close relationship we never had, always leads me towards another memory, but this one is draped in darkness and fear. I am sitting in the back of the Commer van, primitive by today's standards and now an object of curiosity at shows of vintage vehicles. It is 1965, and my sister, who was born a couple of years after me, is also lounging in the back, reading. We are bumping

Anna Volk and Doris, Bühl-am-Alpsee, 1950s

Me, Anna Volk, Clare and Doris, Bühl-am-Alpsee, 1960s

along the roads of Germany, my parents in the front with the windows rolled down and my father's right elbow resting on the door ledge – his forearm red and blistered from sunburn. At the time, long convoys of British and American troops, the beefy residue of the force that had occupied Germany in 1945, still rumbled along the autobahns Hitler had built to transport his own armies and munitions.

Every time calamity struck our Commer van – when a gasket blew, or a water-pump failed, or a fan belt snapped, or a hole gaped in an exhaust pipe, or the engine began to knock, we would decamp to a small hotel in the nearest town while the mechanic waited the three or four days it took for the part to be shipped from England and my father fretted about the delays and expense. But for now, the Commer is behaving. I am eagerly scanning the small circular stamps on the licence plates of German vehicles, each of which begins with an abbreviation of the place of registration. For anyone from Britain, the German licensing system has an organised charm, easy to interpret. In Britain, the opaque approach requires a decryption machine to unravel. In Cardiff, for example, the alphanumeric system always includes two letters – either BO, KG, or UH. On the autobahns and streets of Germany it was simple. I soon learned that F stood for Frankfurt; N, Nuremberg; D, Düsseldorf; K, Köln (Cologne); M, Munich; S, Stuttgart; A, Augsburg; H, Hanover (not, I had learned, Hamburg). The two- and three-letter designations indicate smaller towns and villages. The ones still lodged in my memory are in Bavaria or were places to which strands of my father's emotions were tethered: GAP, Garmisch-Partenkirchen; MM, Memmingen; OF, Offenbach; WU, Würzburg; WO, Worms; NES, Bad Neustadt.

Then there are KE and KK. These Ks still cause me confusion and I must keep reminding myself that Kempten, KE, is in Bavaria and Kempen, KK, is in northern Germany, in what had, at one time, been Prussia. It was here in KK, a small town in the Rhineland, tucked between the Ruhr to the east and the Dutch border to the west, that my mother had spent her childhood.

In my memory our small camper van is rattling through the pastures surrounding KK, about twelve miles from the Dutch border, ground that had been fought over by French, Hessian and Weimar troops during the Thirty Years War and occupied by the French in the 1920s. We enter the fringes of Kempen and it takes just minutes before we are slowly circling a small park. My mother is staring intently out of the window and my father turns the wheel in the direction her finger points. She shrinks lower in her seat. She instructs my father to circle the small park again. She sees a man and says she recognises

Alfred and Doris's Commer camper van

him. She points at a house and says that was her home. And then she is a bundle on the floor of the Commer, crouched above the wheel well, hissing to my father not to stop but to speed up. Get out of Kempen. Get out of the Rhineland. Get out of Germany. Get out of the past. *Get out.*

My father wanted to return to a place he associated with solace, affection and family. My mother wanted to flee. My father had lost his parents, Max and Minnie – Maximilian and Hermine – Moritz, and much of his entire family, and there was nowhere he could call home. My mother's parents – Salli (an abbreviation for Salamon) and Louise Rath – had escaped to Cambridge in Britain, though they too lost most of their family and friends. For my mother, Salli and Louise remained a central part of her life for thirty years after the war and their house in Cambridge offered a semblance of home. We went to the little town in Bavaria repeatedly. After that one brief passage through Kempen, the small town in the Rhineland, we never returned. A few minutes had been enough to unleash the pain of the past.

LUDWIG, AS IN ALFRED

NOW THAT BOTH MY PARENTS ARE DEAD (having chosen cremation rather than burial perhaps because in Wales there was no graveyard where they could be surrounded by other familial bones), I'm puzzled by the fact that, until I embarked on this book, I knew only the barest outline of their lives in the years before I was old enough to form recollections of my own. Neither of them was willing to delve into their pasts, let alone ponder how their emotions had been shaped by their childhoods.

Part of their reticence may have stemmed from the reverence they ascribed to the murdered members of their families. These people had disappeared from their lives before they themselves were old enough to rebel – although the irreverent, mildly anarchic streak of children who became teenagers in the sixties and seventies was hardly a leitmotif of young, middle-class Germans of the prior generation.

Much of my father's unwillingness probably sprang from shyness or the apprehension, always present in the mind of a storyteller, about boring an unreceptive audience. I have often wondered whether the way they coped with their early experiences was to bury them in silence. My father's inner thoughts were as carefully secreted as a set of codes stitched on a small piece of cloth between the lining and outer layer of a spy's raincoat. His frustrations or anxieties would occasionally erupt as fearsome tantrums and he would stalk out of a room clenching his fists and slamming the door. But he had nowhere to retreat to and would soon return in sheepish silence. His inclination was to back down from confrontation and eventually revert to compromise.

A reserved and introverted man, he became increasingly meditative and melancholic as age, loss of hearing, and, perhaps, accumulated disappointments, including the break-up of my sister's marriage after her husband became inexplicably enchanted by a faith healer – an acrimonious saga that involved, among other things, ascribing magical properties to crystals, allegations of libel and perjury, hearings in the High Court and misery on the home front – took their toll. The bitterness of the battle – something most people only encounter when an unlikely story about otherwise respectable people appears in the tabloids (as my sister's did) – weighed on my father during the decade before his death.

One day during the first summer of the pandemic, while I was working in the library of Borgo Pignano, which had been closed because of the virus and travel restrictions, I got an email from a business acquaintance in California who had moved with his family to England. The one-line message, written in the terse style characteristic of the sender, asked, 'Are you any relation to the L. A. Moritz who wrote the book on ancient grain milling?'

As it happened, I had been yearning for the culinary expertise of L. A. Moritz because I had volunteered to help edit the English product descriptions of the gift hampers containing the wines, olive oil, pastas and other products that we make in Borgo Pignano that were being prepared for sale on our website. But I needed an expert to help me understand the heritage of the heirloom seeds, which at harvest time we mill and turn into flour or pasta. When I confirmed to the sender of the email that L. A. Moritz was indeed related to me, I was gratified to learn that he considered my father's book, *Grain Mills and Flour in Classical Antiquity*, a seminal work in the history of technology because it demolished some of the myths that had grown up around the early centuries of grain milling. My correspondent thought it so vital a work that he kept copies in both California and England.

Many of the books from my father's study are now shelved in Borgo Pignano's library. The cloth- and leather-bound works contain the thoughts of philosophers such as Aristotle, Plato, Socrates, Mill, Burke and Kant and reflect the mature studies of a man who, as a boy, had been educated at a German gymnasium, St Paul's School in London and Merton College, Oxford. They are also the legacy of someone gifted enough to teach philosophy, Latin, Greek, Hebrew, ancient history and religious history at one of the world's great universities, as well as introductory courses for advanced mathematics.

Grain Mills and Flour in Classical Antiquity was published by the Oxford University Press in 1958, and, to my father's delight, republished the year before his death. It was based on his doctoral thesis, a topic suggested by an Oxford scholar who had worked during the war at the Ministry of Food, where he had been involved with bread production and supply. My father's research delved into the history of ancient mills, flour, and bread-making techniques. It was the kind of work welcomed by academics who specialised in the area and by the small circle of people fascinated by the history of progress.

My father never wrote another book, although he made regular contributions to academic journals. Among his other subjects were the letters of Cicero, the Odes of Horace and the philosophy of the Stoics. Had he been reared sixty years later, these gifts would have served him well in an era where the most valued languages are those that control computers. He had a poet's devotion to brevity, metre and precision, and a mathematician's patience for puzzles – characteristics of the best programmers.

Instead of writing books, my father busied himself with university life. He was promoted to a senior lectureship, then after a secondment to West Africa where he became the first professor of classics at the University of Ghana, he clambered up the academic ladder in Cardiff – becoming a full professor, dean of faculty and, eventually, for about twenty years, heading the administration of the university. He had a lifelong deference to authority; L. A. Moritz was not one to spoil for a fight.

His pastimes were cerebral, not physical or social, and he was not adventurous. I don't recall seeing him or my mother drunk or complaining of a hangover. Mildly tipsy was as far as they dared venture. His idea of exercise amounted to a walk, mowing the grass with a gas-powered lawn mower or, later in life, kneading dough for upper-body strength or cutting and sewing his own bow ties. It was my mother, not my father, who might have delivered the right hook. My father was prone to vertigo, had difficulty following the flight of a ball, paid little attention to televised sports and even less to the swinging sixties. One weekend afternoon, the year in which I bought my first record, 'She Loves You', we were sitting with friends when everyone was asked to write down on a slip of paper their favourite Beatle. All but the best-educated person in the room had a ready answer. It was the first examination my father had failed.

His disdain for physical exercise was more than compensated for by mental mobility drills – and in this he was a medallist. His exchanges with the dwindling number of Latin and Greek scholars included snatches of both languages. Among his papers I found his Greek translation of *Sing a Song of Sixpence*. He enjoyed composing limericks and doggerel, of which one lamented the decline of the postal service – a problem he attributed to a newly created job category:

> It's a job for both summer and winter.
> For fog, snow, rain, sunshine, or hail:
> I'm employed in the Postmaster's office
> As a delayer of second-class mail.

The *Times* crossword, the daunting Mephisto puzzle of the *Sunday Times*, cryptograms and, later, bridge were his natural habitats. The magical properties of polygons or etymology could occupy him for hours. He was too modest to ever note that in a compilation of the mind-numbingly difficult Brain Teaser puzzles published by the *Sunday Times*, he was the only person to have contributed more than one. I was startled to find that in one of my father's numerical puzzles, the two characters, whose ages formed clues, were Anna and Minnie – the names of his nanny and his mother. I'm sure that no subscriber to the *Sunday Times* would have imagined that there was something deep within my father, as he sat in his study in Wales smoking his pipe and creating the puzzle, that had taken him back to a time in his childhood when the world had seemed serene.

As his professional activities tapered off, my father increasingly turned to his synagogue, and it became the centre of his life, in which he not only helped administer its affairs but also gave many talks. He became the tutor to a generation of boys and girls preparing for their religious rite of passage. Before my father reached the compulsory retirement age, he also obtained satisfaction from volunteering at the Citizens Advice Bureau, where he derived amusement from domestic conundrums such as one about how to divide a horse between a couple whose marriage was falling apart.

But it was my father's knowledge of the early use of various grain in diets that I needed in Borgo Pignano, as I tried to understand the differences between the grains we plant in the surrounding fields, so that I could assemble some punchy prose for our website. My father had the temperament required to unravel complexity – something for which my slapdash, impatient temperament has little tolerance. I just wanted the answers. As I tried to sort through the differences between rye, wheat, barley, spelt and farro, and understand how they are used in porridge, semolina, pasta and bread, I knew that my father would have been able to trace them back to their earliest mentions in Latin, Greek and Hebrew. He would have been able to quickly and easily explain why Borgo Pignano's whole grain – which contains bran, germ and endosperm – is so much more nutritious than the endosperm alone, the latter being the caloric portion that is the principal constituent of factory-produced white bread. And had I still been perplexed, he would have quietly implored me to 'use my loaf'.

A few days after my father died in 2003, I accompanied my mother to a solicitor's office in Cardiff to sort through the details of their estate. It was an encounter that illustrated the difference between my parents. While my father navigated life with his mind, my mother pursued it with a dark gusto. She compensated for feelings of inferiority in a donnish milieu by outdoing all the academics with energy and an Olympian irascibility. She shrugged off any compliment that she received – about her looks, her dress, her garden, the flowers she had bought, anything. She did not engage in effusive displays of affection, joy or happiness. She was capable of great verbal violence and the people most liable to be contaminated by exposure were, in order of danger, her closest family, her more distant relatives, friends, acquaintances and politicians. By contrast she would treat a gardener or a cleaning lady with great kindness. My mother was belligerent, always led with her chin, had a propensity for blurting out whatever was on her mind, made hasty judgments and was even quicker with censorious verdicts. She was a specialist in nursing grudges and not forgiving slights. Finesse, subtlety and guile were not in her armoury. On the rare occasions when she was moved to offer some form of praise, it almost always came as a backhanded compliment. She engaged in neither whimsy nor irony.

Many of these traits, particularly her sensitivity about being treated as a foreigner in the city she had called home for fifty years, were on display while we were discussing my father's will in the solicitor's office. The lawyer was a small, bald man who wore a pinstripe suit and a loud purple tie. He began the meeting by cleaning his spectacles on the inside lining of his suit jacket. Then, in the manner of a customs clerk taking inventory of the contents of a suspicious-looking truck at a border crossing, he pulled out a long form and asked, 'National Insurance number?'

'I'm sorry?' said my mother.

'Your husband's National Insurance number?'

'I have no idea,' my mother replied.

'Oh, well then, his name please?' asked the solicitor.
'Alfred.'
'Alfred?'
'Yes.'
'That's his first name?'
'No.'
'I thought you said his name was Alfred.'
'It is.' My mother corrected herself, 'It was.'
'But it wasn't his first name?'
'No.'
'What was his first name?'
'L,' said my mother.
'L?'
'Yes. That was his initial.'
'Ah, I see. His initial. What did it stand for?'
'Ludwig.'
'Ludwig,' the solicitor confirmed, then paused. 'What sort of a name is that then?'
'That was my husband's name.'
'Ah, so his first name was Ludwig.'
'No. His first name was Alfred.'
'Ludwig, as in Beethoven?' asked the solicitor.
'No,' said my mother. 'Ludwig, as in Alfred.'

A few months later she fired off a tart letter to the editor of the *Sunday Times* following the publication of an article about the opening of a new arts centre in Cardiff. The curtain-raiser was being produced by Bryn Terfel, the Welsh opera singer, who had expressed doubts about whether Michael Howard, then the new leader of the Conservative Party, who was born about fifty miles from Cardiff and happened to be the son of two

Jewish parents (whose last name had been Hecht), was actually Welsh. My mother's letter (which went unpublished) unleashed the same tension between her ferocious desire to assimilate without losing a sense of self: 'My children were born in Wales, and I consider them Welsh, and so do officials when they realise that my son has done well in the USA. No doubt the same goes for Michael Howard. May I suggest that Bryn Terfel stick to his lathe and do what he does well and not meddle in genetics.'

In the fifty-four years they spent together, my mother had permitted little to interfere with my father's work and the household machinery was her preserve. It was she who ventured into the attic to remove the snow when it blew in beneath the tiles during the winters. It was she who made marmalade and jams every year, making sure her freezers were stocked with sufficient supplies to successfully survive a blockade of all shipping lanes. She also had the courage to try to learn to play the piano as an adult. In her eighties, she gamely took up the recorder, and in her final year, pottery.

After we came back from West Africa, she returned to the pursuit she had taken up as a young woman and taught young children. She spent almost twenty years teaching Indian and Pakistani immigrants (for whom she had a deep and abiding sympathy, particularly those who appeared at school with bruises but refused to explain the cause) at a series of elementary schools in some of South Wales's toughest neighbourhoods.

It was she, a natural adventurer, who opened my eyes and ears to museums, art, classical music, the opera and the theatre. It was she who, in the age before yoga and Pilates were in vogue, kept herself fit by playing squash. My affection for fresh flowers and for the opening hour of street markets comes from my mother. Every time I visit the farmer's market behind the Ferry Building in San Francisco, or the Saturday market near the amphitheatre in Volterra, or Borough Market in London, I think of my mother, large wicker basket in hand, staging an assault on the markets of Cardiff, and merrily bantering with the grocers, butchers and fishmongers. These outings displayed an aspect of my mother that she mainly kept under wraps.

My mother had a far deeper sense of the misfortunes of others than my father. She was as magnificent and professional as a volunteer as she was as a complainer about the small things. Much of this revolved around their synagogue, some around a charity shop where she volunteered for close to thirty years, and there was not a hospital bed she would not visit. She was stoical, courageous and resilient in her attitudes towards the more difficult setbacks of life. But bleakness hung over everything. She defined the three stages of life by the history of her teeth, of which she said, 'They hurt when you get them, they hurt when you have them, and they hurt when you lose them.'

Given her disposition, I never understood why, before she went to bed, my mother insisted on opening all the curtains in her living room so that the following morning she would be greeted by daylight rather than darkness. Was it an expression of hope, a deeply suppressed sense of optimism or a yearning for a better day? When her only granddaughter once asked her to select her most enjoyable decade, she answered, 'What do you mean, "Which decade?" They were all terrible.'

Sifting through the photographs and documents my sister had sent, I found an image from 1960 in which I am seated behind a large menorah during a Chanukah party, tucking into the sandwiches, cakes and biscuits that had been made and

Me, Chanukah party, Cardiff, 1960

served by the female congregants in the basement hall of the synagogue that had started life as a Baptist chapel. By 2014, when my mother turned ninety, that cold, damp hall had been renovated and was warm and cheerful.

Before the celebration, during a Saturday morning service, my mother had, for the first time in her life, received the priestly blessing from the rabbi. She had refused any assistance and gamely navigated the steps that led to the lectern, clutching onto a handrail with one hand and gripping her cane with the other. The invocation, which bridges religions and cultures, is universal. It never moved me more than on that morning when the rabbi raised both his hands above my mother's bowed head, as she clutched the side of the lectern – stooped but indomitable.

After the service, and after the congregants had moved to the basement hall where a buffet lunch had been laid out to celebrate my mother's birthday, I was standing amid the extended family that my parents had created for themselves. Some sixteen members of our own family had been mustered (all but two born in Britain after the war) but most of the other guests were refugees from Nazi Europe or descendants of refugees from the pogroms of the nineteenth century. This was the group of people who had come to provide my parents with a sense of family and community, which the war had otherwise obliterated.

A few hours before I received an email from my sister, on Guy Fawkes Day (when Britons traditionally light bonfires to commemorate a failed plot to destroy the Houses of Parliament), 5 November 2019, saying that our mother had died at the age of ninety-five in the London nursing home where she had lived for the previous year, I had already dreamed that she was dead. I was less surprised to learn that my mother had died than by the fact that I knew. I cannot explain the premonition and I don't remember having experienced one before. Somehow, I knew that unlike her father, Salli, my mother had not expired while putting on her shoes, unlike her mother, Louise, she had not died as she sat alone on a park bench, and unlike my father she had not gasped for a final breath while sitting in the passenger seat of a car. For once, she had got her wish – she died in her sleep. Across the hallway, a woman who had survived Auschwitz died a few days later.

Perversely, my mother would have felt cheated by so narrowly missing out on the pandemic – the global calamity she had been expecting since adolescence. She died about two weeks before it began. My mother would have relished spreading the word of the deadliness of the virus because she could be relied upon at breakfast to recite the tales of misery she had heard on the radio during her sleepless hours. Not a morsel of bad news escaped her attention. Before she took a sip of coffee, we could depend on her to convey the news of a famine in Namibia, a flood in Bangladesh, a suicide bomber in Tel Aviv, a coach full of tourists careening off an Alpine road, summary executions in Saudi Arabia, an oil spill off the French coast, a typhoon threatening to decimate a Caribbean island, a strike of London Underground train drivers, the defeat of the Welsh rugby team and a forecast for heavy showers later in the day. But she missed out on Covid-19, the first catastrophe to afflict the entire world since the end of the war that had made her a refugee.

By the time my mother's body had been returned to Wales and received its ritual washing, and relatives and friends had assembled at the same crematorium where, sixteen years earlier, I had spotted the name Alfred Moritz scrawled in charcoal on the side of my father's casket, all was regimented. The mourners, most of them ghosts from my childhood – stooped, thinner and armed with hearing aids, sticks and walkers – were bundled up against the wet, cutting wind that blew in from the Bristol Channel. They had filed into a reception room where the frailest secured the chairs and others gamely stood. My mother's penultimate fear (the ultimate one being the manner of her death) had been that nobody would show up for her funeral. It was one of the ways her insecurity (and sense of competitiveness) had expressed itself in her final years. She should not have fretted. So many people turned out and, in the Jewish custom (which on the surface seems incongruous at a funeral), wished me a long life that, if their wishes come true, I might live until I'm 10,000 years old.

I was pressed to recall all the connections and remember the names and relationships. There were mourners whom I was meeting for the first time and others whose familiar frames had withered. All the while I found myself being gradually pushed towards the wall and felt a growing sense of claustrophobia, as if I was on the verge of suffocating. I kept looking for the exit, and then I realised the source of my anxiety: I was packed into a small chamber with a couple of hundred Jews, all of whom were being funnelled towards a corridor leading to a crematorium.

This memory makes me think of being in a university classroom in Philadelphia in 1976, where, once a week, I formed part of a seminar group discussing the novels of the Penguin series 'Writers from the Other Europe', edited by Philip Roth, who, dressed in a tweed jacket, button-down shirt, knitted tie, flannels and polished brogues, was sitting in front of this small crescent of students during a stint as a visiting professor. We were discussing a novel by Tadeusz Borowski, a Polish author whose parents had been deported during Stalin's Great Terror and who had acquired his education in an underground school in Nazi-occupied Warsaw before being imprisoned at Auschwitz and Dachau. Seven days after the birth of his daughter, Borowski, just twenty-nine years old, had taken his own life by inhaling gas from a kitchen stove. It was he who had written the short story collection that was the subject of Philip Roth's class, *This Way for the Gas, Ladies and Gentlemen*.

BELOW THE SURFACE

AS MY YEARS IN AMERICA TICKED BY, Sequoia's success increased and there were occasional mentions of me in articles about companies with which I was involved, my mother grew increasingly uneasy. Whenever I was mentioned in a newspaper listing of wealthy people, she only commented on the story if I had slipped in the rankings. Similarly, after we acquired Borgo Pignano, my mother remarked, 'Why can't you be like everyone else and buy a normal house?'

Much of my parents' reluctance to dwell on the past may have been a by-product of trying to demonstrate that, except for their heritage, they were as British or as Welsh as their neighbours. Maybe it all boiled down to wanting to remain inconspicuous. They knew full well the consequences of being singled out, of being labelled as different, of having a 'J' stamped on their passports, of being stripped of jobs, possessions and relatives, and forced to wear a yellow badge on the left breast of their clothing. My father and mother did not want to stand out. They wanted a comfortable life and were eager for my sister and me to do well scholastically and to progress thereafter. It was good to obtain high grades, but it was not fine to be cocky about the achievement.

Both my parents carried the emotional shrapnel of their parents' wounds. For my father, this meant the memories of the parents he last saw when he was fifteen years old, while for my mother it was the sense of displacement, of being a foreigner in a strange land, of her father Salli's disappointment that he had no sons. They thought psychiatry was a self-indulgence for well-heeled Americans. They were not capable of looking inwards and had been imbued with the British way of carrying on with a stiff upper lip. They could not convey their grief in words and though they paid homage to the horrors during the weekly prayers for the dead, their sense of loss locked them in an emotional straitjacket. It was this inability to grieve that was almost certainly the cause of their anger, outbursts and lack of empathy for those closest to them. Their emotional security had been destroyed long before I was born.

As I was making notes for this book and thinking about my parents, I was reading the second volume of *The Lives of Lucian Freud*, written by William Feaver and published by Bloomsbury in September 2019. Freud, too, was a refugee who made a life in Britain. In this book, I chanced upon a review of an exhibition of his work: 'What makes Freud's paintings so enthralling and so relevant to our lives is the drama just below the surface, a battle between who we strive to be and who we become, between our parents and ourselves, between our minds and our bodies, between life and death.' You can detect these dramas in one of his last self-portraits. It's a small work, and I was drawn to both what was contained within the frame – an unsparing examination of a life's experiences – and its title, *Reflection*.

The dramas of Freud's life – art, womanising, gambling, children – often made the newspapers. In contrast, all the emotional tumult of my parents' lives played out in private. The critic of Freud's exhibition was, I thought, describing the consequences of inherited despair. We all live in the past and present at the same time. My parents did and so do I, although, as I age, I have become increasingly conscious of the debilitating effects of the past on my behaviour.

Rereading hundreds of letters my parents wrote between the time I left Wales as a nineteen-year-old and the years when telephone calls became cheap enough for us to exchange a few minutes of conversation once a week, I was struck by the absence of emotion. They make for a distinctly flat read. My father could not even tiptoe near intimacy – it was treacherous ground for him. His matter-of-fact recital of weekly events made me recall an evening before I left Wales. He and I were watching an interview with Albert Speer, Hitler's favourite architect and the Nazis' Minister of Armaments, who, having escaped a death sentence at Nuremberg, was promoting the publication of his memoirs on the BBC. My father watched the figure on television – who seemed like a genial German college professor with a good command of English – but said nothing. He did not stalk out of the room or turn the television off in anger or condemn Speer. He just watched and listened, as he completed the *Times* crossword and smoked his pipe. For us, an intimate conversation amounted to discussions about the British budget, the declining cost of computing or the life cycle of electric shavers. Once, while bidding farewell after I had visited Britain, he said, 'I don't want to make a speech, but you know what I mean.'

My mother had less fear of territory my father considered forbidden. She was more willing to address tensions she saw in my marriage, to scold me for bursts of temper or urge me to take more vacations. My parents meant well with their letters, just as my mother meant well when she spent hours preparing meals that were her way of expressing affection, but which were subsequently often presented with surly resentment.

In the letters, there would be news about relatives and the state of the roof on the synagogue. In winter there would be updates about frozen pipes, crumbling garden walls, ways to eradicate moles from beneath lawns (by inserting smoke bombs), broken water heaters and the lack of grit on icy roads. On other occasions there would be mentions of vandalism – car robberies, stolen radios, broken phone boxes. Every summer the talk turned to water-rationing, the need to carry buckets of water from the toilet to irrigate the garden, lawn treatments and the harvesting of raspberries and strawberries, as well as exotics such as white asparagus, chicory, radishes, runner beans and Jerusalem artichokes. My mother could be relied on to cut to the quick. On the charms of a relative's girlfriend she observed, 'She is a big girl with lots of acne.' After watching *Shoah*, Claude Lanzmann's nine-hour documentary about the death camps, when it was released in the mid-1980s, she noted of the Polish peasants featured in interviews, 'Looking at the country folk I was astonished to see what poor mouths they had. That great socialist state does not seem to practise dental hygiene.'

My parents were always on high alert for anything that was a threat to the established order – militant trade unionists, 'Ban the Bomb' protestors, the Irish Republican Army, Welsh separatists or waterlogged music festivals. They never forgot the consequences of extreme statements, disruptive minorities and physical intimidation. During the pre-Thatcher years, every national dislocation was mentioned – train strikes, printer strikes, lorry driver strikes, bus strikes, post office strikes, journalist strikes, as well as college politics and the closures of steel mills, coal mines and automobile and television factories. For them there was nothing more disconcerting then the prospect of chaos, and clips of large marches or angry picketers would inevitably prompt my father to growl. Inwardly, I suspect they feared the consequences of the collapse of the orderly society in which they had found sanctuary.

As the years passed and the age of retirement dawned, there were more outings to concerts, operas, plays, museums and country houses, and more notices of doctors, dentists, newsagents and favourite shopkeepers closing their practise or business and choosing an easier life. There were references to the arrival of the transatlantic discount airlines and girls with safety pins piercing their earlobes, and the rumoured facelift of the television presenter David Frost. Every so often my mother would trip across an accomplishment of someone I might have known at high school or encountered at Oxford and on reading one update, I could almost hear her asking herself why I had not been able to accomplish something as distinguished as having written the best fellowship thesis submitted to the Institute of Taxation.

And then came the litany of illnesses, deaths and funerals, with my mother making special note of weeks during which she had been fortunate enough to entertain herself by attending two burials. She lingered too as she reported the death of a man who had suffered a massive heart attack having just returned from a holiday in the Virgin Islands. In the following breath she mentioned that this man's first son had died in an aeroplane crash while the second had met his end in a motorcycle accident. Such were the bulletins from Wales.

My mother had a waspish tongue, which my father never did. Here are some examples – the first from the beginning of

1978 when I was in the second of my two years at the University of Pennsylvania. 'Your tremendous ambition in wanting to participate in everything and greed for possessions like cars and stereos drives you on. I am not saying or maintaining that ambition is a bad thing but that one must keep things in proportion. You must allow yourself time to think and enjoy your surroundings. That seems rather an odd suggestion to make to you when I have always thought of you as a selfish bastard!' In 1980, she upbraided me on another topic: 'Looking at your letter just shows how little progress you have made in handwriting. You will always have to be near a typewriter.'

A paragraph dispatched after she and my father had visited San Francisco at the end of 1992 made me pause. At the time, Harriet and I had two boys under the age of four, I was apprehensive about my standing at Sequoia, and Harriet was drained by the demands of motherhood and a week with my parents under the same roof. My mother issued a prescription: 'As you know I was deeply shocked by the very nervous state you were in. I strongly advise you to seek professional help. As Jake and Will grow older and become conscious of your nervous disposition, they too will react, and it will leave marks on them. If you do not take advice, you will destroy not only yourself but those around you.' I couldn't squabble with her assessment, and I followed her guidance. It was one of the better decisions I made. Perhaps my mother's insight reflected how people often see others more clearly than themselves.

I occasionally scold myself for not pushing and prodding my parents for more information about who they were. Should I have tried harder? Should I have insisted? Should I have composed a long list of questions and compelled each of them to sit for tape-recorded interviews? I never subjected my parents to the sort of interrogation I always employ with those I interview for jobs. I never asked my father or mother about an incident from the past that they wish they could eradicate, or about the person who had the most influence on their lives, or their worst failure, largest disappointment, or the details of how they met, or what they recalled of the moment they climbed onto a train in Munich or stepped down to a platform in London, or any of the thousands of memories that shape a person.

Shame on me for not asking if their dreams and nightmares occurred in German or if, in the hopeless confusion, sometimes murdered ancestors spoke in English during the night-time hours. As a boy and even as a young reporter, I had not learned enough about the art of interviewing – of listening intently, of allowing silence to pry open the gates, of not intruding, of holding my breath, of maintaining eye contact. I was relieved then to find a letter that I wrote to my parents when I was in my late thirties, in which I apologised for behaviour that might have hurt them, while also imploring them to reveal more about themselves.

I had mailed the letter to Wales shortly after reading the bound and laminated account of childhood composed by my father's brother, Ernest. The letter contained the following passage:

> When you used to say and, I suppose, still say, 'You don't know how lucky you are!', you've been more right than I would care to admit. I think I have always sensed that life for us in the 60s and 70s was worlds removed from what life was like for you in the 30s and 40s, but Ernest's recollections make the comparisons far starker and blatantly apparent.

I also don't think I ever fully appreciated the scale of your accomplishments and triumphs until I understood the way all the cards were stacked against you. This week of soaking in an intimate, family history also helped provoke a fair amount of rumination and underlines the fact that my behavior towards you has not always been what it should have been. I suspect most children are guilty of that, but I'm equally sure I have been more guilty on more occasions than most. Without much trouble I can think of a couple of dozen occasions when my behavior must have seemed cold and reprehensible.

So why does this happen? It's not for lack of gratitude – because I've never doubted that you were always prepared to make whatever sacrifice was necessary to help me on my way. I think it's because parents always need to make judgments about their children and vice versa. Those judgments, whether they occur within the confines of a small French farmhouse (as they did two summers ago), or as they did just last October, are almost bound to ignite everybody's rockets. So this time, as we get ready to make another trip, I am jam packed with all sorts of noble intentions about how I shall not pour salt on old wounds and how I will bite my tongue if I find myself receiving lectures more suitable for a 12 year old.

That said, I also want to say one other thing. I don't think you have ever believed or taken seriously my urging for you to put down on papers some of the things that happened in the years before I arrived. When I made those requests in the past, I did so because I was genuinely interested in what had happened to you. Now, maybe you don't relish digging up the past and I can quite understand if that's the case. However, even if you only have the slightest inclination to do so I would urge you to follow your instincts. You can be assured that you will find one very avid reader right here.

I uncovered my second plea for an account of the past in an email that arrived in Wales on Sunday, 5 January 2003 – the day before my father died. My mother had printed this email, which I had sent to my father's Yahoo! account, and I later discovered it among her papers. My father had been frail for several years and on visits during this period I had often thought that our farewell was the final goodbye. I had no idea that, when I wrote this email, it would be the last time I corresponded with him. The message was my response to the brief appendix he had composed to a memoir Ernest, my uncle, had written in which, beyond trying to paint Max, his own father, in a softer light, he had said little that I hadn't already known. Perhaps my father read the email in the hours before his death. Perhaps the email went unopened. I don't know, but I do know that I begged him to talk about himself and, I suppose, to explain what shaped him.

> Well, I suspect you are surprised, but your memoir [the appendix to my uncle's narrative] has been read with great interest here and has spurred a lot of questions. We'd all be interested in hearing more about the schools that you attended and the subjects you were asked to study and the quality of the teachers and the rigor of the curriculum. We're also interested in learning more about your father – since this was the first time that I was ever aware of his 'nervous breakdowns'. They must have been very upsetting to you and other members of the family. Did he ever talk

about his horrible experiences in World War I? Do you know what he actually did during the war? Did he have a uniform hanging in his wardrobe? Did he belong to some military association that had reunions in the post-war years? What were these breakdowns like and what effect did they have on you and Ernest? Did he ever seem happy or content or was he bearing scars that were always impossible to conceal? Do you think that because he was a judge you, in later years, were interested in the law? Did you have any special friends that you recall from Munich or from your schools in Munich? Did any of them ever resurface in later life? And then what happened afterwards? What do you remember of the introduction and immersion into St. Paul's and the gradual mastering of the unfamiliar and the foreign language? It must have all seemed very odd and strange and lonely. Please tell us something about your life at Oxford, the start of the war, your work in the factory, events and people you remember from the war years. I'm sure there will be other questions – but these are the main ones.
Love, m

When writing my final letter to my father I had not thought to ask, 'When did you start dreaming in English?'

Like most children who, in their later years, relive aspects of their lives, my familial accounting is tinged with remorse. There are aspects of my younger self (which even now surface occasionally) that I loathe: bursts of temper; abrasive tendencies; insolence; an inclination to dwell on what is wrong rather than all that is right; impatience; a propensity to automatically be suspicious of others. The list goes on.

While I am less inclined than my parents to hide my private thoughts, I know I have inherited their reticence, their unease with conspicuous behaviour and my father's congenital shyness. It's too easy for others to mistake a capacity for performance with an outgoing nature. I always tend to sit towards the back of a meeting room or, as others jostle for pole position in group photographs, retreat to the outer fringes.

And so, reared in an atmosphere that contained the after-effects of two terrible wars, I imagine that, until I learned better, I unwittingly conveyed these to the third-degree victims – my wife and sons – who now also bear the scars and residues of horrors perpetrated generations ago and far away.

JONES THE JEW

ONE LEG OF MY JOURNEY back to the past began about twenty years ago, in London, when I was browsing the display table near the entrance to Hatchards bookshop in Piccadilly, and spotted *Austerlitz*, by W. G. Sebald. I had not read any of his works and quickly learned that Sebald had a voice and imagination different from anything I had previously encountered. Sebald died shortly after *Austerlitz* was published when, aged fifty-seven, he was struck by an aneurysm while driving near Norwich, in the east of England. He left behind a body of work that occupies territory between life and dreams, between the past and the present, between memories and photographs, between Britain and the aftermath of Nazi Europe. It is cloaked in solitude and loneliness – for Sebald was a German who spent a lifetime struggling to come to terms with his homeland. His books hover between dawns and twilights – the hours when the world emerges or recedes.

The principal character of *Austerlitz*, after whom the book is named, recalls how he was brought as a four-year-old from Prague on a Kindertransport train to Liverpool Street station where he was met by an austere couple, a vicar and his wife from North Wales. The boy was renamed Dafydd Elias, and subsequently raised in a small village. As an adult, having reverted to his original name, Austerlitz made his way back to the Czech Republic and, unable to detect the borders between the distortions of memory and fact, relived his life as a child. As I read *Austerlitz*, I came across the following passage recounting the memory of Dafydd Elias's boyhood in Wales:

> I had never heard of an Austerlitz before, and from the first I was convinced that no one else bore that name, no one in Wales, or in the Isles, or anywhere else in the world. And since I began investigating my own history some years ago, I have never in fact come upon another Austerlitz, not in the telephone books of London or Paris, Amsterdam or Antwerp.

Austerlitz reads much like an autobiography and, for me, like a once-removed second cousin to the history of my own family. Austerlitz was raised in Wales. Like my own father, Austerlitz's father was named Maximilian and, again like my father, Austerlitz went to Oxford and became an academic. Austerlitz's Oxford College, Oriel, is located between Merton, where my father studied, and Christ Church where, decades later, I was admitted. *Austerlitz* is so sensitively composed that I was shocked to discover that the author himself was the son of a man who had enlisted in the German Army in 1929, eagerly joined the Nazi party, participated in the invasion of Poland and served for the rest of the war. Sebald, it turns out, had been born and raised in a small town within brisk walking distance of Bühl-am-Alpsee, the village that played a large part in my life as a boy and occupies an even larger part of my memory.

As a boy in Wales, like the fictional Austerlitz, I had never heard of a Moritz other than my uncle's family in Manchester. There were none that I knew of in Cardiff and none that I had heard of in Wales. Once a year, when a new telephone directory landed on our doorstep, I immediately flipped the pages to the 'M' section, hoping that we would not be alone, that there would be another Moritz listed, that we would have company.

I did eventually come across many people named Moritz in a telephone book, but only much later in life. I found them in an online archive of the directories for Munich from the 1930s, which listed six people of our name, including a doctor, an innkeeper, a graduate student and a piano teacher. My grandfather was there, listed as Maximilian Moritz, and his telephone number was given as 37 23 47. The telephone had been installed to help my grandparents follow what my father once described as 'the latest developments'. The same number was repeated in the directories for 1938 and 1939. In 1940, there was no longer a listing.

When, during a lunch in San Jose, California, in 2001, the First Minister of Wales asked, 'What's a nice Jewish boy like you doing in Silicon Valley?', my skin shrivelled and all my feelings about being Jewish and different from others in Wales in the 1960s came flooding back. He posed the question as a conversation opener for a discussion with him and other members of a Welsh delegation about the mysteries of Silicon Valley. He used pauses in the conversation to ask me why there were no great Jewish rugby players and why I, as the son of Jews, had not become a doctor.

Later still, dwelling on his questions, I couldn't help but wonder whether part of the reason a nice Jewish boy like me was in Silicon Valley was that, while I was growing up, my schoolmates, their parents, my teachers, the shopkeepers, the man who hired me to deliver newspapers, our dentist and doctor and the people my parents had hired – once they had sufficient money to do so – to hang wallpaper, or tend to the garden, or replace the roof tiles, or repair their cars, had all been asking themselves (for, on the whole, they were too diplomatic, too restrained, and too tactful to say it out loud), one of two questions, 'What's a nice Jewish boy like you doing in Wales?' or, 'Moritz. What sort of a name is that then?'

These people were, for the most part, Anglican, Protestant, Methodist or Presbyterian in a country that, at the time, was far from multicultural. A few, and they were also considered oddities (but not as odd as the Jews), were Catholics or Quakers. In Britain in the 1960s a first name was known as a 'Christian' name. My schoolmates were called Ian, Rosemary, Catherine, Evan, Hugh, Harry, Rhys, Gareth, Morgan, Robert, Hywel, Sandra, Felicity, Sian and Dewi. They were certainly never known as Mordecai ben Aharon ha Levi – which is what my own name is in Hebrew. Moritz was so much of a marker that I sometimes used to say that my family came from Switzerland since, at the time, it seemed to me that there was only one thing worse than being Jewish in Wales, and that was being German in Wales.

The local shopkeepers also had thoroughly Welsh names. The tobacconist's belonged to Miss Morgan (its interior guarded by a taxidermized black bear clutching a collection box for the Salvation Army between its ossified paws). Two of the nearby shops (one with a small post office counter and the other a general store) were each operated by a Mr Williams – one known as Mr Williams the Top and the other Mr Williams the Bottom. And in between Mr Williams the Top and Mr Williams the Bottom were the greengrocer, Mr Bowen, and the chemist, Mr Thomas. Years later, I was at a dinner with an editor of an American business magazine whose wife, to my surprise, was born in Pontypridd, about twelve miles from where I grew up. After moving to Wales, her father, whose last name had been Rabinowitz, decided it would help him assimilate if it was changed to Jones. Thereafter he was known as 'Jones the Jew'.

The distance between being a Jew in Wales and an Anglican, Protestant, Methodist, Presbyterian, Catholic or Quaker in Wales was illustrated by a wooden panel, topped with a small electric light that was always illuminated, in the chamber of the synagogue to which my parents belonged. Tidy gilt lettering marched across this panel, listing the names and hometowns of the relatives of the congregants murdered during the Shoah: Bortstieber, Cohn, Epstein, Folkmann, Gottschalk, Gross, Gunz, Hersch, Hornung, Kamerase, Karpf, Kotlan, Magid, Mandler, Mayer, Pinkus, Polak, Riemer, Rosenthal, Schindler, Seidner, Silberschatz, Stach, Steidler, Stoger, Ullmann, Weil, Wiznitzer, Wurm and Zander. They were from many of the places from which the Nazis had deported Jews: Brod, Vienna, Brussels, Breslau, Brno, Prague, Žilina, Berlin, Fischach, Frankfurt am Main, Munich, Ingolstadt, Hamburg, Enschede, Jarosław, Brunswick, Bleijerheide, Tarnów, Stříbro, Klatovy, Weiden, Nuremberg, Aachen, Brotzen, Cologne and Trebnitz.

A few of the Jews in this converted chapel had changed their names. An optician named Rosenberg had become Mr Montrose. Mr Grunebaum, who ran a men's clothing shop for his father-in-law, became Mr Greenwood. As if, with their foreign accents that no form of anglicised name would ever conceal, they, or any of us, were going to deceive the people in Cardiff about who we were or where we came from. We were Jews. My family even advertised the fact that we were the only Jews on the block by the mezuzah pinned to the right-hand side of our front door. We were Jews and we were living in plain sight. My friends did not have grannies and grandpas with names like Josef, Mendel, Fritz, Fanny, Sigmund, Emil, Gertrude, Siegfried, Gustav, Pavel, Zdenka, Erna, Lieselotte, Karoline, Mariska, Judis, Regina, Herz, Moshe, Heinrich, Elas, Leopold, Bona, Grete. They called their grandmothers Gran or Nan and their grandfathers Gramps. Not Oma. Not Opa. And definitely none of them had an Opa like mine whose name, when spoken, seemed like a girl's – Salli.

The First Minister's question transported me across the ocean and the decades. Being a Jew in Wales where every slight, though small or unintended or inconsequential and rarely delivered with real malice, nonetheless reverberated within me. Finding a swastika carved on the inside of the lid of my wooden school desk while I was in elementary school. Or the high school English class where, when we were made to read from *The Merchant of Venice*, the teacher amused himself by assigning me to play the part of Shylock and the other Jewish boy the role of Tubal.

The experiences that lodged the deepest were the Church of England services that marked the start of each school day. That was when the handful of Jewish students, sequestered during the prayers in a nearby room, could hear the fullthroated renditions of 'Christ Triumphant, Ever Reigning'. After the singing stopped, we did not sidle into the back of the hall. We were paraded down the aisle to take our seats in the front as if the head teacher was saying to the other boys, 'Here come the circumcised.'

In my last year at high school, after I had been appointed head boy – one of those positions that doesn't exist in American high schools – I had to stand on the stage during these assemblies alongside the senior teachers. As the hymns rang forth and as the prayers were read, I often looked at the school organist who was seated directly beneath us. He was a Welsh speaker who taught English, lived with his mother, and was completely incapable of quieting the classroom titters as he struggled to explain the mysteries and beauty of *Paradise Lost*. Despite his diffidence, as his feet skittered across the organ's pedals playing the melodies that he knew by heart, he would fasten me with his gaze and stick his tongue between his lips as if to say, 'You're a Jew and I know it.'

LABOR OMNIA VINCIT

SOMETIMES WHEN I WAKE in the middle of the night and want to read, I move to our guest bedroom where we have hung a collection of etchings, dry points and oil paintings made by artists commissioned by Kenneth Clark, Director of the National Gallery, to present a portrait of Britain during the two world wars. A picture of a man, painted in 1946, hangs above the bed – the figure is seated, wearing a pale-green uniform and a khaki beret tilted to one side of his head. The man is relaxed, his hands folded gently on his lap, and he has a wistful stare – the gaze of someone imagining a place warmer than the one in which he is confined, as befits an Italian prisoner of war cooped up in a camp in the north of England.

There are other images: of biplanes with open-air cockpits banking over the patchwork fields of Flanders; of drenched soldiers, their shoulders hunched, marching doggedly in the rain; of shattered houses in Arras with roofs staved in from shelling; of a desolate straight road undulating between bare fields towards a high horizon; and of a bandaged soldier screaming in agony as a surgeon tries to remove a shell fragment from his skull. A sketch shows three figures, wrapped in blankets, sheltering from the bombing of London in an Underground station, and there is also a stark etching of a ship in dry-dock being painted in camouflage. But invariably my eyes come to rest on one of the few splashes of colour – a gouache by Graham Sutherland, of the mouth of a blast furnace, which captures the ferocious noise and intense heat generated inside a steel mill operated by the Guest, Keen and Baldwins Iron & Steel Works. The flames of puce, magenta, violet, orange and yellow that streak from the mouth of the furnace resemble a coiled tongue springing from a beast of the underworld. The work was made in Cardiff, eleven years before I was born, in a factory whose towers I could see from my bedroom window.

The fathers of some of my schoolmates worked at Guest Keen which, in the 1960s, became part of British Steel. The mill drew most of its payroll from the other side of Newport Road – the unofficial dividing line between those in Cardiff who, unless they were exceptionally lucky, rarely had a chance to advance, and those of us with hope, living less than a mile away, near an orphanage and local landmark named the Home for Waifs and Strays.

The borderline that separated me from the other side of Newport Road were rows of red-brick houses along streets named for imperial triumphs. Our own street celebrated the victory at Waterloo while others commemorated battles at Kimberley, Mafeking, Agincourt, Marlborough, Blenheim, Alma, Melrose, Balaclava, Trafalgar. At the far end of Waterloo Road lay a world from which – had I been born to different parents and raised in a different manner – I would not have ended up in California, or at Sequoia, or participated in the formative stages of some of the greatest technology companies of the past century. One thousand yards was the distance between what became possible and what would always have been impossible – between the life as a millworker and the world beyond.

On the far side of Newport Road, the man of the house drew a wage packet, not a salary; wore overalls to work, not a suit and tie; his accent was Welsh, not English; his home was rented, not owned; he smoked cigarettes, not a pipe; he ate white bread, not rye, let alone challah or pumpernickel; his newspaper was the *Daily Mirror*, the *Sun* or the *Daily Express*, not *The Times*, the *Guardian* or the *Daily Telegraph*; the television was tuned to ITV, not the BBC; the unheated living room was called the parlour and used only for mourning or at Christmas; his summer holiday was taken in Tenby or Saundersfoot, not Bavaria; and he left school at fourteen.

Whenever a fresh wind blows through the open window of this bedroom in San Francisco, I pull the duvet tighter and the gouache with the mouth of the blast furnace transports me to the late 1960s, to the first floor of a state-run school in Cardiff. I am sitting in a classroom with about thirty boys wearing dark shoes, grey trousers, grey sweaters, white shirts, ties with cerise diagonal stripes on a dark background and blazers whose breast pocket is adorned with a triangular crest, topped by a single chariot wheel supporting a pair of wings and garlanded with the motto *Labor omnia vincit*. (Now, when I read it, this seems almost like the Latin version of the phrase the Nazis hung above the gates of many of their concentration camps: *Arbeit macht frei*.)

The windows to the north look over a two-tier playground where we congregate during breaks when weather permits. The southerly windows offer a view of a rugby field, frequently either waterlogged or frozen, over which two grey concrete towers, shaped like monstrous salt and pepper shakers, vent steam generated by the adjoining power station. On this rugby field, during World War II, barrage balloons, pumped with hydrogen, were tethered and floated high in the air in an effort to prevent the German aeroplanes from making accurate bomb drops; it was also where three of the young women in charge of this equipment were killed in an air raid while a fourth, with her left arm and shoulder blown off and her face gruesomely disfigured, crawled from the inferno to tell of what happened.

In the room overlooking the rugby field, the teacher tries to teach Latin declensions to boys for whom the prospect of the language of a Catholic mass as a gateway to the Romance languages holds all the appeal of cleaning encrusted mud from the spokes of a bicycle wheel. This teacher, then in his early sixties, was a lifelong servant of the school. He had enrolled as a pupil and, but for his years at university and war duty, spent his entire career journeying by bus every day, teaching five different disciplines to an advanced level, and shepherding the students whose families could afford it on two-week trips to distant Europe over the Easter holidays. He provided career guidance, patiently conducted rehearsals after the end of the day for the plays staged each year before Christmas, and decades earlier, had taught many of the ninety-four boys who, in 1940, aged between sixteen and eighteen, were conscripted and sent to places from which they never returned and whose fates he relayed in the 957-page school history he wrote in retirement. His former students had been: killed on reconnaissance for Coastal Command over Heligoland; killed at El-Alamein; killed in a bombing attack on a convoy near Sierra Leone; killed on night operations; killed over Hanover; killed over Kiel; killed in an air crash in Egypt; lost in a raid over Munich; lost off

Bari; lost in the Aegean; lost in the Norwegian campaign; lost over the Bay of Biscay; had died from wounds at St Valery; died from wounds in Singapore; died of beriberi while a prisoner of war building the Siam–Burma railway; drowned in the bombing of a Japanese prisoner-of-war ship; drowned during the North Africa landings. In the 1960s, the echoes of World War II were still fresh enough that my schoolfriends and I would occasionally burst out and sing,

> *Hitler has only got one ball,*
> *Göring has two but very small,*
> *Himmler is rather sim'lar,*
> *But poor old Goebbels has no balls at all.*

The school, a victim of changing demographics, was eventually demolished in the 1990s and its recreational fields replaced by a quilt of neat yellow-brick houses with sharp-peaked roofs dotted with grey satellite dishes and recycling bins in the front yards. The roads in this small development were named after former teachers of the school, which is how my Latin master became memorialised as a street sign – Foster Drive. The three vital accoutrements for any man, according to the teacher who lent his name to Foster Drive, were: a short back and sides; a strong pair of walking boots; and the ability to ballroom dance. It was this same Mr Foster whom I called on every time I returned to Wales to see my parents and at the end of each year, he would send me an aerogram filled with his tiny script, which described visits from former pupils, his progress on a book about the theatre in Cardiff and the declining health of his wife. His final airmail to me was found on his kitchen table after he died and sent to California. The coldest hour of the day, he had once explained, was always the hour before dawn, and none had been colder than the hour he had spent in the dark waiting for the order that took his company of Welch Fusiliers across the River Rhine in March 1945 – near the little town in the Rhineland that my mother had once called home and which Salli, my maternal grandfather, referred to as his *heimat* – a German word that means 'hometown' but whose direct translation fails to capture the emotional consequences of being deeply rooted in a place that you feel you understand and where you sense you belong.

YOU WANT IT DARKER

ONE AFTERNOON I WAS WORKING from Borgo Pignano, which had been closed because of the pandemic, when I had an urge to drive to Florence – to Tempio Maggiore, the city's main synagogue. I wanted to attend a Kol Nidrei service, which ushers in Yom Kippur – the most important day in the Jewish calendar. Tempio Maggiore, with its noble turquoise dome and architectural echoes of Romanesque, Byzantine and Moorish influences, could be lifted straight from some of the paintings David Bomberg made in the early 1920s of the rooftops of Jerusalem. Twenty-five years earlier, during a vacation when our sons were still occupying a double stroller, I had rushed to Florence for a Friday evening service, leaving Harriet in our summer rental. The memory of that evening made me think of two other synagogue visits – during both of which I had burst into tears. I am hard pressed to think of any other occasion – including the deaths of my parents and some of my closest friends, or indeed the births of our children – when I have cried.

The first: I was eleven years old, in 1966, sitting in the front row of what was then Manchester's grandest synagogue. My father and Ernest, my uncle, were presenting a scroll in memory of their parents, Max and Minnie. The congregation still observed many of the traditions of the great German liberal synagogues: the men exchanging their bowler hats for yarmulkas as they entered the sanctuary; the women complimenting each other on their outfits; the rabbi – a tall, imposing man with an East London accent – presiding with a regal confidence while leaving the conduct of less important portions of the service to juniors. My uncle sat with his fellow beadles and officers of the synagogue in tails and top hat behind the rabbi.

The scroll presented that morning in Manchester had been read by the congregation of the sixteenth-century Pinkas Synagogue in Prague, which today is still surrounded by graves packed as tightly as porcupine quills. The scroll had been one of 1,564 pillaged by the Nazis between 1939 and 1945 from the Jewish communities of Bohemia, Moravia and Slovakia. After the war, it had fallen into the custody of the Czechoslovak government. In the early 1960s, these scrolls were transferred to London, including the one acquired by my father and uncle. The certificate accompanying what became known as the 'Moritz scroll' in the Manchester synagogue recorded that it was 'A permanent memorial to the martyrs from whose synagogues they come... to spread light as harbingers of future brotherhood on earth'. I remember thinking that the tinkling bells of the silver finials atop the rollers of the scroll rang in memory of the two people that stared from the wall of my parents' bedroom and broke into sobs. When my father enquired whether I was all right, I said that my knee hurt.

Back in Borgo Pignano, I had forgotten that the virus had closed Tempio Maggiore and as I started searching for links to virtual services in Florence, Siena, Rome, Milan and Turin, I realised that borders no longer mattered and Kol Nidrei would be screened for the next eight or nine hours from the tiny Jewish congregations of Munich, Berlin and Frankfurt and from all the places of prayer of the Jewish diaspora –

Manchester, London, New York, Rio de Janeiro, Johannesburg and San Francisco, to name a few. And so, for several hours, I kept a window open on my computer and skated across time zones to listen to different interpretations of Kol Nidrei.

The opening prayer of Kol Nidrei was being sung across the globe by the Jews of Zoom, who were wearing rubber gloves and face masks and standing in front of the open arks of synagogues, cradling their Torahs. I have listened to the prayer's music on countless occasions. The melody first became a staple for the start of the eve of atonement in Otto von Bismarck's Berlin after it was scored by Max Bruch. The interpretation of Bruch's that most haunts me is not the version embedded on vinyl by Pablo Casals, or by Al Jolson, Neil Diamond or, more improbably, Perry Como or Johnny Mathis, but a recording made in the 1960s by the cellist Jacqueline du Pré with her husband Daniel Barenboim and the Israel Philharmonic Orchestra.

From the opening notes, the world seems to be closing in. Shadows, dark clouds and danger lurk but there are some short, sweet passages and to me these could form the soundtrack for some of the photographs I had uncovered in the cartons shipped from Britain – family picnics on summer days before a thunderstorm, boys taking a sled run just before nightfall, couples slumbering in deckchairs on a beach before the tide turns. But there is no escaping the sense of doom and melancholy after the last note sounds. It was this melody that the Jews of Zoom sang as they stood in New Orleans, Pensacola, Altadena, Denver, Huntsville and Tucson. Here was the melody – adapted, modified and refined for centuries from its roots in the itinerant Jewish communities of the lands that eventually became known as Germany before it became part of the liturgical fabric. This was one of the melodies that gave so much comfort to my father after he arrived in England. Synagogue was the one place that felt like home.

The second memory that was stirred up as I sat watching these Kol Nidrei services on Zoom from a Tuscan hilltop took place in Cardiff the year before my Bar Mitzvah, when I was permitted to accompany my father to Yizkor (the memorial service) – the most solemn part of the Yom Kippur holiday. The September days on which Yom Kippur fell were often hot, and the prayer chamber – bitterly cold for much of the year – was invariably stuffy and uncomfortable. In the hour before the start of the memorial service, children were banished to the social hall, every pew became full, and eventually there would always be some congregants who'd be left to stand at the rear of the seating in the balcony.

I had no idea what these congregants had endured or were recalling during each Yom Kippur. There were daughters and granddaughters of the dead who were now mothers and grandmothers themselves, sons and grandsons who were now fathers and grandfathers – many of whom were sobbing, or blowing their noses, or staring silently towards the ceiling. I do not remember my father showing any sign of emotion or ever mentioning what was passing through his mind as the rabbi, dressed in white to mark the solemnity of the holiday, recited the names of the concentration camps.

I did not grasp that these Jews – gathered in the converted Salem Welsh Baptist Chapel in South Wales – were the most recent casualties of fifteen centuries of brutal antisemitism: pogroms; inquisitions; banishments; dispossessions; murder. Nor did I know that the security and protection of the law offered to Jews by the UK was a gift that few other nations provided. The grief ran so deep, the anguish so profound, that the weight of these emotions felt heavy enough to sink that former Baptist chapel beneath the earth's crust. Even now I remember where they sat: the woman who, according to my mother, in the middle of the night put the nightmares of the Shoah aside by emptying her dishwasher and washing its contents by hand; the two cousins who had fought for the Irgun, an underground movement that smuggled refugees into Palestine and conducted assassinations; an elfin dandy who was a Member of Parliament but only attended on the High Holy Days and who had fought to decriminalise homosexuality and who, in his later years, wrote a book about fellatio; 'Montrose', the optician, whose wife had hidden in Holland throughout the war but, unlike Anne Frank, had escaped detection. There was a man who, with his brother, built the largest leather watch-strap company in Europe. Another made artificial Christmas trees. One couple ran a deli as their parents had done in Austria. There was a man who made rolling garage doors until he killed himself; another, who distributed chickens to the curry parlours of South Wales, also performed the ritual washing of the bodies of the dead. There were brothers who distributed Swiss sewing machines, and several doctors, including an anaesthetist who pioneered the use of ventilators for children with polio.

The Kaddish, the prayer for the dead, always had special meaning on Yom Kippur. As a boy I knew that the Kaddish was not a prayer for children, or at least not for children like me, whose parents were both alive. I knew that the prayer did not contain the word 'death' but did contain a plea for peace.

After the father of a boy in my school had died, a junior rabbi was summoned from the Orthodox synagogue to recite the Kaddish in the classroom, in which the handful of Jewish students were gathered while the familiar sound of Christian hymns drifted from the morning assembly. I had stood in silence, watching with envy while the cleric – wrapped in his prayer shawl – and the boy mumbled the words of the prayer. I had not known whether I was more eager for, or more terrified of, the day when I too would say the Kaddish.

Now, when I hear Leonard Cohen's 'You Want It Darker', the line 'Magnified, santified/ be thy holy name' always makes me think of the Kaddish. This refrain is the same as the one that was chanted by the Protestant, Methodist and Baptist students in the adjacent assembly hall at my school as they recited the Lord's Prayer, 'Our father, who art in heaven / Hallowed be thy name / Thy kingdom come / Thy will be done.' At the end of 'You Want It Darker', Cohen sings the response Abraham is supposed to have given when God calls on him to sacrifice his son Isaac, 'Hineni, hineni / I'm ready, my Lord.' *Hineni* is Hebrew for 'here I am'.

Hineni also happens to be the title of a book, published in 2012 in Wales, of photographs and recollections of some of those very people who, fifty years before, had stared at the ceiling, wiping their eyes during those memorial services in the former Baptist chapel, but who were now nearing the end of their lives. The book had been assembled by a team of volunteers and my mother stares out from one of its pages – she and her companions providing evidence of the resilience of the human spirit and the power of defiance.

And it is *Hineni* that reminds me of a party held at the

Newark Public Library to celebrate the eightieth birthday of Philip Roth, whom I had first encountered when I was a student at the University of Pennsylvania, and who subsequently became a friend. The birthday ceremony opened with a salutation from the local high school's marching band, included tributes from several distinguished writers, and concluded with Roth reading a chapter from *Sabbath's Theater* (published in 1995 by Houghton Mifflin), a work haunted by death. The hardback cover of the book is illustrated by an Otto Dix painting from the netherworld of the Weimar Republic. It is a book about the reaction of its subject – a profane adulterer – to a world in which everything is perishable, and in which everyone whom one loves will return to dust.

For me, *Sabbath's Theater*, rather like the Kol Nidrei prayer, connects different eras and places. It illustrates the gulf between growing up in Wales, with its tiny Jewish population, and being raised, like Roth, as a third-generation immigrant in a country an ocean removed from the immediate proximity of Nazi terror. Roth's book, about the depraved and libidinous Mickey Sabbath, like many of his works, draws heavily on the author's own heritage. By the time Roth was growing up in the 1930s and 40s in a Jewish neighbourhood in New Jersey, his family was firmly rooted in America. His parents spoke with American accents, and Roth was reared in a part of the US where there were millions of Jews and where the descendants of immigrants, with all their 'tribal instincts', far outnumbered those who had arrived a century or two earlier. The Jews, the Italians, the Irish, the Germans and the Poles were Americans too, even if, for some of the entitled WASP citizens, they would always be hyphenated Americans.

I felt the gulf between Cardiff, and Wales – with its tiny

Jewish population – and Roth's Weequahic in the passage that he read during his eightieth-birthday celebration at Newark Library, which described a visit to the cemetery where Mickey Sabbath's grandparents, parents, brother, aunts, uncles and cousins were buried. Even the New Jersey cemeteries were full of Jews and, in Mickey Sabbath's case (and, for that matter, Roth's too), Jews from his own family. By contrast, the portion of the cemetery in Cardiff set aside for Jews was small. When I was a boy, we had no family member, not even a distant one, whose bones rested in that graveyard. Today, I cannot help but think that the absence there of any headstones bearing the names Moritz, Rath, Gompertz or Mayer (the original last names of my four grandparents) emphasised the fact that we didn't belong and gave rise to questions such as that posed previously by the First Minister of Wales, what *was* a nice Jewish boy like me doing there when our family's bones and ashes lay elsewhere?

Roth's Sabbath wanders among the headstones, reading their names. Quite by coincidence, the first four words read by Sabbath as he strolls through the graveyard are 'Our beloved mother Minnie' – the very name by which my father's murdered mother had been known. At the end of this meditative ramble, Sabbath places stones on the graves, which, in the Jewish tradition, convey a message of love and recollection from the living to the departed. The stones signify life. As he reached the last sentence of his reading, Roth looked down from the dais at his audience, and spoke three final words, 'Here I am.' *Hineni.*

★

Five years later, I watched Roth's casket being lowered into his grave in the cemetery of a small liberal arts college on the banks of the Hudson. He had chosen not to be interred with his relatives in New Jersey, but next to souls with whom his ghost could converse. As people drifted away from the gravesite – where friends had read passages from his work – towards lunch at the house of the college president, I stopped at another headstone. It was that of Hannah Arendt – a Jewish scholar born in Germany in 1906, who had studied with Martin Heidegger, the Nazis' pet philosopher, and who had been his lover before fleeing to New York, where she rose to eminence.

By the time I came to be standing at her headstone, Arendt had been lying for decades in the earth to which Roth had just been committed, and upon whose casket I had scattered a trowel of dirt. But in 1961, she had been sent by the *New Yorker* to Jerusalem to cover the trial of Adolf Eichmann, one of the architects of the 'final solution', and had written a famous book, published in 1963 by Viking Press, based on that reportage – *Eichmann in Jerusalem: A Report on the Banality of Evil*. One of the thousands of exhibits entered as evidence in the trial was a photograph of my grandfather Max's brother – my great-uncle, Oskar Moritz. It showed him standing near his cousin, Mira, at the rear of the bus that took them on the first stage of the journey to their death.

Oskar Moritz and Mira Marx, departing from their last bus journey, 25 April 1942, Würzburg

COUNTING SWASTIKAS

THE QUEST TO MAKE SENSE of my past took its first tentative steps not during the pandemic, but at the start of the 1970s when I was a boy and my maternal grandparents, Salli and Louise Rath, were still alive. At the time I had stopped after I had exhausted the memories and knowledge of my immediate family, because I knew nothing about genealogy or how to conduct research, and because I had plenty of other distractions. For over fifty years I have kept the results of my investigation tucked inside a grey folder that has accompanied me to every apartment and house in which I have lived since leaving Wales. There are about forty sheets of crudely assembled paper marked with the copperplate gothic script of my grandmother, my father's readily legible hand and my clumsy jottings. One sheet has eight thin, horizontal pencil lines spaced three quarters of an inch apart. Roman numerals inscribed in blue ballpoint to the left of each line – from I to VIII – signify a preceding generation of my father's family, tracking people whose last names were Sommer, Mayer, Fulda, Carlebach, Stern and Wolff, and who spawned a family named Moritz. A similar page traces my mother's side of the family. I was punctilious about capturing the raw data for my investigation – name, date of birth, place of birth, name of spouse, date of marriage, and names and birthdates of children. But most of all, although my grandmother and father were unaware of my ghoulish interest, I really wanted to find out when and where each of these people had died.

Other boys might have collected stamps or trading cards, but I was counting swastikas. I was not curious or mature enough to find out who these people were or where they lived and worked. I did not know enough to ask whether they had finished school or attended university. I did not know if they sat behind a desk, stood behind a counter, or followed a horse across a field. I did not know whether they were upstanding citizens or heinous villains. I did not know if their marriages were happy, how they amused themselves, or if they were plagued by ill health. I did not know if they read newspapers, whether they were regular synagogue attendees or harboured any political leanings. I had no clue about the lives they may have led. I didn't care. And I also didn't care too much about earlier generations who had expired long before the Nazis came to power. I was cataloguing death of a particular kind. This is why, in my juvenile and macabre way, I marked the knowledge I sought most with a little swastika drawn in red crayon. 1941, 1942, 1943. Belsen, Dachau, Theresienstadt, Sobibor, Auschwitz – the places where my ancestors had been murdered.

According to Jewish tradition, on 20 September 1954, eight days after I was born, in the small dining room of my parents' house in Wales, which was then heated by a coal fire, I was circumcised, and among many others of my family:

Max Moritz, my grandfather, would have been 72.
Minnie Moritz, my grandmother, would have been 62.
Oskar Moritz, my great uncle, would have been 67.
Rosa Moritz, my great aunt, would have been 61.

Freddy Moritz, my first cousin once removed,
   would have been 33.
Andreas Rath, my first cousin once removed,
   would have been 76.
Rudolf Bruch, my first cousin once removed,
   would have been 54.
Auguste Bruch, my first cousin once removed,
   would have been 53.
Ilse Bruch, my second cousin, would have been 22.
Herman Moses, my first cousin once removed,
   would have been 76.
Bertha Carlebach, my great-grandmother, would
   have been 85.
Friedericke Cohn, my aunt, would have been 64.

Yet by the third Monday of September 1954, Max Moritz, Minnie Moritz, Oskar Moritz, Rosa Moritz, Freddy Moritz, Andreas Rath, Rudolf Bruch, Auguste Bruch, Ilse Bruch, Herman Moses, Bertha Carlebach, Friedericke Cohn and several dozen more distant relatives had been slaughtered and the few family members who had survived were hundreds, if not thousands, of miles from their homes – in Paris, France; Vevey, Switzerland; Santiago, Chile; Montevideo, Uruguay; Hartford, Connecticut; New York, New York; Eugene, Oregon; Dunedin, New Zealand; Los Angeles, California; and São Paulo, Brazil.

And I had just lost my foreskin.

LIVES IN PHOTOGRAPHS

INSIDE MY FIRST PHOTOGRAPH ALBUM, with its soft, faded red cover, are two small black-and-white, deckle-edged photographs glued to stiff black paper. These are photographs of the market square of Miltenberg, Bavaria, a town on a bend in the River Main. I took the pictures as an eight-year-old boy on a hot July day in 1963, the year Cliff Richard appeared in *Summer Holiday*, the Russians launched the first female cosmonaut into space, and the Mercury capsule flew for the last time. It was also the year I used my pocket money to buy my first forty-five, as well as the year in which, on the third Saturday of November, the BBC Home Service carried the news to South Wales that John Fitzgerald Kennedy was dead.

After I took these photographs, my father led us through the town and up a hill to an old iron gate that marked the entrance to an overgrown cemetery with crooked headstones inscribed in Hebrew. I had no sense then, or even now, of the emotions and memories stirred up for my father by the visit to this small town where his father, Max, had been born and where, as a boy, he used to come to visit his grandparents and other relatives. But I remember, as intensely as if I had been there a moment ago, my father wrestling with the gate, and the long grass tickling my shins as we wandered among the graves.

Miltenberg, 1920s

Ernest, my uncle, was more willing to relive the past. 'It took me a generation before I could visit Miltenberg without feeling haunted,' he wrote in his family-circulated memoir, published in the 1990s. 'The town was there, as it had been for centuries, unchanged, almost untouched by time: its rose-colored sandstone buildings; its half-timbered gables, its castle on the hill, its walls, gates and towers – they had all survived intact. But its Jews were gone, murdered or scattered to the four corners of the earth.'

Almost sixty years later, I found an image of the market square in Miltenberg from the late 1920s in one of the albums shipped from my mother's house in Wales, which was almost identical to – but far crisper than – the one I had taken in 1963. By then, I had already found on the internet a photograph of a small leather-goods shop in Miltenberg showing Max's brother, my great-uncle, Oskar, standing on worn stone steps in front of a heavy wooden door and an open window, framed by white shutters and a sill bearing four potted plants, and topped by a sign that read 'Lederhandlung, S. Moritz & Sohn'. He is flat-footed in a three-piece suit with a watch chain hooked to his waistcoat and a jacket with sleeves that are too long. He is balding, has grey hair at the temples, a high forehead reflecting the sun, round glasses – a little like the reflection I see when I shave. Sitting on the stoop beside him is a young man in shirt sleeves with blond hair, drawing a scene of the small town with its wood-framed houses and steeply raked streets.

A Brazilian friend, following the Portuguese custom of addressing people by their last names, sometimes calls me Moritz. Whenever he does, I think about *Max and Moritz*, a darkly humorous illustrated book about the pranks and adventures of a couple of boys, published in Germany in the

Oskar Moritz, Miltenberg, 1920s

1860s, that remains popular. This book title always makes my mind hop to Oskar's brother, my paternal grandfather, who, at birth, was named Marx Moritz – both, as it happened, common last names in Germany. This led to so much confusion that he later changed his name to Maximilian.

The man born as Marx Moritz, who became Maximilian (Max) Moritz and was murdered as Maximilian Israel Moritz (after the Nazis insisted that every Jewish man and woman take Israel and Sara as their middle names), is one of two figures who were pictured in a framed black-and-white photograph that hung on the wall opposite my parents' bed. The photograph of Max and Minnie, taken on their wedding day in 1920, was the only picture in the room, which had windows that rattled every time a bus passed by. It dangled, permanently askew, from a single picture hook until shortly after my mother, at the age of ninety-four, was carried from the room on a stretcher. When the photograph was removed, it revealed a patch of wallpaper that looked like a splash of sunlight. Max, like Oskar, was also balding, jowly and plump but in the photograph wore a stiff, high-necked collar and bow tie and had a small moustache; Minnie was petite, had tightly drawn dark hair and wore a demure dress. My entire sense of Max and Minnie was derived from this formal portrait. They were dressed for another age – alien and distant. The only person in our immediate household who had known them was my father, although I doubt whether he had really known them either, since he fled Germany before he was of an age where Max would have felt safe confiding in him his private thoughts or memories. Besides my father, I only knew six people who had known Max and Minnie. There was Ernest, my uncle; Minnie's sister, Helene (known as Leni); and four nieces and nephews. Those were the only members of my father's family who had escaped to Britain. Except for my father remarking that a particular day marked the birthday of Max or Minnie, or their wedding anniversary, I don't remember him ever discussing them. He never did know the dates or exact circumstances of their deaths.

It was my father who turned the photograph I took on that hot summer day in 1963 of the market square in Miltenberg into substance. For reasons of economy, my father developed his own black-and-white film. At night, he would convert the bathroom into a makeshift darkroom by drawing the curtains tightly, rigging a blanket over the door, assembling a second-hand enlarger and projector, and putting a couple of emulsion trays – in which he mixed developing and fixing fluid – on a shelf. He dried the printed images by pegging them to a cord strung over the bathtub and, after waking the following morning, would immediately inspect his handiwork. I would now do much to understand how he reacted as the images of the little town where he had spent his holidays visiting his own grandparents, and uncles, aunts, and cousins, re-emerged thirty years later in an emulsion tray in Wales. Maybe they made him wistful. Maybe they tore him to shreds.

Most of my family, both in Bavaria and the Rhineland, were descendants of the *Schutzjude*, or 'protected Jews' – people beholden to the landowners of rural estates. For the 900 years before my grandparents were born, the Jews of Germany had been perennial scapegoats. They were expelled in the fifteenth century, returned a couple of hundred years later and again fled for their lives in the seventeenth century during the Thirty Years War. The *Schutzjude* were forced to pay taxes whenever they moved to a new region; obliged to provide preferential terms to their landlords whenever they traded cattle or horses; often paid rent for their housing in tallow (rendered ox fat which, like wax, was used for candles); and were forbidden from trading on Sundays or Christian feast days. They were also bound by a law that restricted the right to grant property to the firstborn child, to prevent Jews of subsequent generations from owning property and insinuating themselves in the country.

The birth and marriage records of my family peter out in the mid-eighteenth century. The earlier generations' ancestors, assuming they lived in one of the German states, would at various times have been ordered to wear special badges on their clothes; forbidden from holding public office; banned from walking on public streets; and frequently had their books burned. They would have been prohibited from eating with Christians, entertaining Christians in their homes, employing Christians, engaging in intercourse with Christians, marrying Christians, acting as doctors for Christians, inviting Christians to their celebrations, representing Christians in courts of law, and acting as witnesses against Christians. They would also not have been allowed to draw up legal contracts, to buy or rent property to Christians, or to exclude Christian descendants from their wills, let alone receive academic degrees, or become lawyers, druggists, notaries, painters or architects.

All these ancestors were a world removed from the 'Court Jews', whose trading and credit expertise, together with their connections in foreign countries, was valued by the leaders of the four kingdoms, six archdukedoms, five duchies, seven princedoms and three free cities that made up Greater Germany and who called on them to finance wars, import precious commodities or engage in diplomatic undertakings.

When Max Moritz and Salli Rath, my mother's father, were born, overt antisemitism was still ingrained throughout much of Europe. It wasn't until the passage of the Constitution of 1872 that the last barriers to free movement for Jews in the German Empire were swept away. In Rome, for example, the Vatican continued confining the city's 4,700 Jews within a few dank and squalid streets while making them pay their taxes and foot the bill for the church officials who supervised the ghetto, where they also conducted missionary work. At the time of Max and Salli's births, Miltenberg and Kempen's Jewish communities amounted to about 3 per cent of their respective town's overwhelmingly Catholic population. Their families eked out livings as travelling salesmen selling leather to cobblers, and, in some cases, furs, or as small-time shopkeepers, cattle dealers and butchers – *kaufmanns, geschäftsmann, viehhändler* and *metzger*.

I'm forever astonished by the thought that this would have been my world had I been born just three generations earlier – isolated, circumscribed and bereft of opportunity save for the trades permissible for Jews: leaving school at fourteen, slaughtering a chicken every Friday, marrying a woman from a nearby town or village, and perhaps hammering nails into shoes, hawking furs and leather, selling cheap jewellery or trading cattle while closely adhering to the constraints of Jewish ritual and the Jewish calendar. This was the world into which both Max and Oskar were born and it came to feel even closer after I uncovered a photograph of Max with his mother, Karoline Sommer, a woman born in 1853, for whom the boundaries of life probably did not extend much beyond where her legs or a horse-drawn cart could carry her. She died in 1938 – just sixteen years before I was born.

Max Moritz and his mother, Karoline, 1920s

Some other Jewish small-town merchants and peddlers managed to leave Germany in the mid-eighteenth century for the US. I know many of their descendants in San Francisco, where the current generation of the Haas, Hellman, Goldman, Koshland, Bransten, Dinkelspiel, Strauss, Stern, Steinhardt and Fleishhacker families are the beneficiaries of the wit, ingenuity and drive of their immigrant forbears. The San Francisco hospitals, aquariums, clinics, auditoriums, museums and libraries that bear their names, along with the large number of civic organisations that they support, leave me hoping that, had my German ancestors also left Bavaria and the Rhineland and settled here, they too would have been as generous towards the place they eventually called home. But my family stayed in Germany.

Though the treatment of Jews in the Germany in which Max and Salli were born had been improved by the lingering after-effects of Napoleon's extension of civil liberties into his conquered territories, they still must have felt as foreign – or perhaps more foreign – than I did in the Wales of the 1960s. Even after Bismarck had unified Germany – a decade or so before their births – the German political model was but a shadow of the parliamentary or republican systems that had emerged in the UK and US: the Kaiser retained the power to appoint the head of government, the Reich Chancellor; the powers of the two-chamber diet were circumscribed; and the bureaucracy was held firmly in the clamp of civilians and soldiers drawn from a landed aristocracy that was suffused with inherited prejudices. Germany, or the German regions, had always been under the thumb of authoritarians – whether the names were Frederick the Great or Otto von Bismarck. Jews were excluded.

NON-ARYAN MEMBERS

THE MAN NAMED MARX MORITZ, who changed his name to Max Moritz and was murdered as Maximilian Israel Moritz, was the first and only member of my father's immediate family to receive a higher education and was, as far as I can tell, the first to break free of the confines of a small-town existence. In 1908, he qualified as a lawyer. After four years cooling his heels in an outpost of the German judiciary, he became the third public prosecutor in Memmingen, a modest-sized town about seventy-five miles west of Munich. He was almost immediately blackballed from one of the town's popular social clubs and word of his exclusion was picked up by the local newspapers, one of which editorialised sympathetically that 'Even in the twentieth century, some portion of "better society" still pays homage to peculiar views.' Although Max's judicial personnel file was stocked with letters of support, he was shuffled off to Ansbach, near Nuremberg, to avoid embarrassing the local hierarchy. Some months later, he was felled by a severe fungal infection, plunged into a deep depression and was granted three months of medical leave.

Shortly afterwards, in 1915, thirty-two-year-old Max was called to take his place in the 1st Reserves of the 6th Bavarian Infantry Regiment in Fürth, becoming one of several members from both sides of my family who fought for the Germans during World War I. The men went as soldiers, the women, including both of my grandmothers, served as nurses. All four of my grandparents lost close relatives during the war. Perhaps Max went reluctantly. Perhaps he, like so many on both sides of the four-year war that devoured a generation, thought that the war would be brief. Maybe, like many of the 100,000 German Jews who fought for the Kaiser, Max was eager to show that he was a true German – assimilated, loyal, willing and prepared to demonstrate gratitude and allegiance to a country that had lowered some of the barriers that had confined them to the fringes.

Some 12,000 German Jews died in World War I, and around 7,000, including Max, received an Iron Cross for bravery. But their service did not extinguish the prejudices. In 1916, Max was deployed to the trenches in the Vosges, a range of low mountains separating part of eastern France from Germany, and promoted, first to sergeant, then to platoon leader and finally to lieutenant. He was subsequently dispatched to the hell that was Verdun – the bloodiest battle of all the gruesome fights of the twentieth century. Verdun lasted for ten of the twelve months of 1916, and was fought along a front that, in normal conditions, could be walked in less than three hours. The town itself had no military value. It was chosen by the Germans, who were determined to bleed their enemy dry, because they knew the French would feel impelled to defend a town that had been a symbol of defiance against intruders for over 1,000 years. Two million five hundred thousand men were thrown into the battle, of whom 714,000 were killed, wounded or permanently disabled. Sixty million shells fell on the surrounding nine French villages over 300 days. By the time the subsequent snows arrived, the villages were declared 'dead for France'. For the soldiers on both sides, life was reduced to a perilous existence in the muddy and frozen filth of the trenches, as depicted in the works of the British artist C. R. W. Nevinson, whose etchings and paintings provide a graphic commentary on the annihilation that took place.

During the Battle of Verdun, in which Max's regiment was almost eliminated, the German Army was investigating whether, as portions of the public and press alleged, Jews were shirking war service or profiteering. In a reference Max requested in the early 1930s to prove his worth to the Nazi-controlled judiciary, his army commanding officer, though struggling to express himself within the orthodoxies of Jewish stereotypes, expressed admiration for Max's conduct alongside much younger, less educated soldiers, and his willingness to volunteer for patrols. 'In accordance with his soldierly achievements,' the officer wrote, 'he should also have been proposed by me for promotion to officer. I only did not do so because I already had the attitude at that time that the officer corps must be free of non-Aryan members.' The officer wrote that Max had never shirked his duty and said, 'I confirm that he never tried to get any command outside the trenches which was usually the case with Jews.' He concluded, 'Particularly noteworthy is his modest demeanour, which is not common among Jews.'

The chasm between the loudly trumpeted smears and the reality of German Jewish participation in World War I sprang to life one night during the pandemic when Harriet and I were lighting Chanukah candles, while our two sons joined by Zoom. That same afternoon I had found, among the boxes shipped from Wales after my mother died, an envelope containing about fifty black-and-white photographs that Louise, my maternal grandmother, had stashed in one of the cigar boxes in which she put her keepsakes.

Louise had arranged these images of her brothers and cousins in chronological order and they told the whole miserable story of that war. There they were as youths, brimming with confidence, posing as part of a troop or in a studio clad in dress uniforms with swords. Here they sat as soldiers astride gleaming steeds in a cobbled courtyard or pictured behind a ceremonial mascot. Then they were at the front: standing casually beside mobile kitchens set up before horse-drawn wagons; or with elbows resting on a table littered with empty plates and a dozen drained wine bottles; or taking sponge baths

Minnie (standing second from right, front row), World War I

in a trench on a sunny day. Then, gradually, the images turned bleaker. Soldiers stood sentinel on snow-covered mud or were huddled in cramped dugouts lined with logs and sandbags. I lined up the pictures taken inside hospitals. In one, a group of doctors and nurses stood behind men on crutches or with their arms in slings while another, a double amputee, sat covered in a blanket in a wheelchair. In another, taken in a hospital ward, nobody is smiling. The soldiers, swathed in bandages, lie on their beds with their heads tilted towards the camera while nurses, dressed in nuns' habits, do the same. I know why this photograph affected me. It is almost identical to another that rests on a shelf in my office in San Francisco. This shows Minnie, my paternal grandmother, as a nurse, with a look of resigned sadness on her face as if she is expressing her dismay at the surrounds, the crippling wounds of her charges and the futility of war. Another photograph also lingers with me – Louise's brother, Emil, with several of his platoon in a muddy dugout huddled around a Christmas tree, trying to make the best of the grimness. I thought about this as we lit our Chanukah candles in front of a warm fire, insulated better than most from the virus that was killing many thousands by the day.

The wounds of World War I ran so deep that two of the boys born soon after the war were given the name of the brother of Minnie, my great-uncle – Ludwig Alfred Mayer – who had been killed in March 1915, aged twenty, while fighting for the Germans in a mountainous area in the west of Ukraine. A boy born to one of Minnie's sisters was named Alfred. Two decades later this Alfred, having survived Auschwitz, walked across much of Europe and eventually raised a family in Tel Aviv. The other Alfred, my father, was given not just one but both names of the man who would have been his uncle. And so,

Max Lewy, *Ludwig Alfred Mayer*, 1915

even at birth, my father had death and grief stapled to him. His must have been an echo of the grief felt by Ludwig Alfred Mayer's own father, (my great-grandfather, Carl Nathan Mayer), who had a bronze medal struck bearing his son's image on one side and, on the reverse, depicting a soldier trying to lift a wounded comrade. Ludwig Alfred were the names my father bore until he lay dead in the passenger seat of a car with its emergency lights flashing, while parked on double-yellow lines, outside his doctor's office.

I don't know of a better way to capture the experiences that Max and others must have endured during World War I than to ask what it took to transform strong, healthy men into the jolting, quivering figures in the short black-and-white movies made in hospitals and treatment centres at the time. These are not slow-motion movies, although they might appear as such to the casual observer. These are movies of what happens to a man who has been so traumatised by what he has witnessed that his mental wiring has been permanently shorted. Their limbs appear to have minds of their own; their eyes seem frozen; their only form of locomotion is a strange dancing gait. Some are missing half their faces. And these were the 'lucky' ones – those who survived.

For me, etchings and paintings rather than short, grainy, black-and-white films, have become a form of memorial to my grandparents. It's these familial connections to World War I that originally drew me to the German and Austrian artists – members of what art historians label the *Neue Sachlichkeit*, the New Objectivity – who sought to capture the horrors and casualties of war without a stroke of artificial gloss. The works of artists such as Beckmann, Dix, Grosz, Kirchner and Kokoschka illuminate significant aspects of the lives of Max and Minnie, and Salli and Louise – both the war years and the shattered Germany that was left after the Treaty of Versailles was signed in 1919.

It is the Dix etchings that affect me most. They show the cast-offs of war – men who were abandoned or neglected by German society and forced to live on the streets – maimed, deformed, crippled, mangled. In one etching, a destitute quadruple amputee sits on a sidewalk propped against a wall, trying to sell matches to passers-by. The stockinged and pinstriped legs of his fellow citizens rush by, and he is ignored by all except a dachshund, who urinates on him.

In *The Taxis of the Marne*, a novel about the German occupation of France during World War II, first published in 1957, Jean Dutourd writes about the links between the two world wars. Two sentences hit home: 'War is less costly than servitude. The choice is always between Verdun and Dachau.' For my grandfather, the man born as Marx Moritz, who became Max Moritz and was murdered as Maximilian Israel Moritz, there was never a choice between Verdun and Dachau. He endured both.

Verdun to Dachau. I knew enough about the history of the 1920s and early 1930s to understand the reasons why German society unravelled between the end of World War I and the opening of the Nazis' first concentration camp, but I had never contemplated what it must have felt like to my father, who was thirteen, and my mother, who was eleven, when the first detainees were herded into Dachau.

My father was living with his parents in an apartment in Munich, just eleven miles from Dachau. My mother was in the family home when the Nazis' first crudely fashioned dragnet trawled the Rhineland for Jews, political dissidents and others they deemed a threat. I never heard either of my parents mention those events. No matter what happened during those nights in 1933, both Bavaria and the Rhineland had a part to play in the journey from Verdun to Dachau.

I have a better sense of my father's childhood in Munich during the period in question than my mother's in the Rhineland. Maybe this is because Munich was where Hitler began his rabble-rousing, mustered a following, polished his diatribes and eventually rose to power – a passage that has been studied endlessly and described in so many historical accounts. But I doubt whether that's the real explanation. Much more of it is due to the way in which I was able to uncover the arc of Max's life through his personnel records, which tracked his slow rise and sudden fall as a civil servant in the Bavarian judiciary. It was like uncovering the signposts leading to oblivion. By contrast, I found nothing much in the archives of my mother's father, Salli Rath, beyond records of purchases of pastureland he acquired, which he either used to raise the cows he traded or leased out to other farmers. For me, Salli's character only came to life in the letters and documents of the late 1940s and early 1950s.

The root of my curiosity about Max and Minnie must be because, unlike Salli and Louise, I never knew them. The unfiltered accounts of their existence ended with the outbreak of war in 1939. For me they were never more alive than they were in the photograph that hung in my parents' bedroom. They were silent, distant and always in black and white. Who were they? What happened? Why did they not escape? Why had I never known them? This unfamiliarity impelled me to start rooting through my intermittent diary entries. I found no forgotten revelations of my father about Max and Minnie but I did chance upon a reference to Dachau in an entry I wrote in 1979 about a flight from London to Chicago, during which I must have had a conversation with the person sitting next to me – an American salesman for IBM returning from a jaunt to Munich's Oktoberfest. This salesman's comments clearly hit home as I jotted down his remark, 'Munich was a jewel. I didn't get to Dachau. But then you cannot see everything. I had to leave something for the next trip.'

It's more than forty years since I made that entry recording the off-key reflection. But the reference to Dachau, while I was working in my first full-time job as a twenty-five-year-old correspondent for *TIME* in Detroit, clearly triggered an emotional reflex. It's only recently that I have come to terms with the impulse that made me note it down.

In early 1919, when Max was discharged from the army and transferred to Munich, he found a city riven by the after-effects of war. He, like other returning veterans, exchanged an organised, fortified battlefield for a chaotic, urban one. The humiliation of the war ended whatever unifying influence the German royal family still possessed and the consequences must have been apparent to Max and all Germans. Max was living in a small apartment in a city where food shortages only heightened the sense of hopelessness, and hunger was so acute that people ate carriage horses. In their place, zebras, camels and elephants from the municipal zoo were harnessed to wagons. At the same time, the Spanish flu had crippled any semblance of everyday life – schools, churches and public facilities were all closed and so many tram drivers fell sick that the public transit system all but collapsed.

Neither Max nor other veterans returning to Munich tasted any reprieve. The Munich they had known before the war must have seemed like heaven compared to this city, where separatist gangs jockeying for power roamed the streets with pistols and machine guns, and extremists, from both left and right, sought control. For a time, the city was ruled by a Soviet-style government containing several Jews, which provided fuel for rightist arguments that Jews were the source of all evil. The Bavarian prime minister ordered an expulsion – only narrowly averted – of the Jewish community, whose members had been labelled as Marxists, socialists, Bolsheviks and communists. Eventually, troops arrived from Berlin and aided by the Freikorps (a Nazi spawning pond), using tanks and artillery, stamped out the rebellion with a savage ferocity but only after hundreds had been shot, bayoneted and tortured.

The war and chaos in Munich took a toll on Max. Within weeks of returning to work, while also being hounded by his landlord for rent payments, he became suicidal. He was admitted to hospital where he spent several months, until a friend took him home and nursed him back to a fragile stability. Max's fresh bout of depression and the accompanying insomnia roughly coincided with Sigmund Freud's identification of what is now known as chronic post-traumatic stress disorder – victims reliving their horrors in graphic nightmares and simultaneously being subjected to internal disorders. Max's screams in the middle of the night were one of the few memories my father relayed about his childhood. The emotional shrapnel of World War I buried itself in my father, even if he refused to acknowledge it, and he unconsciously transmitted this to me – shards of traumas from more than a century ago. Three generations have each discovered that there is no such thing as 'Goodbye to All That'. There never will be.

In the fifteen years between Verdun and Dachau, Max and Minnie enjoyed only about five years of relative stability. In Munich, the Spanish flu and resulting tumult were followed in the early 1920s by hyperinflation and in 1929 by the Great Depression, which was as savage in Europe as in America. The hyperinflation was catastrophic for all Germans, save for those who owned houses, buildings or land that retained their value. Max, along with members of Minnie's family, had entrusted their life savings to the government by buying war bonds. At the peak of the hyperinflation, the money that Max brought home from the courthouse on his payday was worth less – eventually far less – when Minnie ordered groceries the following morning. Some of Minnie's relatives were forced to move from spacious apartments into cramped digs, Minnie's small dowry was wiped out and Max had more reason to fret over the household budget and how it would sustain his family of four.

I found a small photograph that captures this brief interlude – between the taming of hyperinflation and the arrival of the Great Depression – in the childhoods of the two Moritz brothers, when life may have appeared tranquil to the majority of German Jews. The idea that a pogrom, conducted on an unimaginable scale, could happen in a country where there were now not just Jewish farmers and shopkeepers, but also doctors, lawyers, writers, composers, artists and judges (including one, in Munich, who fastened his oxyacetylene lamp to the front of his bicycle before pedalling off early every morning to the courthouse) was utterly unfathomable. I can easily imagine how neither my father nor his brother ever gave it a second thought. I say this because I remember my father marvelling, after man first landed on the moon, that he had been born before Lindbergh flew across the Atlantic. The idea of being alive before man flew between New York and Paris was as inconceivable to me as it must have been for my father and mother to imagine living in Germany in the 1860s, as their grandparents had done, when many avenues were closed to Jews. No wonder they thought pogroms only occurred in distant lands and just affected groups of orthodox religious zealots with a tendency towards mysticism who lived in villages without running water or electricity or who were crammed into tenements in urban ghettos.

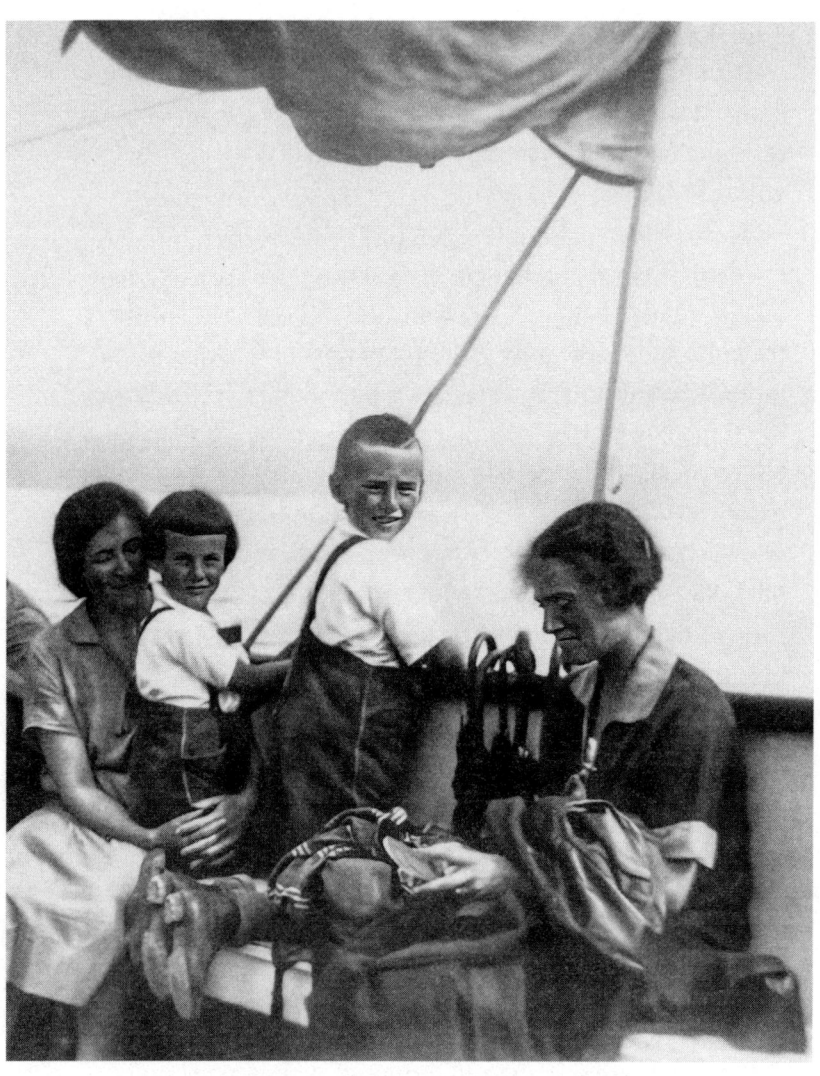

Anna Volk, Ernest, Alfred and Minnie, 1926

The photograph that had caught my eye is of two little boys and a pair of women, and it was taken on a steamer the year before the stock market collapsed. The woman in the foreground of the photograph is Minnie, my grandmother, with her sons' coats on her lap. There is a soft smile on her face – the sort that envelops a parent amused by the antics of small children. It is a mother's smile, suggesting contentment and unalloyed happiness – or perhaps that's just what I want to read into it. It is the only photograph I have in which Minnie is smiling. Behind her, a small boy – my father – is leaning over the ship's rail, from which several umbrellas also dangle. In the background, a younger boy is nestled in the embrace of a young woman. This boy is my uncle, Ernest, and the younger woman is Anna, the Moritz brothers' nanny, whose thick, dark hair is swept into a neat bun and whose hands are sturdier than Minnie's.

INTELLECTUAL DEBRIS

THE IDENTIFICATION CARD issued in French in 1920 to a twenty-nine-year-old woman with an innocent-looking smile and a pile of rich, dark hair revealed how Louise Gompertz, my grandmother, became one of many Germans living in the Rhineland who were caught in the tussle between nations following the end of World War I. The card was printed in French rather than German because the victorious Allied powers, particularly France, on whose territory the bulk of the war had been fought, became so agitated by Germany's delinquent payment of the reparations stipulated in the Treaty of Versailles, that French and Belgian troops marched into the Rhineland in 1923. The *permis de circuler* that I discovered in the boxes shipped by my sister was a consequence of the fact that Louise's hometown, Rheinberg, and Kempen, the hometown of the man she married in 1921, the cattle trader Salli Rath, were trapped in an area that had been cleaved from Germany by the Allied forces to serve as a buffer zone to impede any future German ambition in France, Belgium or the Netherlands. The French occupied all the towns and villages inhabited by Salli and Louise's respective families and seized the coal mines and timber supplies that lay just to the east in the Ruhr. It was in this area, inhabited by his ancestors for about 150 years, that Salli Rath came to pursue the other trade where there were few barriers to Jews – cattle trading. This, even though he was born with badly impaired vision that rendered him blind by his late teens. Eventually, Die Viehhandelsgesellschaft Gebr. Rath (the Rath Brothers Cattle Trading Company) became one of the more prosperous in the region. Louise's family too had been in and around Rheinberg, about sixteen miles to the east of Kempen, for at least the same amount of time as Salli's. Louise's father, Leopold Gompertz, was a volunteer member of the local fire department and, like his own father, a butcher. A formal photograph of Leopold shows a lean man who might have just dismounted from a horse and strode into a saloon in the American West. Leopold died, aged eighty-six, in 1933, three days after Hitler seized power.

The occupation of the Rhineland provided fresh fodder for the hate-filled tirades of the man with the dark toothbrush moustache whose gift for stirring up crowds and radio audiences was developed in Munich's beer halls. This became another 'wrong' that he would 'right', along with the exploitation of workers and farmers, the control of Germany by outside powers, the threat of Bolsheviks and communists and other radicals of the left, the jelly-boned stance of the traditional rightist political parties, the hyperinflation that wiped out the savings of a generation and, above all, the demonic conspiracy of world-wide Jewry. These causes had led to the chaos in the streets of Munich that Max Moritz had returned to after World War I and also gave rise to Hitler's failed attempt to seize control of Bavaria and subsequently topple the government in Berlin. The Beer Hall Putsch in Munich of 1923 resulted in Hitler's confinement in Landsberg prison from which he emerged a martyr after serving a small portion of his sentence. The road from Verdun to Dachau also ran through Bebelplatz, a cobbled square in the centre of Berlin, which lay beneath a hotel room in which I stayed during a business trip in 2013.

Louise Gompertz French I.D. card

Salli Rath, Bachelor Days

Leopold Gompertz (Louise's father), early 1920s

It had been all too easy for me to check in to the hotel and let the friendly receptionist sweep away all the yesterdays; to forget that the building, like many, hid a dark history. A polite bellman had led me to my room where he showed me the safe, reminded me that there was complimentary Wi-Fi, pointed out the in-room fridge, ice bucket, bottles of water on either side of the bed and the desk drawer containing a power point with international adapter and USB charger, before enquiring whether I wanted an explanation of how to operate the smart television and interactive entertainment. He did not make mention of the history of the building, which had been erected as the headquarters of Dresdner Bank. The top floor now housed the Gutmann Suite, named after Eugen Gutmann, the founder of the bank, who, born a Jew, had later decided life would be easier if he became a Catholic. Gutmann's son, also Friedrich, was deemed Jewish by the Nazis and transported from Haarlem in Holland (where he had moved after marrying a Dutchwoman) to Theresienstadt, where he was beaten to death. His wife Louise was later murdered at Auschwitz. Buildings can resemble people: their exteriors say nothing and explain less. It's what happens inside – sometimes deeply buried – that matters. The hotel website brushed aside the inconvenient moments of the building's history in one sentence: 'Once the headquarters of the esteemed 19th century Dresdner Bank, it's a place where heritage and stylish modernity meet.' Instead, it celebrated the placement of the hotel's spa in the former bank's jewel vault.

Somewhere in this building, between the Gutmann Suite and La Banca, the restaurant in which a cosmopolitan breakfast buffet was laid out every morning, the managers of the 'esteemed 19th century Dresdner Bank' had decided to fire Jewish employees, cut their pensions and file the reports they received from the bank's Polish affiliate, which maintained custody of the assets that belonged to the dead. It was here too that they approved the acquisition of a 26 per cent interest in the construction company that built the twin gas chambers of Auschwitz-Birkenau.

It was on 10 May 1933, in the square below my hotel window, that students carrying large Nazi flags and dressed in white short-sleeved shirts and culottes, their teenage temperaments inflamed by the oaths they had taken 'to entrust to the flames the intellectual debris of the past', led a column of men in brown uniforms, as well as many citizens of Berlin, past a bonfire. The marchers threw books plundered from libraries, schools, universities and private homes, and written by 'decadent' authors – both Jews and non-Jews – such as Ernest

Hemingway, Jack London, Helen Keller, Sigmund Freud, Albert Einstein, Heinrich Heine, Bertolt Brecht and Heinrich Mann, into the flames. The Bebelplatz bonfire burned on the eve of my father's twelfth birthday.

Near the flames on that night in May 1933, Reichsminister Goebbels, standing on a low stage behind a podium draped with the Nazi swastika and surrounded by radio microphones, announced that 'the era of Jewish intellectualism is now at an end'. Henceforth, the German language was only to be employed by Germans, and Jewish writers were to only write in Hebrew. It was a scene that prompted the poet Heinrich Heine to remark that wherever books are burned, people will also eventually be burned.

In the hundred days that preceded the book-burning, Germany's political edifice had disintegrated, which, for 1 per cent of the population – the 566,000 Jews – brought trouble, particularly for those in the professional classes or with political ties the Nazis deemed questionable. The military service of Max and Oskar offered little protection. The Reichstag building in Berlin was torched, 40,000 Nazis were sworn in as auxiliary policemen and Hitler was granted emergency powers, which he soon converted into dictatorial rule. The Nazis staged a boycott of Jewish shops and businesses and issued their first decree defining the differences between Aryans and others. The Gestapo was formed. The Communist party's headquarters were raided, homosexuals were pursued, the publication of pornography was deemed illegal, Nazis seized control of state governments, the public health insurance system was prohibited from paying Jewish doctors, the number of Jewish students in public schools was limited to 1.5 per cent, Nazi Brownshirts invaded the offices of trade unions and consumer cooperatives,

Hitler's birthday was proclaimed a national holiday and Jews were forbidden from attending trade fairs. Hitler did not squander any time as he laid waste to Germany. When societies crumble, they do so like clay-brick houses during an earthquake.

Amid this barrage of assaults on liberty, Heinrich Himmler staged a press conference announcing the opening of a 5,000-person detention centre in Dachau on the site of a World War I munitions factory, about eleven miles from where Max and Minnie were raising their family. Oskar was arrested in March 1933 and imprisoned in Dachau in May – the same month that books were burned in Bebelplatz – along with hundreds of others whom the Nazis felt harboured dangerous political leanings. It was Oskar's membership of the progressive Social Democratic Party (SPD) that made him a marked man, and he consequently became prisoner number 1491, 'for glorifying communism'.

Tens of thousands eventually died in Dachau, which became a training ground for many of the Nazis who later murdered millions. But it was not one of the industrial killing centres established after the Nazis married the concentration camp to the gas chamber. Dachau was formed as a detention centre for political prisoners or other dissenters – communists, social democrats, clergymen spreading inconvenient messages from their pulpits, Jehovah's Witnesses, homosexuals, Romani and, of course, Jews. In the month prior to Oskar's arrival, the first summary execution of Jews in Dachau had taken place when four men, thinking they were about to start another day's work, were shot without notice.

★

Oskar was detained in Dachau for over two years, without the right to a legal appeal or trial. He was among those who became part of the Nazis' primitive fascination with eugenics, which began in earnest in German South West Africa (modern-day Namibia) at the start of the twentieth century. One of the principal German practitioners was Eugen Fischer, who headed the Kaiser Wilhelm Institute of Anthropology, Human Heredity and Eugenics in Berlin, and whose poisonous racial theories found their way into Hitler's *Mein Kampf*, Dachau and other concentration camps.

Fischer and his disciples at the Kaiser Wilhelm Institute were influenced by earlier work in Germany and also by ideas regarding 'racial purity' that had been imported from the US. The American South was the epicentre of racist pseudo-anthropology, a legacy of American slavery and a tool for assuring a permanent underclass. There were racial provisions governing immigration, enforced sterilization and studies of eugenics backed by prominent US endowments and individuals. It was easy for the Nazis to fined precedents within the US for some of their policies.

The most notorious of Fischer's students was Josef Mengele, many of whose grotesque medical experiments at Auschwitz were conducted in collaboration with the Kaiser Wilhelm Institute of Anthropology. Another was the son of a graveyard gardener, Hans Lichtenecker, a failed artist who had got his start in this dark pursuit in German South West Africa. There, in 1931, with the help of local police who rounded up subjects, Lichtenecker had noted the particulars of local inhabitants. He had taken their fingerprints, removed hair samples, made plaster casts and recorded their voices on wax rolls with a stylus. The recordings made by this kitchen table anthropologist remained untouched for seventy-five years until they were translated and made part of a ghoulish exhibition in Vienna. In these recordings, the tribespeople, speaking in their local tongue, could be heard to say, 'We are being abused again' and 'I just scream like a dog in a trap'. Another said, 'I couldn't hear or see anything that was happening. But I couldn't breathe through my mouth. My ears were sore, sore, sore.'

Some years later, Lichtenecker turned up at Dachau where he pursued his anthropological studies with zeal. He applied the same crude techniques he had used on the Namibians to Oskar Moritz, proprietor of Lederhandlung, S. Moritz & Sohn, located on the marketplace of the little town on the bend of the River Main. The archives of the museum in Dachau preserve a fifty-page notebook in which Lichtenecker recorded data from

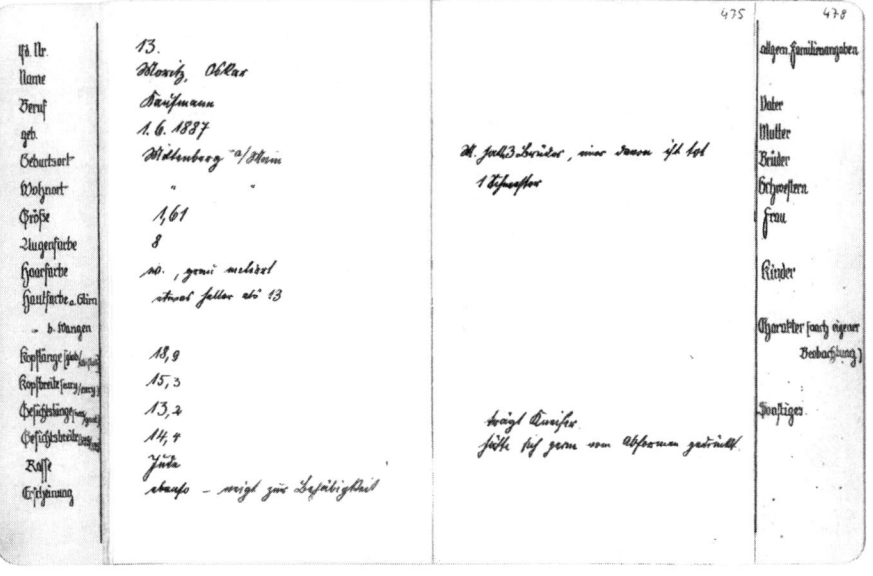

Pages from Hans Lichtenecker's Dachau notebook

fourteen prisoners whose skulls he measured as part of the Nazi attempt to classify the races and determine intelligence.

Oskar was prisoner number 13. His race was noted as 'Jewish' – the other categories used by the Nazis to classify whites being 'South-eastern European', 'Mediterranean', 'Alpine' and 'Nordic'. Oskar's eye colour was accorded an '8'. The skin colour on his forehead was deemed slightly lighter than '13'. His head length – measured in centimetres – was '18.9', his head width '15.3', his face length '13.2' and his face width '14.4'.

In one of the notebook's eight photographs, prisoner 9 – Anton Brand, a Czechoslovakian manual worker, dressed in a white smock – is seated, slumped forward and pictured in profile. Brand is classified as 'Mediterranean-Oriental'. A footnote to this entry observes, 'B. is not a political prisoner but was sent to Dachau from a workhouse. B. is unclean and a big filthy pig.' Standing behind Brand is an SS man and prisoner number 3, Ferdinand Merkel, a mechanic from Munich pigeonholed as 'South-eastern European'. He holds a small frying pan. Seated at Brand's knee is Christian Brautigam, prisoner number 2, a stonemason from near the border with Czechoslovakia who had been an artilleryman in World War I and who is classified as 'Mediterranean'. Merkel and Brautigam stare at the camera, each with a look of resignation on their faces. The two prisoners had been conscripted to apply melted wax from the frying pan to the skulls of their fellow inmates.

Brand's head slumps forward, covered in layers of thick wax. The image reminds me of the disfigured head of Almásy in the movie *The English Patient* (1996) after he was enveloped in flames in a plane crash. There is no photograph of Oskar, but he too must have gone through this procedure, part pseudo-scientific experiment, part ritual humiliation.

Arresting small-time shopkeepers and volunteer members of the local fire brigade, like Oskar, only took hammering on front doors but purging the civil service of Jews required more time and paperwork. By the time the books were burning in Bebelplatz, Oskar was already in Dachau while his brother Max Moritz – veteran of World War I and decorated with an Iron Cross – still placed his faith in the system that, despite his twenty-four years in the judiciary, continued to confine him to the junior ranks. One assessment, from 1925, signed by sixteen judges from three tiers of the court, noted that he '… has a sharp, sure judgement, an excellent grasp and comprehensive knowledge. He also has great business acumen at his disposal… He towers above other capable civil servants. He is suitable for promotion as a judge and public prosecutor even in a very large office and in Munich.' Yet the promotions did not come, and it wasn't until 1930 that he became a counsellor at the Munich District Court and was appointed to supervise the training of fresh lawyers. A year later, his performance report noted that Max had 'a high sense of duty; he has great responsibility and independence, is wise and moderate… He is of untiring diligence and zeal. His achievements are excellent in every direction. There are no shortcomings. Moritz is suitable for any promotion.' The unanimous overall verdict, again signed by several higher judges, was 'Very particularly capable'.

But by the end of 1931, the tone of the reports changed. For Max, the ceiling was caving in, and, despite his requests, after 1931 there were no more promotions. A month before the book burnings of 1933, Max was demoted, although his war service gave him a temporary stay of execution. He was forced to submit a detailed questionnaire to see whether he complied with the new 'Law for the Restoration of the Professional Civil Service'. In it he revealed that he had been a member of the SPD (the same political affiliation that helped doom Oskar) since 1919. Max had joined the party at the behest of the friend who had helped him recover from his breakdown after his return from World War I. Apart from attending a handful of meetings, he explained, he had done nothing more than pay his annual dues. These statements carried about as much weight with the Nazi authorities as the references he supplied from his military superiors and his observation that, as a Jew, he could not demonstrate his patriotism because he was forbidden from joining the Nazi party. Eventually he was granted an audience with Hans Frank, who had taken part in the Beer Hall Putsch in 1923 and had subsequently been struck off the roll of solicitors in Munich. After the tide turned, Frank became Hitler's personal lawyer, the pre-eminent legal authority for the Nazi party and, by the time of his encounter with Max, was the Minister of Justice in Bavaria. It was then that he offered Max the choice of taking a post in a village north of Munich or retiring with a pension at the end of November 1933, shortly after his fifty-first birthday.

The effect on this servant of the Kaiser and the Weimar Republic was profound. Max suffered another collapse and confined himself to his bedroom for several weeks. He had become a refugee in his own apartment. The world in which he had been reared, the universities in which he had been educated, the army for which he had fought and the judiciary where he made his career had all abandoned him. He had been tossed aside by the country of his birth. He began taking solitary bicycle rides and swimming in the open-air municipal pools, until they were declared off limits to Jews. After that, he found solace in rituals — spending hours fussing over the household accounts, but more fruitfully, gradually immersing himself in the religion he had largely left behind during his thirty-year quest to become assimilated. He armed himself with copies of the authoritative religious commentaries and busied himself with the affairs and some of the committees of his synagogue as well as the broader Jewish community in Bavaria.

During the 1930s, there were occasional periods of respite and hope. One came in August 1935 with the release of Oskar from Dachau. Max had written petitions for his younger brother's release and Minnie had bravely made pleading telephone calls to the office of Reinhard Heydrich, the Gestapo chief in Munich. After his release, Oskar returned to Miltenberg where his wife, Rosa, and his young employee, Leopold Halberstadt, had assumed responsibility for the shop and leather-goods business. Despite his apparent freedom, Oskar was thereafter subject to constant surveillance by the local Gestapo — who viewed him as a ringleader — and was targeted by gossips and whisperers.

For Max and Minnie, the one place they found some respite from the world that was closing in on them was with Anna and Sepp Volk in Bühl-am-Alpsee. It was there that they, along with their sons, spent the four summers between 1933 and 1936 — the last they enjoyed together. In the summer of 1933, this little village had not yet fallen victim to authoritarianism but, a year later, the black spider on its white-and-red background was fluttering from flagpoles beside the lakes and, by the summer of 1935, the swimming area of Der Grosse Alpsee, like the public pools in Munich, sported a sign that read, 'Jews not welcome'. The Moritz brothers — my father and uncle — found that they were also no longer welcome in the homes of friends from previous summers.

Anna shrugged off the asides from neighbours and Sepp brushed off the comments of fellow workers in the railway yards urging them to refuse accommodation to Jews. They welcomed the four Moritz visitors from Munich, until the four became two (after my father and uncle started attending school in England) and until the summer when visits were no longer possible.

THE SWIMMING BATH

AS I RETRACE HOW MY FATHER and uncle got out of Germany to be educated in England, what comes to mind is not the soul-searching my grandparents, Max and Minnie, must have undertaken before they decided to seek shelter for their sons in a foreign country, nor the scurrying around Munich in search of the unfamiliar items of clothing required of a British school, nor my father's suitcase, which contained a Hebrew Bible and prayer shawl. It is also not the uncertain farewell at the München Hauptbahnhof, his crossing of the English Channel, or his enrolment in St Paul's School. It is a wedding reception in a London hotel in the mid-1960s.

The ballroom of the Mount Royal Hotel in Marble Arch was, when I was eleven, the grandest room I had ever seen. The enormous floor was carpeted, chandeliers hung from the two-storey-high ceiling, round tables were topped with white cloths and crowded with silverware while glasses of different shapes and floral arrangements almost obscured the distant bride and groom at the head table. Near the groom sat his father, Arnold Meier – a diminutive figure, clad in a dinner jacket, reduced to an even smaller dimension by the geometry of the ballroom.

Arnold's second wife, whom he married in 1955 after his first wife died, was named Trude. She was one of Oskar Moritz's three children, had been born in Miltenberg and was a first cousin of the Moritz brothers. Arnold's marriage to Trude and their subsequent life in Manchester meant that for my father, and especially Ernest, my uncle, Arnold became a lifelong presence. Arnold was almost twenty years older than the Moritz brothers and had fled Germany – where he had taught modern languages – in 1933. In England, he started teaching at Whittingehame College, a Jewish boarding school about three miles from Brighton Pier. This school eventually became a refuge for Ernest, and it was there, during vacations, that my father met Arnold.

As the thirties progressed, the safety of their children became of paramount concern for Max and Minnie, Salli and Louise, Oskar and Rosa and all the other Jewish parents caught in Nazi Germany. The only six adults of this generation to whom I was directly related who were guests at our small family gatherings in the post-war years were Ernest, my uncle; Erika, my mother's sister; both children of Leni, Minnie's sister; and two of the three children belonging to Oskar and Rosa. Their third child, a son, born in the same year as my father and known as Freddy (although his real name was Manfred), had been sent to a Jewish agricultural school near Hanover to prepare him for a life in Palestine. Oskar had made three payments into an account at the Jewish Transmigration Bureau in New York to help his son escape from Germany. On 15 December 1941, Freddy was deported to the ghetto in Riga, where he was murdered.

When my father became the first of the Moritz brothers to be delivered to a school in Britain – St Paul's School in London, 'founded in honour of "Christ Jesu in puerida, and of his blessed mother Mary"', he was unable to speak more than a few words of English. He arrived with Max, my grandfather, on 20 April

1937 – Hitler's birthday – with his tuition at St Paul's having been guaranteed by Jeanette Franklin-Kohn, a British benefactor. An intimidating figure, Franklin-Kohn, who when younger had been a keen supporter of the suffragette movement, had, to the displeasure of her family, married a Jew and moved to Düsseldorf. After Hitler came to power, she and her husband returned to Britain, where she became a saviour for dozens of young refugees, providing both money and introductions to schools. My father was placed in digs and it was from these lonely rooms that he wrote a postcard in German and copperplate script to Minnie, my grandmother, announcing his arrival in England. 'I just want to tell you that we arrived safe and sound at Liverpool St. last night. There was no one at the station, but we found our way around anyway. Last night we slept in a hotel and this afternoon I moved into my quarters. It's 10 minutes to the school.'

My father always had a solemn streak, which must have been apparent at an early age because, in 1931, when Max was fruitlessly applying for promotion, he had explained to his superiors, 'I am limiting my application to Munich because my eldest son, at his request and on the advice of his teachers, is to prepare himself for the rabbinical profession. He must begin this preparation now and cannot receive the necessary instruction in any other Bavarian city as well as here...' By 1934, when my father had his Bar Mitzvah, the time of life when a Jewish boy is supposed to become accountable for his actions, the impulse to be a rabbi had worn off. It was also the year Jews were banned from enlisting in the German military and forbidden from performing in theatres throughout the country.

The semester before my father appeared on the doorstep of St Paul's, he had been a student at Munich's Maximiliansgymnasium. He always said that most of the teachers there treated him and other Jewish students sympathetically, even as they were ostracised by some of their classmates. He never mentioned that Hans Frank, the Nazi lawyer who ended Max's career, and was later known as the 'Butcher of Poland', had graduated two decades earlier from the same school. My father chose to believe that the final report card he received in Germany, garlanded with stellar grades, was an expression of his teachers' contempt for the Nazi regime. My uncle, who also attended the Maximiliansgymnasium, was much less charitable and recalled several teachers who maliciously singled out Jewish students.

Before arriving in Britain, my father had received a handful of English lessons from a private tutor in Munich. It wasn't until I came upon an affidavit written in German, submitted by my father as part of a reparations claim thirty years after arriving in London, that I got a glimmer of how much rested on his ability to quickly master the language. His stay at St Paul's, rather than repatriation, hinged on whether he could pass his exams and obtain a scholarship that would cover his school fees. For the first few months of his stay in Britain, my father paid seven shillings and sixpence for each of the four hours of tuition he received every week from a young grammar-school teacher.

Decades later, when he sometimes amused himself by putting ruminations to verse, my father made light of acquiring the mastery of a tongue that had been essential for all that lay ahead. The opening stanza of one, which he titled 'Is English Difficult?', reads,

> We'll begin with a box, and the plural is boxes,
> But the plural of ox should be oxen, not oxes.
> The one fowl is a goose, but two are called geese,
> Yet the plural of mouse should never be meese.
> You may find a lone mouse or a whole set of mice,
> Yet the plural of house is houses, not hice.
> If I speak of a foot and you show me your feet,
> If I speak of a boot, would a pair be called beet?

Towards the end of his life my father remembered that one of his proudest scholastic moments had been when, for the first time, he had felt confident enough to raise his hand in one of the classrooms of St Paul's and participate in a discussion. A few months later, he wrote a date in red ink in the gothic script he had acquired as a student in Germany (but which he later abandoned in favour of the handwriting taught in British schools), in the margin of a one-sentence announcement in *The Times* of 4 November 1937 that St Paul's School in London had awarded a Senior Foundation Scholarship to L. A. Moritz.

Less than two years after posing his first question in English, my father – by then familiar with the importance the English attached to Shakespeare, rowing on the Thames and cricket, and proud of the alacrity with which he learned that Napoleon, much venerated by the Jews of Germany for the way he separated the church from the state, was considered an enemy of the British – attended his third, and final, prize-giving. The ceremony occurred on the same day that the Nazis shuttered the last Jewish enterprises in Germany. Visitors to the awards ceremony – my father had none – were invited to view an exhibition of wall paintings in the Art School and were informed that, after the awards, 'The first round of the Inter-Club Swimming Relay

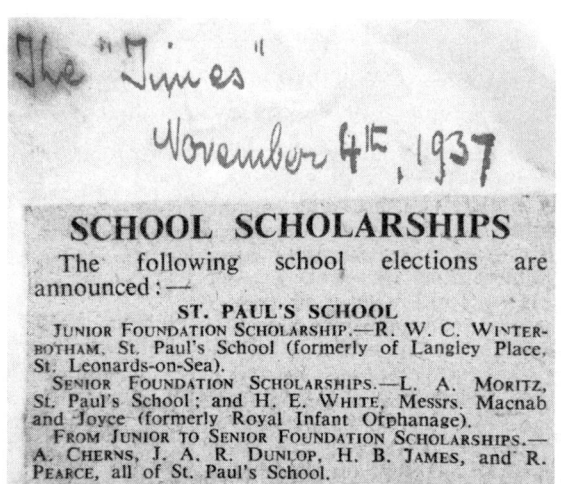

The "Times" November 4th, 1937

SCHOOL SCHOLARSHIPS

The following school elections are announced:—

ST. PAUL'S SCHOOL

JUNIOR FOUNDATION SCHOLARSHIP.—R. W. C. WINTERBOTHAM, St. Paul's School (formerly of Langley Place, St. Leonards-on-Sea).

SENIOR FOUNDATION SCHOLARSHIPS.—L. A. MORITZ, St. Paul's School; and H. E. WHITE, Messrs. Macnab and Joyce (formerly Royal Infant Orphanage).

FROM JUNIOR TO SENIOR FOUNDATION SCHOLARSHIPS.—A. CHERNS, J. A. R. DUNLOP, H. B. JAMES, and R. PEARCE, all of St. Paul's School.

Races, and the semi-final round of the Inter-Club Water Polo, will take place in the swimming-bath.'

Before the visitors could adjourn to the swimming-bath there was a celebration of the accomplishments of old boys, some of whom had become members of the Colonial Administrative Service in Nigeria, Tanganyika (now Tanzania) and Malaya (West Malaysia). Another had become commissioner of education in India, one the mayor of Malmesbury, while two had received the Order of the Nile and another the Chevalier of the Legion of Honour. There was also a performance of Aristophanes' *Frogs*, in which Charon was played by the eighteen-year-old L. A. Moritz. But for my father, the highlight of the day came later, when he was presented with the school's second most prestigious award, the Sleath Prize for Latin Prose. The high master wrote on his final report card, 'Only a scholar of great courage could have faced so manfully his difficulties of the last few years.'

> # ST. PAUL'S SCHOOL.
>
> ## APPOSITION, JULY 6TH, 1939.
>
> *ented by* BRIGADIER H. CLEMENTI SMITH, D.S.O., Master of th[e] Company and Chairman of the Governors of St. Paul's School.
>
> **Governors' Prize.**
> GREEK VERSE.
> J. CHADWICK.
>
> **Sleath Prize.**
> LATIN PROSE.
> L. A. MORITZ.

Reading this comment made me think of the author Jan Morris, and a passage I encountered while reading *Pleasures of a Tangled Life*, a long out-of-print collection of her essays, which I had ordered shortly before she died in 2020. In the years prior to her death, she and I had enjoyed an occasional email correspondence based on shared connections – with Wales, our Oxford college, and a long-dead literary agent.

Hers was an extraordinary life. A transgender woman, she had been, as the then twenty-six-year-old James Morris, the only journalist to accompany the expedition that had climbed Everest for the first time, and her newspaper, *The Times*, had broken the news on the morning of Elizabeth II's coronation. At the height of her literary powers, she had written a three-volume history of the British Empire, *Pax Britannica* (1968–78), capturing the journey of conquest and retreat between the birth of Victorian ambition and the death of Churchill. I had read many of Jan's forty-five books, including two – a set of diaries and a wistful memorial to the Japanese battleship *Yamato* – which she had published in her ninety-first year. I stayed up much of one night reading her collection of essays and saved one for last. It was titled 'Jewish Friends'. The opening anecdote reads as follows: 'The first Jew I ever knew was a boy of my own age, a refugee from Vienna who came to live with us for a time shortly before World War II. He was the most brilliant person I had ever met. He spoke not a word of English when he arrived but seemed to pick up the entire language in a month or two.'

I felt an immediate connection with Jan's parents who, like so many in Britain, had done everything possible to help these young refugees, and, of course, to the comparisons between their Viennese schoolboy and my father, and my uncle, Ernest. (Max brought Ernest to England two weeks after depositing my father at St Paul's.) Unlike my father, Ernest had not secured a scholarship and Max was counting on the good graces of a school on England's south coast. A fortuitous and unexpected meeting on Bond Street between Max and an émigré acquaintance solved the problem. This friend underwrote Ernest's first year of education. Later, Ernest came to attribute his belief in the Almighty to this encounter that saved him from the flames.

The school Ernest attended, Whittingehame College, had been established by Jake Halevy, a lifelong admirer of the British prime minister Arthur Balfour, the author of the declaration that favoured the establishment of a permanent home for the Jewish people in Palestine. So deep was this admiration that he had named his school after Balfour's ancestral home in Scotland. Its modernist buildings had been designed by a Bauhaus architect but the school reflected the ways and habits of Eton and Harrow. While the uniform of boaters, white trousers and cricket sweaters was foreign for the Jewish refugees, the familial sanctuary it provided to Jewish refugees was far warmer – including bridge games and ballroom-dancing lessons – than anything that could be provided at St Paul's. Whittingehame's founder and his wife provided year-round boarding for the boys who had no home to which they could return.

Whittingehame also provided a launching pad for Arnold Meier, whose son's wedding had introduced me to large hotel ballrooms, and in one of those photographs you can find lodged in the deep recesses of the internet, I found an image of him handing out gas masks at the college shortly after war broke out. Until it closed in 1967, Whittingehame was a haven for other Jewish refugees who were forced to flee during the 1950s from Egypt, Syria, Lebanon, Iran and Iraq.

Arnold went on to become an exemplar of the devoted educators of the post-war period, a man so loyal to his pursuit that he spent fifty years teaching modern languages in Manchester at one of Britain's great grammar schools during an era when schoolteachers still occupied exalted positions. In the 1950s, he also began organising exchange trips with a school in Cologne, centred around football matches, to kindle a sense of fraternity and decency among a younger generation.

While Ernest saw Max and Minnie once more (after he travelled to Munich during a school break), my father, who spent vacations at Whittingehame preparing for his entry examinations to Oxford, never saw them again.

A POSTCARD FROM DACHAU

EVEN THOUGH IT WASN'T RECORDED in the log of family birthdays and the anniversaries of weddings and deaths kept by my parents, there was one birthday they never forgot: Hitler's. My father had arrived in London on Hitler's birthday in 1937, and through some strange coincidence, my mother first set foot in England on Hitler's fiftieth birthday – 20 April 1939. As a teenager I remember that on 20 April whenever I entered the small kitchen for breakfast, she would immediately ask, as if posing a question for a general knowledge quiz, 'Do you know what day it is?' Just as quickly she would supply the answer: 'Hitler's birthday.' She did this with enough gusto to suggest that she had baked a cake for the occasion.

My mother's arrival in England occurred about five months after Kristallnacht – the night of 9 November 1938 – which brought terror to the apartment occupied by Max and Minnie in Munich, the house where Salli and Louise lived in the Rhineland and to every Jew across Germany. If Salli and Louise needed further encouragement to spirit my mother and her sister to safety, Kristallnacht must have provided a fresh impetus.

The newspapers in Miltenberg, the little town on the bend of the River Main where Max was born and Oskar kept his store, were full of ominous rumblings in the days leading up to Kristallnacht. One was an announcement of a roll-call for a tribute to the dead that would take place in the town hall that evening. The subsequent violence was ignited by an incendiary broadcast speech from Joseph Goebbels, which drew on the strains of antisemitism that had existed within portions of the Catholic Church, subsequent Protestantism and, in their most virulent form, had been pinned on a church door in Wittenberg some 400 years earlier by Martin Luther. 'Their synagogues should be set on fire,' the priest had written. 'Their homes should be broken down or destroyed.'

Goebbels vehemently echoed this, screaming instructions into the radio microphones that carried his voice into Miltenberg, Kempen and throughout Germany. In Miltenberg, the local police were ordered to stay at their posts. Then, one of the town's pharmacists, who was the head of the local *Sturmabteilung*, the roughneck security forces employed by the Nazis to terrorise and intimidate their opponents, was given the order to administer Goebbels' command. The mob was unleashed and the local synagogue, along with its adjoining school, was set ablaze. Thugs in civilian clothes hammered on the doors of Jewish houses and apartments, rousing sleepers from their beds and seizing the men, whom they took to the town courthouse. By the following morning even schoolchildren were permitted to help destroy the interior of the synagogue. The vandals hurled the torah scrolls into the street, smashed ornaments and pelted the teacher at the Jewish school with stones when he tried to retrieve his clothes, which had also been tossed into the gutter. The night of Kristallnacht, Leopold Moritz, a brother of Max and Oskar, suffered a stroke, was incapacitated and eventually died.

Years later, after most of the Jews of Miltenberg had been slaughtered, a rough inventory was made of the damage. At

Hauptstrasse 162, just yards away from where, on the hot summer day of 1963, I had taken the two small black-and-white, deckle-edged photographs glued to stiff, black paper inside my first photograph album, the shop windows of Lederhandlung, S. Moritz & Sohn were broken and Oskar's leather goods and shoemaker's tools lay strewn on the cobbles, while the proprietor himself had been arrested and frogmarched off. For my father and uncle, by then schoolboys in England, the news about Oskar's arrest, the ransacking of his house and the destruction of the synagogue in Miltenberg travelled quickly. 'We were desolate. It was as if someone had died,' Ernest wrote decades afterwards.

In Kempen, where Salli had become the head of the small synagogue after its incumbent (who had been ousted from his post as a lawyer and forced to peddle ties to earn money) had fled for safety in Holland, other dark characters also went to work. Decades later, after Salli and Louise were both dead, a remnant of Kristallnacht migrated to our home in Cardiff – a painting that hung above a bookcase housing dozens of orange-, red- and green-spined Penguin paperbacks, on the landing of my parents' house. The picture, of a train steaming alongside a lake, was painted in umber and olive. When light hit the canvas at a certain angle, a diagonal scar became visible – the result of a clumsy attempt to repair a gouging slash in the canvas made by a thug's knife on Kristallnacht. During that same raid, much of Salli and Louise's silverware was stolen, china and glassware were tossed through the windows and hurled onto the floor, furniture was smashed and bedlinen shredded. Salli was also carted off to prison, in nearby Anrath.

In Munich, all the Jewish families were ordered to hand over the keys to their apartments and houses and leave the city within forty-eight hours. Cars belonging to Jews were

Salli Rath identification card with 'J', 1938

confiscated and the sale of gasoline to Jews was also forbidden. Max, like Oskar, was roused from his bed in the middle of the night. The following day, Orthodox Jews were dragged by their beards down the street, and other Jews were forced to wash the sidewalks and clean up the damage. The destruction was so great that Kaufingerstrasse, one of Munich's main shopping areas, looked as if it had been subjected to aerial bombardment.

About 200 synagogues were destroyed in Germany on Kristallnacht, and around one hundred Jews were murdered, while some 20,000 were rousted from their homes and arrested. Many were sent to Dachau. Salli, thanks to the intervention of a friend, Kempen's district superintendent, escaped that fate and was released from prison after five days. But Max and Oskar were not so fortunate. Two days after Kristallnacht, Max was transported the eleven miles between his apartment and Dachau, where he was registered as prisoner 19633 and lingered in miserable conditions for over a month. It took longer for Oskar to be moved from Miltenberg and he didn't reach Dachau until 29 November, where he remained until five days before Christmas. Oskar's return to the place where he had already been confined for two years made the words of the IBM salesman echo again from my diary entry of 1979: 'Munich was a jewel. I didn't get to Dachau. But then you cannot see everything. I had to leave something for the next trip.'

Dachau are two syllables that I have heard since childhood. So, when, about one year into the pandemic, I woke to a BBC World Service broadcast titled 'Got a Postcard from Dachau', I was immediately alert. The story was about the recollections of a woman whose father had been rounded up and sent to Dachau. I had never thought about the reactions of Minnie, Louise and Rosa when Max, Salli and Oskar were hauled from their beds in Munich, Kempen or Miltenberg, or all those other Jewish wives and children elsewhere in Germany, left behind in their ransacked homes. But the BBC segment brought it all to life. The father of the woman recounting the story had returned in such a state that she and her sisters were frightened by the spectre he had become. The narrator's mother had noted in her diary that her husband was '… so thin, so degraded, so tormented and full of grief. The man who never cries, cried now.'

How, I wondered, had Max and Oskar appeared when they eventually returned to the apartment in Munich and the little shop overlooking the square in Miltenberg? Had they also been thin, degraded, tormented and full of grief? I suspect I know the answer for Max, given the history of his prior breakdowns.

As for Oskar, his appearance is one of those morsels of history that are known to few and, within a generation, vanish.

My parents were spared the sights of the abduction of their fathers on Kristallnacht. The Moritz boys were already ensconced in their schools in England and my mother and her sister, Erika, who was two years younger, were in Berlin. There they had been enrolled during the spring of 1938 in the Private Waldschule Kaliski, which had started in 1932 to prepare Jewish children, many of whom came from fully assimilated homes, for life outside Germany. It had been set up by a twenty-three-year-old polio victim, Lotte Kaliski, and operated until the Nazis closed it in 1939. Students like my mother and her sister were prepped for British and American examinations, while those children who were heading to Palestine were given a grounding in Hebrew. Each afternoon, they learned the skills required to survive as refugees – cooking, gardening, needlework. Among my mother's fellow students were Mike Nichols (then known as Mikhail Igor Peschkowsky), later the director of The Graduate (1967); Michael Blumenthal, who became Jimmy Carter's secretary of the Treasury; Gunther Stent, a prominent molecular geneticist; and Ralph Koltai, who became a set designer for the Royal Shakespeare Company.

In the years after my father died, I asked my mother on several occasions about her memories of Kristallnacht. For her, 9 November was rather like 20 April – it was a date in the calendar that she, and my father, would always note. But my mother remained adamant that she did not remember that night or the following days. When I asked her whether she recalled soldiers or thugs barging into the school, or the sound of sirens in the street, or the breaking of glass, or the smell of smoke,

PRIVATE WALDSCHULE KALISKI
Berlin-Dahlem

Klasse: 4 (U III)

ABGANGS- Zeugnis

4. Vierteljahr, Schuljahr 1938/39
Versetzt nach Klasse: 5
Konferenzbeschluß vom: /

für Doris Rath

Religionslehre		befriedigend	Chemie	//
Hebräisch (Nachholekurs)		gut	Naturgeschichte, Biologie	befriedigend
Deutsch	mündlich	befriedigend	Zeichnen	gut
Deutsch	schriftlich	ausreichend / befriedigend		
Französisch	mündlich	/	Musik	gut
Französisch	schriftlich	Ausreichend		
Englisch	mündlich		Werkarbeit freiwillig	sehr gut
Englisch	schriftlich	befriedigend		
Lateinisch	mündlich		Nadelarbeit	gut
Lateinisch	schriftlich	//		
Geschichte		gut	Leibesübungen	ausreichend
Erdkunde		gut		//
Rechnen Mathematik	mündlich	/		//
Rechnen Mathematik	schriftlich	gut		
Physik		gut	Handschrift	gut

/ versäumte Stunden. Verspätet / mal. Ordnung: //

Bemerkungen:

Doris Rath, geboren am 25. Januar 1924 zu Kempen/Niederrh. Tochter des Herrn Sally Rath,

hat die Schule seit 25. April 1938 von der Klasse 4 (U III) an besucht und das Klassenziel erreicht. Sie verlässt die Anstalt, um eine Schule im Ausland zu besuchen.

Urteile der Leistungen: 1 = sehr gut; 2 = gut; 3 = befriedigend; 4 = ausreichend; 5 = mangelhaft; 6 = ungenügend.

Das Zeugnis ist beim Wiederbeginn des Unterrichts, am / , von dem Erziehungsberechtigten unterschrieben, dem Klassenleiter vorzulegen.

Berlin - Dahlem, den 25 ten Februar 1939

Paul Israel
Leiter

Gelesen: *(Unterschrift)*

Klassenleiter

Doris (Rath) Moritz, school report card, 1939

or whether she and her fellow students had been ordered to a more secure area within the school, she would always shake her head. She would apologise for not being able to conjure up even a sliver of the past and she would always blame her memory. On Kristallnacht, she was fourteen years old – a time of life that can remain vivid even for those whose memories, towards the end of their lives, start fading to black. But there was little wrong with my mother's faculties. She retained her mental acuity, including her ability to rattle off the rap sheet of all the people who had incurred her wrath, until she died in her sleep on Guy Fawkes Day, 2019. Though she could never, or perhaps would never, unlock the memory of Kristallnacht, I believe that it had not disappeared; it was just deeply suppressed. What happened that night, and all the preceding and subsequent events related to it, were lodged forever in her soul.

About a year after my mother died, two incidents made me think again about Kristallnacht. The first was when I watched a video released by Arnold Schwarzenegger, the bodybuilder, movie star and former California Republican governor, comparing Kristallnacht to 6 January 2021 – the day that the mob stormed the US Capitol Building. The former governor meant well with his attempt at an historical analogy but, for me, the comparison obscured more than it illuminated.

Unlike the members of Congress in Washington who, within hours of the invasion, resumed their lives and were wreathed with circles of police and military protection within their debating chamber and offices, the Jews of Germany (those who were not dragged off to prisons and detention camps) were forced to shovel glass, board up broken windows and parade down the centre of the streets with placards hanging from their necks bearing slogans such as 'I am a race defiler'. As for those who were murdered on Kristallnacht, their ashes were sold back to their relatives by the Nazis.

In a strange coincidence, shortly after watching the former governor's video I received an email from Sylvia Landsberg, a British woman and long-time friend of my parents, whom I had known since childhood. She was in her nineties by the time of the email which she had dictated to her daughter from the nursing home where she was living. Her husband, Peter, had also attended the Private Waldschule Kaliski, and he too had been at the school on Kristallnacht. Later, after fleeing to Britain, he became a mathematician and physicist and distinguished himself by becoming one of the early researchers in how electricity could be powered by semiconductor cells – a precursor to the solar panel. Unlike my parents, he was not a practising Jew, although until the end of his life, he was an enthusiastic organiser of the occasional reunions of children who had studied at the school in Berlin.

A photograph of Sylvia was attached to the email. She was looking directly into the camera and had a palish serenity about her. Her features were strong, and her hair was a dusty blond. The image was at such odds with the features of my mother towards the end of her life, which were taut and pursed, and full of tension. As a boy, I remember being struck by the contrast between Sylvia and my mother. Sylvia was tall, fair and striking – the very essence of a fully enrolled, dues-paying member of the master race – and her three children were raised in the Church of England. She was gregarious and confident and had a gaiety about her. Despite their vastly different backgrounds and the contrast in their personalities, she and my mother became close friends and the bond between them was strong.

I was struck by the tone of her email. It was so different from anything my mother had ever sent. Sylvia's message radiated the joy she was extracting from her life, though it alluded to death. She told me she had been thinking of my mother. She wrote that she did not expect to survive the pandemic but had '... learned about mediaeval troubadours (including female ones) and the fin amour of the Cathars. I tasted Leonardo da Vinci's soup, ate Pompeii bread and mediaeval mushroom pasties, listened to Kate Bush, Loreena McKennitt, and "Baba Yetu", a stunning Swahili version of the Lord's Prayer that was in the soundtrack of a video game. Courtesy of my wonderful caregiver, I got to know the music of Zap Mama, Ladysmith Black Mambazo and Miriam Makeba.' I sensed that the difference between Sylvia and my mother was that the former had grown up in freedom, and my mother, in fear.

THE WRETCHED REFUSE

ONE LATE FALL MORNING in 2019, I was walking from an early breakfast meeting at the Bank of England towards Liverpool Street Tube station when I noticed that among the orange icons on my iPhone map for Patty & Bun, Costa Coffee and Wasabi was one in turquoise that read 'Kindertransport Memorial', which commemorates the evacuation of children from Nazi Europe. Their flight was made possible in November 1938 when, in the wake of Kristallnacht, the British Parliament authorised the temporary shelter of refugee children under the age of seventeen, provided they had a guarantor in Britain who could pay for a return trip or a journey to another country. Before Kristallnacht, fewer than 500 children had been granted asylum in Britain, although my father and his brother Ernest, despite being enrolled in English schools, did not enjoy that protection. Their fate, after they completed their studies, had been left undecided. My mother and her sister, however, were members of the Kindertransport, and were among the 10,000 children who came to Britain during the ten months separating Kristallnacht from the outbreak of war.

My mother had attended the unveiling of the Kindertransport Memorial in 2006 but I had never seen it and so made a detour. Like most memorials, it goes relatively unnoticed, and I had the sculpture to myself as commuters criss-crossed the plaza.

The work consists of five children standing around a miniature section of railway track and was cast in bronze by an Israeli sculptor who himself had been one of the thousands of children rescued and absorbed by the UK. Three of the sculpted figures are girls – the eldest of whom wears her hair in a plait and holds a suitcase. The tallest boy, wearing a tie, blazer and short pants, rests a hand on the shoulder of the smallest girl, precariously perched on her small suitcase and clutching a teddy. The smaller boy wears a peaked cap, has a satchel strapped to his shoulders and a valise and violin case at his feet. All five of these bronze heads were smeared with bird droppings but there was no escaping the poignancy of the scene: five uprooted little Jews, arriving bewildered and drained in a city they did not know, in a country whose language they did not understand, with a number written on a card dangling from a label around their necks.

My mother, just like the five figures cast in bronze, had also arrived at Liverpool Street station with a numbered card around her neck corresponding to the number on her suitcase. She had just turned fifteen – old enough to remember the journey she had made with her younger sister, although try as I might, as with Kristallnacht, I could never prise any details out of her, with one exception. One summer in the 1960s we had taken the Commer camper van on a ferry from Harwich to the Hook of Holland and the voyage prompted one of the few memories my mother revealed. She announced that as a girl she had made the same crossing – although in the opposite direction.

I found it hard to understand how my mother had suppressed such a painful journey since I remember scenes from my own voyage to America in 1976, when it was still cheaper to cross the Atlantic – if you were a student and had two or three suitcases –

by sea rather than air. When I came to America, I was about seven years older than my mother was when she and her sister travelled from Germany to England. But my circumstances were entirely different. I was not fleeing – in traumatic circumstances – a country run by a despotic regime. My application for a US student visa had been straightforward. I had a generous scholarship, traveller's cheques in my pocket and a dormitory room waiting for me in Philadelphia. I also spoke the language, knew I could always return safely to Wales and that the world was not on the brink of war. My only uncertainty was whether, after a year, I would be able to renew my visa. It is my arrival in America that I remember most. The liner waited for the tide and the tugboats directly below the Verrazzano-Narrows Bridge. I had risen early to be on the deck and was surprised by the heat and humidity of the August morning, the sight of the Statue of Liberty and the prospect of the skyscrapers of Lower Manhattan through the haze. But it is the shock of being by myself, after disembarking at Pier 90 along the Hudson River, that stays with me: standing beneath an overpass with my bags, at the edge of the busy West Side Highway, wondering how to get to Penn Station and feeling quite alone. There was no comparison, beyond the obvious, with my mother's journey – we had both exchanged one country for another – and yet I still felt alone and forgotten.

These memories prompted me to retrace my mother's journey with the help of a researcher in Cambridge. When she boarded the train in Cologne, less than forty miles from Kempen, the little town in the Rhineland, she was probably aware, even if she did not know the particulars, that the Dutch authorities were sending refugees who had crossed the border without the proper papers back to Germany; that Sweden was the only other country in continental Europe that had shown a willingness to accept refugees; and that a guarantor had been found by the Jewish Refugees Committee to cover the cost of the two Rath sisters' potential re-emigration to Argentina, Uruguay, Paraguay, Venezuela, the Dominican Republic, Palestine, Cuba or Shanghai – a requirement that was a sop to those politicians with protectionist tendencies. Like the other refugee children, she would have waited at the Köln Hauptbahnhof for the D 67 from Vienna with one piece of hand baggage, a suitcase, 10 Reichsmarks, a packed lunch and a German passport stamped with a 'J'. At the time, the railway station was draped in Nazi flags, and the signs hanging from the train carriages read 'London – Hoek v. Holland'. She and the other Jewish children would have been bundled into segregated carriages at the rear of the train, with their parents staring up at the windows, until some walked, jogged and then ran along the platform as the D 67 left Cologne at 3.42 p.m. on 19 April 1939.

The train stopped at Düsseldorf and Duisburg, and then again on the border with Holland, where German soldiers ordered the children to open their bags and took what they wanted. A couple of hundred yards later, as they inched into Holland, women standing beside the tracks handed up cocoa and zwieback through the lowered windows. Then the train went on to Arnhem, Utrecht, Gouda, Rotterdam and the Hook of Holland. I could find no record of the steamer the two Rath sisters boarded – but it would have been one of three owned and operated by London North Eastern Railway – *Vienna*, *Amsterdam* or *Prague*. My mother may even have travelled on *Prague*, the same ferry that the protagonist of *Austerlitz* had boarded. In the novel, Austerlitz, trying to recreate his own journey to England, had to summon up a distant memory and wrote about how he saw himself. By inference, I thought of my mother rather than Austerlitz '... waiting on a quay in a long crocodile of children lined up two by two, most of them carrying rucksacks or small leather cases. I saw the great slabs of paving at my feet again, the mica in the stone, the gray-brown water in the harbor basin, the ropes and anchor chains slanting upwards, the bows of the ship, higher than a house, the seagulls fluttering over our heads and screeching wildly.'

The ship bearing my mother and her sister steamed away from the Hook of Holland at 11 p.m. and docked in Harwich at six the following morning. There, the children boarded the 6.20 a.m. to London Liverpool Street, where they arrived at 8.02 a.m. on 20 April 1939. Meanwhile, back in Berlin, a major military parade featuring 50,000 German troops was taking place to celebrate Hitler's fiftieth birthday.

There was no welcoming inscription at Liverpool Street station like the one adorning the Statue of Liberty in New York Harbor, with its promises of refuge for the 'wretched refuse... the homeless, tempest-tost'. Nevertheless, there was a gulf in the US between those beckoning words and the unwillingness to accept any more of the 'wretched refuse' and the opposition to any increase in the number of German Jews permitted to enter the country. The plea from European refugee agencies to absorb 20,000 children under the age of fourteen above the prevailing quota limits, for two years, was rejected by American politicians, who argued that their country, still freeing itself from the grip of an economic depression, needed to take care of its own unemployed and was duty-bound to its veterans. Others argued that the country should not be inundated with the unwanted of Europe or turned into a gateway for Stalinists or Red infiltrators; that the US was a Christian institution, and any opening of the border

4511

This document of identity is issued with the approval of His Majesty's Government in the United Kingdom to young persons to be admitted to the United Kingdom for educational purposes under the care of the Inter-Aid Committee for children.

THIS DOCUMENT REQUIRES NO VISA.

PERSONAL PARTICULARS.

4335

Name RATH, Doris
Sex Female   Date of Birth 25-1-24
Place Kempen
Full Names and Address of Parents
RATH, Sally e Luise

15, Vorst str.
Kempen - Niederrhein

This side is reserved for official use only:—

LEAVE TO LAND GRANTED AT HARWICH THIS DAY ON CONDITION THAT THE HOLDER DOES NOT ENTER ANY EMPLOYMENT PAID OR UNPAID WHILE IN THE UNITED KINGDOM.

R/e 496,122

BOROUGH POLICE ALIENS 27 JAN 1940 DEPARTMENT CAMBRIDGE

IMMIGRATION OFFICER (6) 20 APR 1939 HARWICH

Doris (Rath) Moritz's entry permit to the UK, 20 April 1939

was, according to one congressman, 'contrary to the laws of God'. Beyond the halls of Congress there were even some American Jews who worried lest the arrival of boatloads of European Jews would spark more antisemitism in the country they called home.

In 1939, my mother was deposited at Liverpool Street station in the middle of rush hour and ushered into a vast underground waiting room. People passed overhead, the sounds of train whistles and squeaking steel echoed through the room, and the air tasted of soot and sulphur, which makes my self-centred loneliness at the edge of the West Side Highway seem as insignificant as it was. For the young Austerlitz, the waiting room was '... one of the darkest and most sinister places in London'. When, years later as a grown man, Austerlitz returned to this waiting room, he felt '... all the suppressed and extinguished fears and wishes I had ever entertained – I became aware, through my dull bemusement, of the destructive effect on me of my desolation through all those past years, and a terrible weariness overcame me at the idea that I had never really been alive, or was only now being born, almost on the eve of my death.'

Like all refugees, my mother was given a small twenty-four-page booklet, issued by the German Jewish Aid Committee, written in English and German. The opening page reiterated the importance of registering with the nearest police station, implied that their stay depended entirely on the sufferance of the British and emphasised that in Britain, 'The Police are your friends and are ready to help you wherever you are.' Among other things, it stressed the importance of not speaking German in public spaces; to talk in a low voice; to refrain from criticising the government; to not join any political organisation; to help and serve others; and – in bold letters – to 'Be loyal to England, your host.'

★

During the pandemic, when a magazine editor, for some obscure reason, asked me to identify the best gift I had received during the lockdown, I immediately thought of something my sister had sent. It was an unused steamship ticket. My sister had encased the pale-blue and burnt-orange second-class ticket – costing £156, for two passengers for a voyage between the Netherlands and New Zealand – in a neat black frame and it now hangs on the wall of my home office in San Francisco. The ticket is as pristine as it was on 14 August 1939, when it was issued in Rotterdam to my grandparents, Salli and Louise, by the Rotterdamsche Lloyd agency.

Tickets to New Zealand issued to Salli and Louise, 14 August 1939

Salli and Louise were supposed to make the first leg of their escape from Europe aboard the RMS *Mooltan*, a 21,000-tonne steamship operated by the P&O line, which was to take them via Colombo (Sri Lanka) to Sydney, where they would then board the RMS *Niagara*, owned by New Zealand's Union Steam Ship Company, and head for Auckland. The ticket hanging in my office is stamped '*Auswanderer*' ('emigrants') in two places and stipulates 'any refund to be made in Germany only' – a sign of the Nazis' desperation for funds. Salli succeeded in exchanging this ticket for another from the same shipping line so that, prior to sailing to the other end of the world, they could visit their daughters in Cambridge. (Salli and Louise had planned to send for my mother and her sister after they were settled in New Zealand.) They were rebooked on a Rotterdamsche Lloyd ship due to leave Southampton on 15 September 1939 but the outbreak of war upset those plans. The ship on which they had been booked was later torpedoed and sunk off the Algerian coast in 1944.

Salli and Louise's decision to leave Germany was complicated by Salli's blindness, by the way he made his living from the land and the fact that both their families had considered the Rhineland home for at least 150 years. Almost all their cousins and second cousins lived between Essen, about thirty miles to the east of Kempen, and Dulken, a village about eleven miles to the south. The Rhineland was home – their *heimat*. Salli owned around one hundred cows and several plots of land amounting to about 160 acres, scattered in the countryside outside Kempen. This provided him with a comfortable income, the means to support his family and, most importantly for a blind man, a sense of independence and dignity. Despite his disability, Salli was able to do most of what a man of the house did – save for reading and navigating unfamiliar territory.

Salli and Louise faced the same dilemma confronting the majority of German Jews who owned property or had qualifications that were not easy to repot. Only a handful of German Jews – eminent scientists like Albert Einstein or well-known figures like Sigmund Freud – obtained shelter with relative ease. Others tried to refashion themselves to become more attractive to the dispensers of foreign visas. But lawyers, doctors, dentists, schoolteachers, journalists and architects usually lacked the necessary credentials to practise their craft elsewhere. Later, these same qualified professionals became less likely to survive in the concentration camps, where the Germans placed a premium on physical strength or knowledge of a trade or craft that could be exploited. Carpenters, plumbers, electricians, mechanics or even those with an aptitude for forgery were the people who stood a chance – not a blind farmer like Salli or a mid-level judge like Max.

In the weeks following Hitler's seizure of power in 1933, which had made many German Jews panic, I do not know whether Salli and Louise were seized by the impulse to emigrate. As the immediate pandemonium subsided, perhaps they made the mistake of other German Jews who placed their hopes in whatever argument they found most comforting: that Hitler would soon be replaced as chancellor; that he could not possibly mean what he said and wrote; that saner voices would prevail; that Germany, whose proudest accomplishments as a nation were advertisements for the virtue of the Enlightenment – the intellectual movement that had promoted the virtues of rational thought – could not possibly abandon those principles now; and that it was impossible to imagine an organised campaign to exterminate the Jews of the world.

As the owner of two passports which, when the world is not gripped by a plague, give me complete freedom to travel, I find it hard to contemplate being trapped in my own home, let alone answering questions such as: How can I escape? Where can I go? Who will welcome me? What will I do? How will I support myself and my family? And, specifically for Salli, how can I sell one hundred cows and 160 acres? Salli was probably more worldly and daring than Max and must have become acutely concerned in September 1935 when the Nuremberg Laws removed German Jews' citizenship, making them stateless in their own country. By the end of 1937, after he and Louise had dispatched their daughters to school in Berlin, they were trying to engineer their own exit.

The news from a meeting held in Evian, the French spa town, during the summer of 1938, some months after the Nazis annexed Austria, cannot have buoyed Salli and Louise's spirits. Delegates from twenty-nine countries and thirty-nine private organisations convened in Evian to discuss what should be done with 'all these Jews'. Some of them suggested the easiest solution would be to relocate them to newly created sanctuaries in British Guiana, Tanganyika, Madagascar or Alaska; or even an island in the southern Philippines.

For Salli and Louise, and other Jews, the Evian conference revealed a world divided in two: countries where Jews were not wanted and countries where Jews were not welcome. France, Belgium, the Netherlands and Switzerland claimed they were already inundated, and the Canadians and other English-speaking colonies pleaded high unemployment. The British, anxious to pacify the local Muslim, Christian, Druze and Bahai populations, declared Palestine off limits, and pro-Nazi lobbies shut most doors in South America. The representative from Trinidad said his small island could not accept immigrants from countries south of Belgium and east of France. The French went so far as to stipulate that doctors who had trained in other countries, no matter how qualified and well-respected, had to complete not just nine additional years of undergraduate and medical studies once in France but also the last year of high school before they would be eligible to practise there. The Dutch, for their part, had started repatriating Jews who had entered the Netherlands without the proper visa.

The US, first choice for most, was particularly hard to enter. Only 508,000 immigrants of all stripes were admitted between

1931 and 1940, compared to 4.1 million in the prior decade. The annual quota for German immigrants – Jewish or otherwise – was 25,957 in the pre-war period (this increased slightly after Austria fell into the Nazi orbit). However, due to the considerable additional requirements such as citizenship papers and immigrant and transit visas, it wasn't until 1939 that the quota was filled for the first time.

It was the events of Kristallnacht, and Salli's resulting five-day spell in prison, rather than the dispiriting news from Evian, that put an end to any debate that remained about staying. Getting out of Germany was the first challenge. Foreign embassies and consulates throughout the country were overrun with Jews eager to obtain a visa. But the odds were long. It was first necessary to find an overseas sponsor who would vouch for them. They had to deal with the pressures of selling their property at distressed prices and obtain an exit permit. And they had to do all of this before the dates on the passport, or the visa, or the exit permit, expired.

Among Salli and Louise's documents, I found letters of accreditation and affidavits secured from relatives who had fled to Oregon, revealing the difficulties of securing passage to the US. One of the affidavits supporting Salli and his family's entry there acknowledged that the guarantor knew 'Salli Rath's English is extremely poor'. In December 1940, more than a year after he had fled to Britain, Salli received a letter from the US Embassy in London, which referred to his earlier application for an entry visa made in Stuttgart and included a sentence, in something approximating English, that would have tested the most fluent of speakers:

A communication is today being addressed to that office asking that your asserted registration be officially verified
in order that you may be given the benefit thereof and your name entered on the waiting list maintained at this office from the date of your original registration.

The options for entry into Canada were not much better and, thereafter, Brazil, Argentina, Chile and Uruguay were all mooted as possibilities. For the Jews of Germany, Shanghai, due to its distance and local tongue, was considered the least hospitable of all venues.

Salli and Louise eventually plumped for a spot that was about as far from the Rhineland as they could get – New Zealand, where fellow farming friends had landed and where, with money he had been lent, Salli hoped to use his knowledge of cattle trading. On 10 July 1939, Salli and Louise received permission to enter New Zealand but they still needed to obtain a certificate of 'non-objection' to leave Germany.

Salli encountered enormous obstacles as he sought to sell his land and cows. It was only thanks to the mayor of Kempen and a lawyer – both of whom were appalled by what had happened to Germany – that Salli was able to liquidate anything. Several of the people who had leased his pastures refused to pay their rent and bidders for the acreage entered lowball offers. The mayor of Kempen offered almost double the sum that a government agency and the leaders of the local farmers' association had made, and it was he who had advanced 10,000 Reichsmarks so that Salli could pay the so-called *Judensteuern* ('Jew taxes') – the *Judenvermogensabgabe* (Jewish Property Tax); the *Reichsfluchtsteuer* (Reich Flight Tax); and

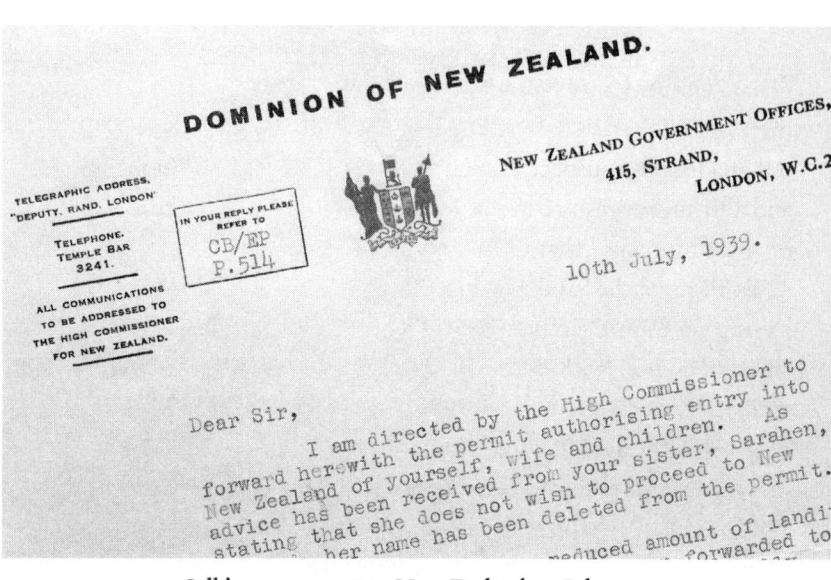

Salli's entry permit to New Zealand, 10 July 1939

the *Golddiskontbank* (Gold Discount Fee) – that Nazis slapped on any Jew who wanted to emigrate. Salli remained convinced that this advance saved his and Louise's lives.

By September 1939, about 400,000 Jews had emigrated from Germany and Austria, leaving around 260,000 in the two countries. The outbreak of war halted emigration to most Western countries and after that, only around 40,000 German Jews escaped (half of whom went to Shanghai, despite the challenges). The remainder were stranded in the grip of the Third Reich, including many members of both sides of my family.

Now, I wonder whether there may just be a simpler explanation for why my father's parents perished while my mother's parents survived. Max was a lawyer, a civil servant and a man who had devoted his entire life to supporting several German governments, which had, at least for some time, provided him with a pension. Salli, by contrast, was largely self-made and, I suspect, had an instinct for self-preservation and a stronger grasp of human nature – or at least the nature of some humans – that ultimately saved his skin.

Both my father and my uncle later wondered why Max, having set foot in England not once but twice, had returned to Germany on both occasions. The immediate answers were straightforward. He had no visa to stay in Britain and Minnie was still in Munich. Later, the answers became murkier. Max may well have clung to the hope that his military service and long membership of the judiciary would render him invulnerable or that more rational hands would wrest control from Hitler, or that foreign powers would not tolerate a barbarous regime in the middle of Europe.

As the Nazi noose tightened, Jake Halevy, the headmaster of Whittingehame, offered an apartment above a garage to Max and Minnie. But they still did not have exit permits or visas to stay in Britain and, according to my uncle, Max fretted that he was too old to start anew, and that none of his legal knowledge would account for much in a country where he didn't even speak the language. Minnie also needed gallbladder surgery. Both my father and uncle said that they felt neither Max nor Minnie had wanted to be a burden on them.

Until the end of his life, Ernest felt deep remorse for remembering that, as a teenager with a venturesome spirit, he had felt relief at the prospect that he would not have to take care of ageing parents. The two final entries made in Max's personnel files in the summer of 1939 illustrated the challenges. These were copies of letters in which he was given permission to transfer his residence abroad until the end of May 1941, subject to revocation at any time, with the proviso that his pension payments were to be transferred in full to a domestic, foreign-currency account.

My mother had a harsher explanation for why Max and Minnie got trapped. She said they were not prepared to accept more straitened circumstances, by following the example of a pair of their Munich friends who had come to England and worked in a factory sewing glass eyes into the faces of teddy bears.

On 25 August 1939, the last Friday of the month and a week before Poland was invaded, my mother wrote to Salli and Louise from Cambridge, just over four months after she had arrived at Liverpool Street station on the 6.20 a.m. from Harwich. It began like an account of a blissful summer day until the note of desperation in the last two sentences:

> *Wednesday we were away all day. We drove to a river. We took our lunch and tea with us and spent the whole day lying by the river. The sun was wonderful and I got quite a tan. Eri* [her sister] *caught three fish, I only caught one. The fish were all thrown back into the river in the evening. Can't you do anything about your emigration? Can't you write if there is anything we can do?*

Today, a trip by car across the now invisible border separating Kempen – in the Rhineland – and the docks of Rotterdam takes about two hours. On 28 August 1939, Salli and Louise were driven by friends to the Hook of Holland. They were among the last of the 55,000 Jews from Europe to gain refuge in England, and arrived at Liverpool Street station on 29 August 1939 – a Tuesday. Two days later, the Royal Navy was mobilised.

Louise's UK refugee cards

Three days later, the Nazis invaded Poland. And five days later, between breakfast and lunch on the first Sunday in September, Britain and Germany were at war. On the same day that Salli and Louise arrived at Liverpool Street, my father's grandfather, Carl Nathan Mayer, died, aged eighty-one, in Frankfurt in a cramped apartment plastered with Nazi propaganda posters where he was cooped up with other Jews. Two days after Carl's death, on 31 August 1939, his daughter and Minnie and Leni's sister, Friedericke Cohn, received her permit to travel to England. It arrived too late. Her destination was not Liverpool Street. It was Theresienstadt.

Between the time Airbnb went public in late 2020 and the day a mob was sent to storm the Capitol Building in early January 2021, a friend sent us a board game called Airbnbopoly, a riff on the old favourite, Monopoly. The familiar railway stations had been replaced with some of the world's busiest airports; neighbourhoods and streets had been substituted with countries, and the priciest city locations with castles and igloos. I read the rules and concluded that I preferred the original British version, where the railway stations of London are labelled Kings Cross, Marylebone, Fenchurch Street and Liverpool Street, where my father had – with Max – first set foot on English soil, and where my mother had arrived with a suitcase in her hand and a label around her neck.

My father, when playing Monopoly, was as cautious with money and fearful of debt as he was in life and favoured three sorts of properties: the utilities (the Electric Company and the Water Works), the railway stations and the cheapest real estate which, on the British version, includes Whitechapel Road and the Old Kent Road. The former and its synonymous district had been London's equivalent of Manhattan's Lower East Side – an area to which immigrants, particularly those of Jewish heritage, flocked. In the case of Whitechapel, Jews had started to arrive there from Amsterdam in the seventeenth century, fleeing the persecution of the Catholic Church, which had made their lives impossible in Spain and Portugal. Towards the end of the nineteenth century, pogroms in Poland and Russia made Whitechapel – situated close to London's docks, the poorest area in the city and the site of Britain's oldest synagogue – the first port of call for Jewish arrivals.

It was also from Whitechapel that Leon Kossoff, one of my favourite painters (an artist who deserves to be mentioned in the same breath as Lucian Freud or Francis Bacon), emerged. He was the son of a Jewish baker and I once foolishly asked him whether he ever missed the smell of fresh bread – not realising, until he answered 'never', that he associated the aroma with penury and unremitting toil.

After learning his craft in the 1950s, Leon never strayed far from the figures in his life and scenes of London that were close to home. He painted views from bridges over railway tracks, entries to Tube stations, and Christ Church, Spitalfields, one of fifty churches built in London in the early eighteenth century in a spree of religiosity ordained by Parliament. The church was a few minutes' walk from Kossoff's father's bakery. Until I received Airbnbopoly, it had never struck me that one of my favourite paintings contains shades of Whitechapel. It is a large oil of Leon's wife Peggy, lying pregnant and naked on a sofa. So proud was Leon of this painting, that it is the only one that he signed in heavy impasto with both his first and second names. Now when I look at the signature, instead of Leon Kossoff, I see the word 'Whitechapel' and I think of how my father, during the holiday breaks he dreaded, was made welcome at Ernest's school in Brighton, which was where, in 1938, they started playing Monopoly. They drew so much amusement from the game that they decided to fashion a German version for the birthdays of Max and Minnie.

The Moritz brothers secured a stray board and stuck labels, bearing the names of Munich streets and landmarks, over the London neighbourhoods. They translated the rule book and Community Chest and Chance cards into German, converted the currency from pounds to deutschmarks, and fashioned houses and hotels from small bits of wood that they painted green and red. I doubt whether either of them contemplated the irony of trying to amuse their parents, who were being stripped of their freedoms, income and possessions, with a game devoted to the accumulation of property. The completed board was sent to, and arrived in, Munich. But in 1938, Max's birthday, which fell in October, and Minnie's, which occurred in November, were separated by Kristallnacht. Before Minnie turned a year older, Max had been arrested and transported to Dachau.

After Max was released, he and Minnie, according to some surviving letters, sometimes spent an evening playing the game their sons had painstakingly crafted. For them, perhaps, dealing the money, or turning over the cards, or moving the small green and red wooden pieces made by their children was a way of maintaining a silent bond between the generations. I hope it was consoling, but it could just as easily have been a source of great emotional pain. As with almost everything, this handmade treasure did not survive the war. And, tragically, the 'Get Out of Jail Free' card supplied by my father and uncle went unredeemed.

THE LOST GENERATION

I WAS IN MY EARLY THIRTIES, learning how to make venture capital investments, when Pierre Lamond, the Frenchman who, for twenty-five years, played an important role in the development of the semiconductor industry and then became a mainstay of Sequoia Capital for two decades, would squelch my enthusiasm to undertake anything by saying, 'I can see you have never been in the army. That teaches you not to volunteer for anything.'

I ponder Pierre's wry comment whenever I consider how my father and uncle attempted to be useful to Britain during World War II. A letter from my uncle dated four days after Britain declared war on Germany, addressed to the Coordinating Committee for Refugees, read,

> Since I, like every Jewish Refugee, owe so much to this country, which has given me shelter from the Nazi persecution, I should like to give my help in some way during this war.
>
> These are the particulars of my person:
>
> NAME: Ernest A. Moritz, age 16½, born at Munich. Studying at Whittingehame College, where I have been since May 1937.
>
> I am a boy scout and know how to type.

> I should be very grateful to you, if you could let me know in what way I can help this country in this time of National Emergency.
> Expecting the favour of your reply,
> I remain,
> Yours faithfully...

On the day that Ernest – who was a boy scout and knew how to type – wrote this letter, my father was waiting to begin college. Once, when I asked my father to name the happiest day of his life, fully expecting the answer to be the day that World War II ended, or when he had married my mother, or when my sister and I had been born, I was startled when he answered, 'The day I discovered I had won a scholarship to Oxford.' This was as close a look into my father's emotions as I was ever permitted. In that sentence, I sensed the pride and relief that he must have felt as a seventeen-year-old living alone in digs, when he learned the news that he had received the scholarship to study at Merton College, Oxford. He saved the clippings from Friday 13 January 1939 announcing his admission as a scholarship student to Oxford – in *The Times*, the *Morning Post*, the *Daily Telegraph* and the *Guardian* – for a lifetime. The scholarship paid for about half his studies, and the rest was covered by a loan he secured from the Education Aid Society, which he paid off until the late 1940s. It was this scholarship that became the second most important visa of his life, following the benevolence that had paid for his studies at St Paul's.

Almost thirty-five years later, in 1973, my father accompanied me on the journey from Cardiff to Oxford. A typewriter, record player and several suitcases sat in the back of the car – a contrast to the single suitcase carried by my father when he had arrived

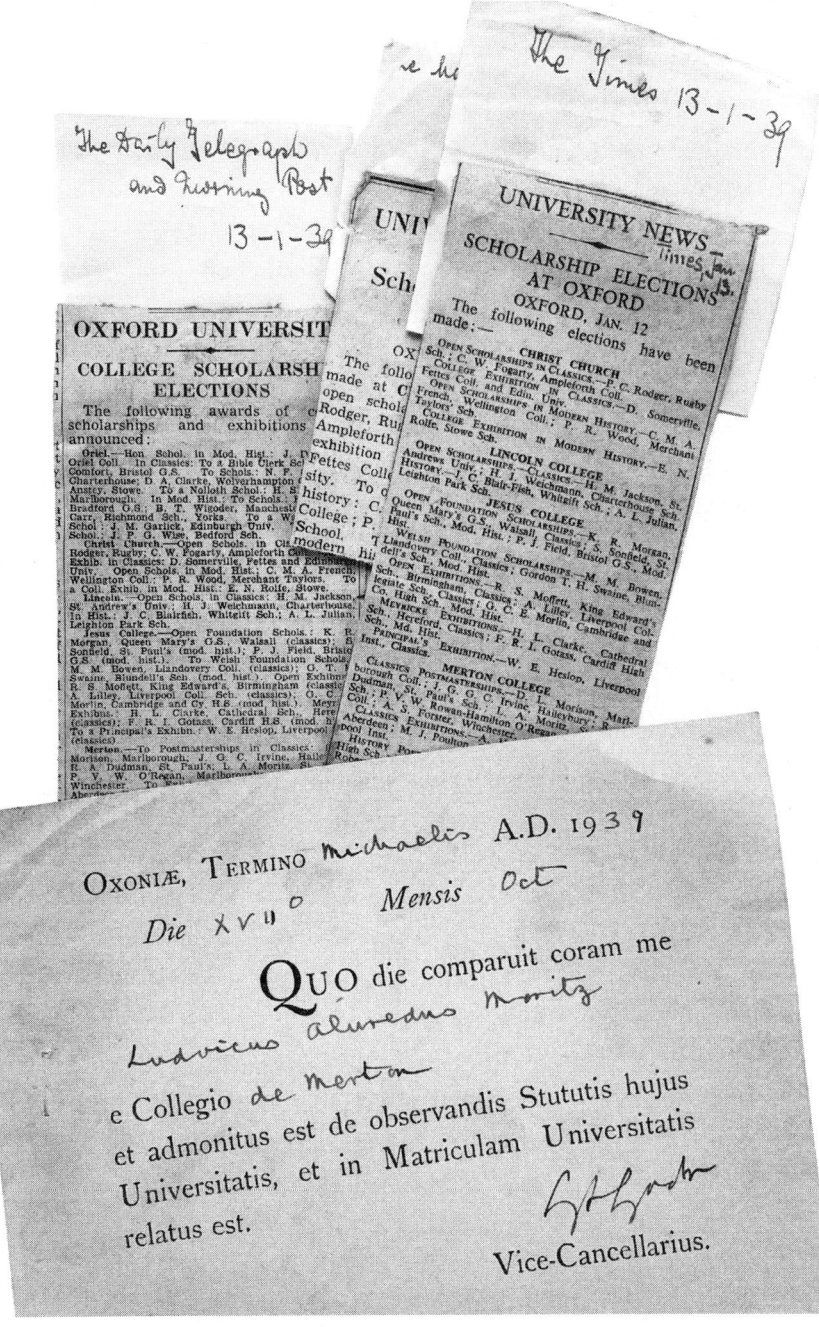

Alfred's Oxford scholarship newspaper notices, 1939

in 1939. We placed my baggage on one of the wooden hand trolleys Christ Church students use at the start and end of each term and set off across the quadrangle. As I pulled the trolley with its small steel wheels across the gravelled paths, I was too self-absorbed to think about how my father felt, as he looked at the fresh limestone buildings and remarked that Oxford never seemed to change, save for the fact that he remembered when all the buildings were coated with soot.

Yet I too remember feeling like a rank outsider during my first few weeks at Oxford. Soon after I arrived, late one night, there were sounds of heavy footsteps racing up a wooden staircase and a loud, fruity voice roaring repeatedly, 'Did he chunder?' *Chunder.* I had never heard the word. I understood the meaning of 'sick', 'retch', 'throw up', 'puke' and 'vomit', but 'chunder' was part of the vocabulary of a foreign world.

It was the vocabulary of the public-school boys – the voices of Eton, Harrow, Winchester, Marlborough and Westminster – who invariably were chosen to recite grace before dinner. In those moments, instead of yelling questions such as 'Did he chunder?' as they did in the still of the night, they confidently boomed, '*Nos miseri homines et egeni, pro cibis quos nobis ad corporis subsidium benigne es largitus, tibi Deus omnipotens, Pater cælestis…*' as they stood behind the lectern to the right of High Table in the sixteenth-century limestone and oak-panelled hall of Christ Church. I also recalled the casual way in which, after dinner in the Hall, they added a bottle of port to the tabs they kept open at the college bar. Some of these students did not think twice about skipping the dinner that had already been paid for and substituting it with a far more expensive dinner in London and a night with a girl, returning, sleepless, in time for breakfast the following morning. Their parents could afford to entertain six of their son's friends for dinner and, as the evening ended, pay the bill without double-checking each entry, and pressing a large note into the waiter's hand. When the Queen and the Duke of Edinburgh visited the college one evening for dinner, they fell into easy conversation with her and treated them like relatives, which, for some, she was. One boy, to my astonishment, had a new BMW with a set of golf clubs lying across the back seat, which stood out when parked alongside the tutors' far shabbier cars.

I doubt whether these particular young men understood the import of the dean's welcoming remarks when we all assembled in the Hall for our introductory meeting, as he instructed us to remember one thing: that it was far easier to attract a new student than one of the 'scouts' – the college servants. He did not pause to describe the lives of these scouts (although mine liked to recount to me how as an army private he landed in northern Norway in 1940 without an overcoat or gloves). Nor did the dean explain how the college gates were locked at midnight and women were banned from rooms; or how other students like Benazir Bhutto, three decades before she was assassinated and twenty-eight years after her father was hanged, and who occupied a perch of impossible privilege, liked to drive around Oxford in a yellow MG; or how Imran Khan, who also became prime minister of Pakistan, was already a Test cricketer by the time he played for Oxford, where he developed a reputation as a charming rake.

In 1973, there were marked differences between the students who enrolled in Oxford. Students like me, from state schools (those that had received a free education), were still in a minority – as were the Welsh and the Jews. But the distinctions were far less pronounced than they were when my father had begun his studies at Merton College and the government provided no support.

When my father arrived at Oxford there were two categories of students: those whose parents could afford the tuition and board, and those, like my father, who subsisted entirely on scholarships. It was still very much the era portrayed by Evelyn Waugh in *Brideshead Revisited* and by the RAF pilot Richard Hillary, who was severely burned when his Spitfire was shot down and, after returning to combat, perished, aged twenty-three, in 1943, just one year after Macmillan published his memoir, *The Last Enemy*. He noted in the book he wrote of his interrupted time at Oxford that he and his friends inhabited a dissolute milieu. 'I venture to think that we differed little in essentials from the majority of young men with a similar education. We were disillusioned and spoiled. The press referred to us as the Lost Generation and we were not displeased. Superficially we were selfish and egocentric without any Holy Grail in which we could lose ourselves.' When I read this passage, I thought of myself tugging the wooden trolley across the quadrangle of Christ Church and realised how I too, at the time, was 'selfish and egocentric', not pausing to imagine, or enquire about, what might have been passing through my father's mind.

In 1939, as my father took his place among the scholars of Merton, the college's art and silverware were being moved to cellars, and windows were being draped with blackout shades. The universal military call-up depleted all ranks, from the college servants to the scientists recruited to conduct urgent research on radar, rockets, nuclear power and sonar. Previous graduates from Christ Church served Winston Churchill as his Foreign Secretary, Marshal of the Royal Air Force and chief scientific advisor, while one, from whom I received history tutorials decades later, was installed as a member of MI6 (where he worked for the Radio Security Service decrypting German wireless transmissions), and for whom he later became a talent-spotter. Another, Hugh Trevor-Roper, was a young researcher at Merton when my father arrived, and whose work *The Last Days of Hitler* was published to great acclaim in 1947.

I thought of this period in 2019, when I was standing in the Oxford University Museum of Natural History beneath the neck of a Megalosaurus dinosaur at a reception for Crankstart scholars, a programme that provides financial support to students from low-income households which Harriet and I helped set up. One of the recipients was describing how the headmistress of her school in Bolton had told her that 'Oxford was not for people like us', and I knew, as I stood in my Italian suit, custom-made shirt and suede loafers with a chauffeured car waiting outside, it would have seemed disingenuous if I had said, 'I know how you feel', or even 'My father would have known how you feel'. Despite my silence on the subject at the time, the empathy I felt was there.

In March 1940, my father's tutor at Merton, where he had begun studying Greats, wrote a reference to help him land a position in the Armed Forces. 'He is easily the best man of his year in this college although considerably younger than most of the scholars of his year. In personality he is quiet, friendly and steady-going and I could not wish to see a boy adapt himself to strange and unhappy circumstances with better fortitude and balance than he has done.' This accolade recognised the talent that my father was always too modest to advertise. Unlike many scholars, he never radiated the arrogance of those who come to spend a lifetime in academe. The Oxford tutor also observed, in an echo of what the German army officer had written about Max during World War I, 'He has none of the qualities which create prejudice against his race or against refugees and is liked and respected by everyone here.' Yet, in the time of national emergency, the country had other plans for my uncle, the boy scout who knew how to type, and my father, the best man of his year.

A LEG OF GOAT

I HAVE ALWAYS BEEN HAUNTED by a painting, made in 1943 by Richard Eurich, one of Britain's war artists who, although gifted, never rose to prominence. The work portrays the heads of five men gazing soulfully into the middle distance. One, wearing round, horn-rimmed spectacles, supports his head with his right hand. Behind him, half-concealed, is a man whose right eye, circled by reddish and purplish folds of skin, is sunk deep into the shadows of his head. The figure to his right is wearing a scarf bearing red, white and blue stripes, which form the brightest registers in the composition and suggest the Union Jack. On his left, a younger man, only half in focus, appears like a phantom summoned from the past.

I thought of this painting one wintry afternoon when rain, carried by gusts from the Golden Gate, plastered bursts against the windows of our home in San Francisco. I was in the middle of aimlessly meandering along the back trails of the internet, prompted more by curiosity than purpose, reading about the Jews who were interned on the Isle of Man during World War II.

An idle click took me to the archives of Tate Britain and there I tripped across thumbnails of 164 black-and-white photographs of internees. There were photographs of laundry hanging on a fence, of a man working at a desk near a window, of a guard patrolling alongside a wire boundary, of the camp commandant, of converted hostelries around a sloping square overlooking Douglas Bay, of men chopping wood, of roll-call line-ups, of shower stalls and of drawings, prints, linocuts and paintings that formed part of one of the regularly scheduled art exhibitions. There was also one of a group of internees and their guards standing in a field.

In the foreground of this photograph, about three dozen men and four British soldiers are lined up behind a low fence loosely strung with two strands of barbed wire – nothing that would present much of an obstacle for fox hunters or deer, or anyone wanting to escape. A copse and a patch of sky in the background suggest a world beyond. The internees are wearing overcoats; a few have hats. A couple of the men hold walking sticks. Some are smiling and, to the left of the photograph, one of the internees rests his hand on the shoulder of one of the soldiers. A figure, half-obscured, towards the centre of the third row, stops me cold. This man is Alfred, my father.

Although I remember one or two mentions of the Isle of Man while I was growing up, until I found this photograph, I had never paused to think of my father as ever being on the wrong side of the law, or an internee, or an 'Enemy Alien'. He was a man who considered a parking ticket as being dangerously close to a prison sentence.

In another photograph, there he is again. This time among a group of seven men standing on a sloping hillside, wearing raincoats and overcoats with their collars turned up against the weather. My father is looking directly at the photographer. He is smoking a bent pipe with a white band around the shaft that forms the brightest tone in the photograph. His hair is windblown and sweeps to the right of his head. He is smiling

Alfred interned on the Isle of Man, 1941

as if he has just shared a joke with one of the men to the right. He is nineteen years old.

Both my father and uncle wound up behind barbed wire on the Isle of Man in 1940 after a river of fear and suspicion about all Germans coursed through Britain following the fall of Denmark, Norway, Belgium, the Netherlands, Luxembourg and France, and the encirclement of the British Army at Dunkirk. Every German and Italian male over the age of sixteen was subject to a British government order to round up 'Enemy Aliens'. In all, 27,000 were interned (although Salli, because of his blindness, was an exception). It was an assortment that included Yiddish-speaking Hasidim, Spanish Civil War veterans, Italian waiters, former government ministers of Prussia, Protestant priests and captured German soldiers and airmen.

Ernest was the first of the Moritz brothers to be detained and, days later, my father was ordered to report to a police station in Oxford. The pair were soon camped out in tents behind barbed wire on a council estate in Liverpool and from there, put aboard ships supplied by the Isle of Man Steam Packet Company. On the Isle of Man, they were billeted in hurriedly converted boarding houses on the Central Promenade in Douglas where, as an air-raid precaution, the windows were painted blue, and the rooms illuminated with red lightbulbs. My uncle's possessions were tucked in the German army surplus backpack with a horsehide clip that had accompanied him to England and which, unlike its original owner, my father's namesake, Ludwig Alfred Mayer, had survived World War I.

The Moritz brothers became absorbed in the small communities that developed in each boarding house, organised throughout the camp under the gaze of a predominantly benevolent military authority. I don't know how much they encountered each other or indeed anything about their feelings of waking up in an unheated room occupied by strangers during wintry weather on an island in the middle of the Irish Sea. They would have read the hand-printed newspapers that circulated, listened to lectures that were given (with enough experts among the interned to assemble a curriculum that would have done most universities proud) and attended religious services. I suspect my uncle who, by disposition, was always more outgoing than my father, probably found the adjustment easier. Yet the Moritz brothers would have been mere cyphers compared to some of the more notable internees, such as Kurt Schwitters, whose originality had made him stand out in the adventurous art scene of Weimar Berlin, where one of his hallmarks were collages assembled from the detritus of cigarette boxes, candy wrappings, used stamps and newspapers. On the Isle of Man, according to the recollections of other inmates, he occasionally sculpted porridge, slept beneath his bed and barked like a dog.

During the summer of 1940, Ernest was among 7,000 internees deported to Canada and Australia to provide more capacity on the Isle of Man. Five ships were designated for this duty and within the span of twenty days, four sailed from Liverpool and one from Greenock, west of Glasgow. Ernest, bound for Canada, was sent from Scotland on 4 July (a month during which U-boats sank thirty-nine ships in the North Atlantic) aboard the SS *Jan Sobieski*, a commandeered Polish steamship, which, just days earlier, had helped spirit British troops away from the Dunkirk beaches and, some weeks earlier, had retrieved other British troops from Norway.

Two days before Ernest sailed, another ship, the SS *Arandora Star*, one day out from Liverpool and also due to travel to

Canada, was torpedoed by a German U-boat, and 805 men drowned. The vessel had been carrying many innocent Italians, rounded up from – among other places – London's restaurants, along with Jewish refugees. Some of the survivors were subsequently placed aboard the HMT *Dunera*, bound for Australia, whose fifty-seven-day voyage between Liverpool and Sydney became the subject of a government inquiry after it was discovered that the internees had been robbed and subjected to beatings and other acts of violence. Several of the *Dunera*'s senior officers in charge were subsequently court-martialed.

Compared to the unfortunates who had been consigned to the *Arandora Star* and the *Dunera*, Ernest escaped lightly, although barbed-wire barriers had to be installed aboard the *Jan Sobieski* to separate the 982 Jewish refugees from the 548 German prisoners of war. The convoy in which the *Jan Sobieski* sailed was escorted by several British warships, including the hopelessly antiquated HMS *Revenge*, which had seen action in 1916's Battle of Jutland, the largest naval battle of World War I. Squirrelled away in the holds of some of these ships, to keep them out of Nazi clutches, were Polish art treasures including a coronation sword from 1320, a Gutenberg Bible, more than a hundred tapestries and several dozen Chopin manuscripts. The British ships, as part of Operation Fish – the largest movement of physical wealth in history – carried gold bars sent for safekeeping by the Bank of England to the vaults of the Bank of Canada.

After landing in Halifax, all the Germans – Jews and Nazis alike – were pelted with tomatoes as they walked along the dockside and subsequently were temporarily confined. Towards the end of July 1940, the Jews were taken to one of around forty camps in which there were Germans, Silesians, Bavarians and

Austrians; academics, artists and musicians; butchers, bakers, carpenters, plumbers, barbers, dentists and doctors; Orthodox rabbis, communists, trade unionists and social democrats; family men, schoolboys and college students.

Ernest ended up in Ripples, the largest of the internment camps, in a remote part of New Brunswick. On arrival, he and others were unloaded from trucks and ushered into a camp behind twin rows of barbed wire, surrounded by floodlights and with machine-gun turrets in each corner. They were surprised to see that the barracks were built on stilts about five feet above ground level – high enough to stand over the snows that came during the perishingly cold winters. The younger internees, including Ernest, spent much of their time hewing wood from the surrounding forests for the fuel to keep the camp warm. They were also given uniforms emblazoned with a large red circle on the back of the jacket to make them easier to spot should they try to escape.

Some months later, the British government, heeding a Canadian request to distinguish between the different categories of internees, sent Alexander Paterson, the UK Commissioner of Prisons and a renowned social reformer, to unravel the confusion. In Britain, Paterson had campaigned for fines and probation instead of incarceration, shorter prison sentences and more enlightened treatment for young offenders. In the early 1930s, during a tour of US prisons, he had been appalled by the harshness of sentences and the primitive conditions. The Canadians baulked at Paterson's authority, and he was obliged to remain in Canada for over eight months to interview and evaluate every refugee, including Ernest. Paterson was disgusted by what he found, took exception to the military – rather than civilian – control of the camps and reported to his superiors back home, 'The uniform an internee is required to wear is both degrading and unworthy of a civilisation that believes in encouraging the individual, rather than treading on his soul. It was disturbing to find distinguished university professors dressed as clowns. The red circle, which is commonly supposed to be a target for the machine guns, is a shabby insult to men who are ready to wear the Red Cross.'

After his interview with Paterson and ten months in the camp, Ernest was shipped back to the Isle of Man for processing and then released – a reflection of the backlash of the British public against the internment of refugees and in stark contrast to the way Vichy France treated Jews, or the US government later treated its Japanese internees. By August 1941, only 1,300 refugees remained in British camps. Following his return, Ernest wrote a letter to Paterson expressing gratitude for his help, never expecting to receive a reply. Instead, he was invited to make contact should he ever find himself in London. One Sunday, His Majesty's Commissioner of Prisons met Ernest outside Sloane Square Underground station before taking him to his home for lunch, where the latter saw an unexpected amount of meat (which was subject to severe rationing) on the serving plate. A friend had sent the Patersons a leg of goat.

THE MUNICIPAL
SLAUGHTERHOUSE

AMONG THE FIVE BOXES containing all the documented heritage of my family that my sister had shipped to me from Wales, I found a notelet and a bulging envelope that contained carefully folded pages of typewritten German. The first is a plaintive message sent – under the auspices and rules of the International Red Cross – from Cambridge written in German by Louise, my grandmother, to Salli's cousin in Kempen, Andreas Rath, on which she had pencilled the twenty-five words she was permitted and had signed it not just with her name and Salli's but also with both her daughters' – as if transmitting four separate messages of concern: 'We are all doing very well. We are sending Hanne, Karla, you and the whole community the warmest greetings and wishes for your well-being.' Several months later, the message was returned in a small envelope, postmarked in Berlin on – of all dates – Hitler's birthday, 20 April 1942. The envelope was stamped '*Zurück*' ('Return') and contained a typed one-line message on a half-inch strip of paper: 'According to police information, the recipient cannot be traced and has moved to…' There was nothing else – no mention of a destination or of Andreas' condition. Just silence.

The folded pages of typed German contained in the bulging envelope were circulated in 1945 among the handful of refugees from Kempen who had been granted sanctuary by the UK.

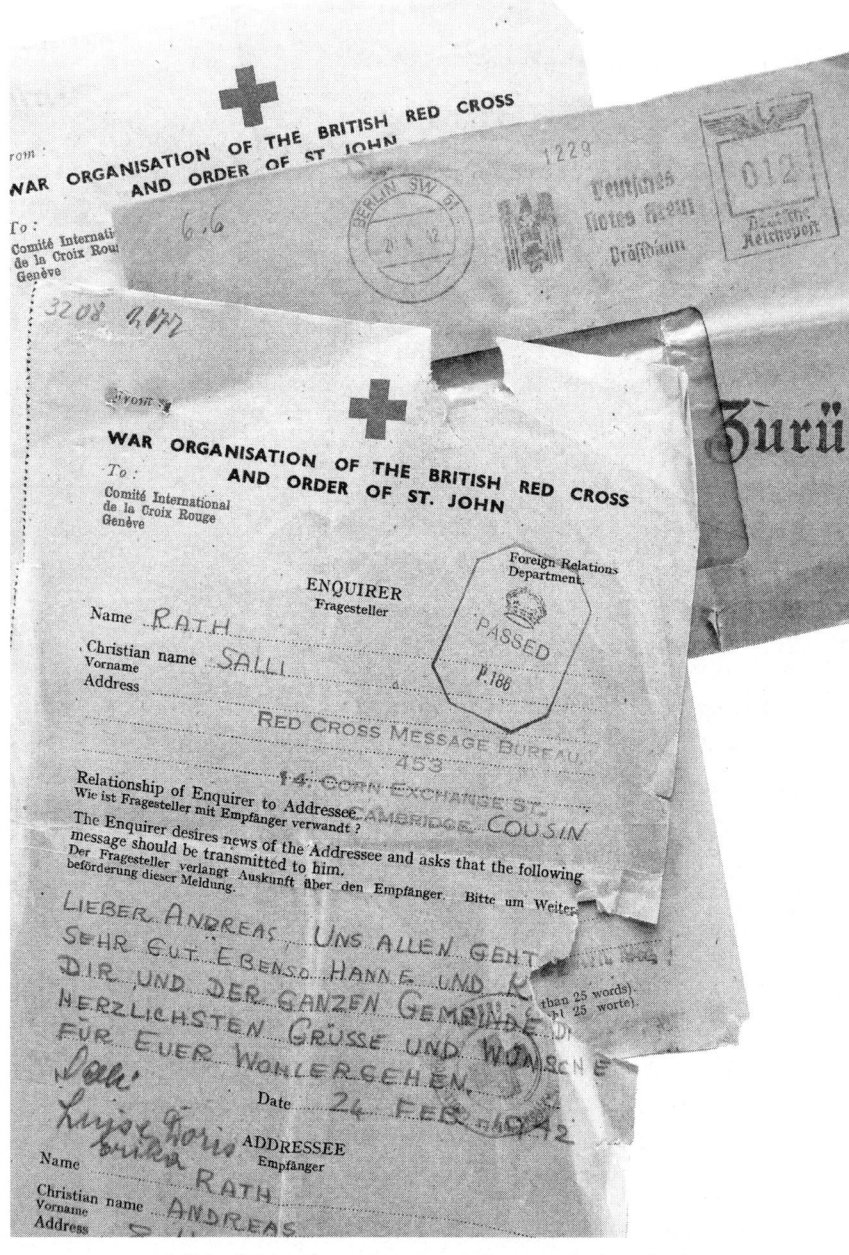

Salli and Louise's vain attempts to contact Andreas Rath, 1942

It contained an account of what had happened to Andreas and the other Jews from the Rhineland and had been written by a friend of Louise and Salli who had fled to Sweden, which was where, after the war ended in Europe, he had been given a gruesome recital of events by one of the few Jewish survivors of the concentration camps. Before this brown envelope was pushed through their mailbox in Cambridge, Salli and Louise had not received any account of the fate of their relatives and friends who had been trapped in Germany.

Like Salli, Andreas' livelihood had depended on cattle – although he was a drover who ushered the cattle between pastures, a bachelor and a man of modest means. Both Salli and Andreas, like their parents and grandparents, had been on friendly terms with other members of this rural community. Yet their livelihoods made them vulnerable to the racist propaganda of the Nazis, which portrayed them as exploiters of hardworking Germans and accused them of deceiving and underpaying farmers, negotiating unfairly and levying exorbitant interest rates.

In early December 1941, word went out to the Jews in the towns and villages of the Rhineland that they had to present themselves for 'evacuation' to Riga, Latvia, along with instructions about the baggage, money and documents they were permitted to bring. They were each limited to provisions for three days, bedlinen, eating utensils and 50 deutschmarks. The only papers they were allowed to carry were passports bearing the stamp 'evacuated'.

Buses and trains brought Andreas and others from Kempen to Düsseldorf on 11 December 1941, where they were herded to the city slaughterhouse, near the city's goods station. There, soldiers rifled through their possessions, relieved them of their valuables and instructed them to sleep on the concrete floor. In the early morning, they were roused and marched towards the goods station – a departure point purposefully selected to conceal the activity from ordinary Germans and curb potential unrest.

Along the way, one man tried to commit suicide by throwing himself under a tram. An hour or so later, an elderly woman managed to disappear from among the 1,007 Jews who were subsequently forced to stand for five hours on a platform, but she was discovered by a domestic servant in a bathroom of a nearby house and returned to the station. Another man, who had the temerity to enquire of a guard when the train would arrive, was clubbed to death in front of the others.

Andreas and his fellow townspeople were among the first wave of Western European Jews sent to the east (mainly to Łódź, Minsk, Kovno and Riga) in the weeks after Hitler had ordered the murder of every Jew on the continent – an edict presaged by the mass shootings of Soviet Jews, which had started in the summer of 1941. The Rhinelanders were being assembled for the improvised rehearsals of mass murder that allowed the Nazis to figure out how to kill Jews not just by the thousands, but by the hundreds of thousands, and then by the millions.

A meticulous report written by the commander of the transport, a former municipal policeman, was discovered after the war. It reads as if the train, destined for Riga and composed of third-class carriages, had been carrying squawking chickens or squealing pigs, rather than men, women and children. The report makes occasional mention of the deportees, but its most animated sections deal with the inconveniences and discomforts suffered by the guards during a journey in which it rained and snowed almost continuously, and which was punctuated by frequent stops to provide right of way to military transport. The commander complains about the dilatory performance of the Deutsche Reichsbahn, the impudent behaviour of some of the railway officials and includes a list of suggested improvements for future transport. He advises that the carriage carrying the guards should be positioned nearer the middle of the train where the heat worked better; that the troops should be equipped with fur coats and boots; and that attention be paid to providing more drinking water for the Jews since they were difficult to control if they were permitted to disembark to gather snow to melt and quench their thirst. As an aside, the report mentions that a boy died in the seventeenth carriage and a menstruating fourteen-year-old girl had suffered a heart attack.

It took the train sixty-one hours to transport Andreas across Germany and Poland to the outskirts of Riga. On arrival, the German commander transferred responsibility for the transport to the Latvian SS (whose cruelty managed to exceed that of its German counterparts) and was himself conveyed by police car to the guest house of the local SS commander. The following day, he recounted, 'Riga is a very beautiful city that could compete with any city in the Reich.' He also noted that it was possible to buy a very satisfying lunch at an affordable price, and that the Latvians did not understand why the Germans went to the bother of shipping all the Jews to the east to be killed, rather than just murdering them at home.

While the German commander was driven by car to Riga, Andreas and his friends and relatives from Kempen remained in the train for another night in freezing weather. After daylight made the ice-coated platform slightly less treacherous, the Latvian guards unbolted the doors, and the passengers – now stripped of their suitcases and restricted to backpacks or handbags – were made to trudge, five abreast, four miles to the ghetto in Riga.

There they found pools of blood on the streets, corpses in some of the houses and apartments, uncleared tables and ovens that were still warm. These were the last traces of the previous occupants of the ghetto, where the 40,000 Jews of the town – about one tenth of its population – had been confined following the German invasion of Latvia in the summer of 1941. On 30 November and 8 December 1941, 24,000 Jews had been forcibly marched out of the ghetto, ordered to undress, toss their shoes and clothes onto different piles and were then machine-gunned beside open trenches in the nearby forest of Rumbula. Except for the slaughter at Babi Yar, this was the biggest two-day massacre of the Shoah until the construction of the death camps in 1942.

The newly arrived men, like Andreas, were jammed into rooms housing twelve to eighteen other people, and then immediately put to work unloading ships in the harbour – a four-hour journey each way, on foot. Others were ordered to cut peat. Some of the arrivals from Kempen and the Rhineland survived the shock of a Baltic winter and life in the ghetto. They became acquainted with the laws of barbarity: instant execution if found in possession of food or money or for failing to open a railcar door quickly enough; bodies left dangling from gallows for three or four days; and a ritual hanging every Saturday, the Jewish sabbath.

Andreas survived for about a year in Salaspils, a concentration camp about eleven miles from the Riga ghetto where he had first been consigned. He was not among the 3,000 considered unfit for work, who were deceived into believing they were being transferred to a work camp and were then murdered and buried in the Bikernieki forest – a name that barely registers as a third-rate corpse-processing facility in the history of the Shoah. He also survived the reprisals conducted by the Nazis after a group of escapees from the ghetto had been rooted out of nearby forests. But he almost certainly starved to death before he could witness the destruction of the ghetto by the Nazis in late 1943, the deportation of the surviving Jews to nearby barracks or the reopening of the mass graves during the summer of 1944, when the Jews who had been forced to burn the remains were subsequently shot.

Two years after the war, the commander of the train that took Andreas towards his death applied to be reinstated in the German police administration, saying in a letter sent to the Head of the Düsseldorf Police, 'I promise that I will also serve the cause with my whole being in the new democracy, just as I did under the governments of Wilhelm II, Ebert, Hindenburg and the Third Reich. I ask that you please employ me again in the police, albeit at the rank of chief inspector.' He was not readmitted to the ranks but received full pension benefits until his death in 1972 in Düsseldorf, the same city where Andreas and thousands of others had spent a night in the municipal slaughterhouse, before being marched to the goods station, where a man had been clubbed to death on the platform and where the Jews were forced to board a train that did not have proper heating for the guards.

A NINETY-MINUTE MEETING

ON A CRISP SEPTEMBER MORNING during a business trip to Europe, in 2017 I set out on a bicycle across Bebelplatz, where the books had burned in 1933, onto the Unter den Linden, past the red awning of the Hotel Adlon, around the Brandenburg Gate, through the Tiergarten and along Bismarckstrasse where, as the minutes passed, the traffic gained intensity as more Berliners joined the early-morning commute. I had no planned route and passed the Berlin Zoo where, in the aftermath of Allied bombing raids, the carcasses of crocodiles, buffalo, antelope and deer provided hundreds of meals for the grandparents and great-grandparents of some of the commuters making their way into the city on that weekday morning.

At an intersection, another cyclist offered to show me the easiest way out of the city and led me onto a cycle path through the Grunewald, where he revealed that, during all but the worst of the winter weather, he cycled twenty-five miles each way to his job in Potsdam, where he had recently been promoted to the post of hotel manager for one of a small group of family-owned hotels.

Along the side of the wide dirt bike path, there were occasional signs pointing towards Wannsee – a name irrevocably associated with one of history's darkest hours. I bade farewell to the young hotel manager at the Havelchaussee and cycled down the narrow road enclosed by pine, birch and oak trees until, tugged by morbid curiosity about a particular house, I reversed direction and threaded my way into a residential neighbourhood.

I propped my bike against the closed iron gates of Am Grosser Wannsee 56–58, through which I could see a straight driveway that looped around a grassy oval in front of a neoclassical villa with arched casement windows and a porte cochère supported by a pair of Ionic columns. Four adolescent putti stood on the parapet. They had long enjoyed a view of all visitors, including the fifteen men who had arrived for a meeting on a Tuesday morning – 20 January 1942 – some six weeks after Andreas Rath had been deported from Kempen.

This meeting, which lasted about ninety minutes (roughly the length of the movies that were later made about it), had originally been scheduled some weeks earlier but the Japanese attack on Pearl Harbor and Hitler's decision to declare war on the US had forced a postponement. Reinhard Heydrich, the chairman of the meeting (whose office in Munich Minnie had called in 1933 to try and obtain Oskar's release from Dachau), was the son of an opera singer and composer and had served in the German Navy until being dismissed for conduct unbecoming an officer and a gentleman. Heydrich had summoned senior representatives from different departments of the Third Reich to this house on the edge of the Wannsee to coordinate and cement his control over an operation designed to eliminate the 11 million Jews who lived in the lands that the Reich controlled or had in its sights. The inventory of Jews that was surveyed even included 4,000 in Ireland and 200 in Albania. Apart from six lawyers, the other participants in the meeting included Nazi officials who had previously worked as a policeman, a travelling salesman, a bank clerk, a wine salesman, a furniture mover and an interior decorator.

The meeting's most junior participant was the man from Latvia responsible for the fate of Andreas Rath and the other Jews of Kempen. He explained the difficulty of disposing of a high volume of Jews when graves had to be dug in frozen ground; the challenge of contending with troops dealing with the psychological consequences of shooting or machine-gunning civilians; and the mechanical complications and inefficiencies associated with operating the gas vans that had previously been used to murder mentally ill children but were now packed tight with Jewish people of all ages.

The minutes of this 'Conference on the Final Solution of the Jewish Question' were purposefully vague and recorded that 'Due to the war, the emigration plan has been replaced with a deportation of the Jews to the east, in accordance with the Fuhrer's will.' The chairman noted that many of the Jews were expected to succumb to hard labour while the others would be 'treated accordingly'. There was no explicit mention of that great Nazi invention: the combination of the concentration camp and the gas chamber.

The fifteen men who attended this meeting eventually met different fates. Some months after its conclusion, Heydrich, by then 'Deputy Reich Protector of the Protectorate of Bohemia and Moravia', died from wounds suffered in an assassination attempt as he was being driven towards his office at Prague Castle in a green, open-topped Mercedes 320 Cabriolet B (which triggered savage reprisals by the Nazis, including the annihilation of the 500 inhabitants of Lidice). Three others died towards the end of the war or shortly thereafter; four were hanged after being tried in Nuremberg; one committed suicide;

two eluded the Allies and were never heard from again; one became a city clerk; one an academic; another a city treasurer; and one was released from prison due to lack of evidence, returned to the practice of law and was subsequently working as a tax advisor in Ulm at the same time that I, some seventy miles to the south, was spending my summer mornings walking up a hill with my father, carrying our breakfast rolls and a churn of fresh milk. This tax advisor died just eighteen months before our eldest son was born in San Francisco.

The Wannsee House became a museum and memorial in 1992 and I noticed on Google that one visitor has given it a two-star review: 'One star for seeing a cat and another star for meeting such cute ducks.'

NO SITTING ON TRAMS

ONE NIGHT DURING THE PANDEMIC I watched *Ida*, a 2013 film by Paweł Pawlikowski, set amid the bleakness of communist Poland in the early 1960s and shot in stark black and white. Before taking her final vows, Ida, a young novice, is instructed by the mother superior of her convent to go and unearth her family history. Ida journeys to meet her aunt – a woman in her mid-forties who is a judge and a notoriously severe upholder of communist justice but, haunted by a life that is slowly revealed, has become a chain-smoking alcoholic and spends her nights picking up strangers in bars and sleeping with them in the spacious apartment to which she is entitled as a senior jurist. The girl learns – from her aunt – that she herself is Jewish and had been sheltered as an orphan by the sisters of the convent. The aunt explains that their family home had been in Lublin and the girl reveals she had been planning to travel to nearby Piaski the following day.

Lublin. Piaski. I rewound the film to make sure I had heard correctly. The subtitles left no room for confusion. I first heard of Lublin when, as a boy engaged in my first, primitive attempts at genealogy, I asked my father where Max and Minnie had been murdered. His answer was Lublin. He never mentioned Piaski, a village fifteen miles to the southeast. My father imparted nothing but the fact that Max and Minnie were killed in Lublin. He didn't describe how, or even if, they had actually reached Lublin, or whether their lives had been ended at one of the extermination centres for which the area around Lublin served as a hub. Maybe my father had always shied away from wanting to know the place and circumstances of their deaths. Lublin was the answer. Lublin sufficed. There was a finality about the name. Neither my father nor Ernest ever expressed an interest in visiting Poland to investigate the circumstances further.

I remember, as a boy, being dissatisfied with my father's explanation about where Max and Minnie died. It was not because of the absence of detail, but because the answer was Lublin. Nobody of my age had even heard of Lublin. I was insulted, angry even, that the Nazis had only seen fit to transport Max and Minnie to one of their second-rate killing centres rather than to one of places whose names are known around the world for their unspeakable deeds – Auschwitz, Bergen-Belsen, Treblinka. As a boy I felt that if they were going to kill Max and Minnie, they should have done so properly. I am at a loss to explain why my immature brain made me think that my paternal grandparents had not been extended a common courtesy, had not been awarded a proper send-off – Auschwitz. Now, I shudder at my childhood vanities.

In the movie, Ida seems to have been stirred by a similar sort of curiosity about the way her relatives met their end, because she says she wants to visit the remains of her parents. Her aunt explains, 'They have no graves. Neither they, nor any other Jews. No one knows where their bodies are.' Yet she drives Ida through the barren Polish countryside to the former family home, now occupied by the Polish peasants who had provided shelter to Ida's mother and to her own small son until, fearful of being discovered harbouring Jews, they murdered them in the woods and buried them in a common grave. The aunt intimidates the peasants and forces them to reveal the grave and exhume the remains. The girl and aunt wrap and cradle the skulls in their arms and drive to Lublin where they inter the bones in the family plot in a cemetery full of tilted gravestones jutting from the undergrowth like malformed teeth.

Days later, the aunt sits in her apartment, stroking the photograph of a small boy she has placed among cracked and torn photographs assembled in an improvised family tree. The following morning, after the man she has picked up in a drunken stupor departs, she eats a slice of bread slathered in butter topped by a sprinkling of sugar and sits in her bath smoking a cigarette and staring into space. Then she dresses in her nightgown, places Mozart's 'Jupiter' Symphony on her record player, and does what so many other Jews had done before in broad daylight, pouring rain or a night snowstorm – holding the hand of a spouse, clutching a child, murmuring a prayer or screaming; she jumps to her death from an open window. This was my reintroduction to Lublin.

As a boy, I had not known that Lublin was the headquarters of the General Government established by the Third Reich to rule over large parts of Eastern Europe and had become the centre of Operation Reinhard, concocted in the house in Wannsee; or that Hans Frank, the governor-general of Poland, that former student of the Munich's Maximiliansgymnasium and Max's former boss, had issued a barrage of punitive decrees from Lublin.

Nor had I known that Jews from elsewhere in Poland and Western Europe had been deported to the villages and shtetls surrounding Lublin until they could be fed into the killing machines. The entire area around Lublin was a holding pen for the slaughterhouses of Treblinka, Chełmno, Sobibor, Majdanek and Bełżec – although the Nazis did not fatten the people they considered pigs. Today, Lublin's official website bears the slogan 'City of Inspiration', and exactly 4,730 words are devoted to its history. Only twenty-two of these refer to the 42,830 Jews who made up about one third of the town's population in 1939, or all the other Jews for whom the name Lublin meant death. The official website does not mention that the Nazis, after occupying the town in September 1939, renamed its main garden Adolf Hitler Park; that they summoned a military band to drown out the wailing of Jews as they watched their books go up in flames; that children were shot along with their teachers in one of the town's suburbs; that patients from the Jewish hospitals were murdered in the nearby forests; or that a Jewish barber who also operated a brothel collaborated with the Nazis and helped consign victims to their death.

Between the summer of 1938 – when Ernest made his last and only trip to Munich, while my father stayed in London to study for his Oxford entrance examinations – and early 1942, when the Jews of Munich first heard rumours about deportation, correspondence between Max and Minnie and their sons had been limited. After war broke out, it was reduced to the occasional International Red Cross postcard.

In early 1940, my father received a typed postcard from the Bournemouth & District Committee for Refugees from Germany bearing a message from Max. 'Mr. Moritz was very happy about the well-being of his children. He hopes to hear soon again about them. The whole family is well, and the children must not worry about them. They have very good contact with their paying guests. Mother has visited her family during the Xmas days. All of them were well. Could the children try to get an affidavit for their parents.' As with the correspondence from my mother in Cambridge to Salli and Louise the year before, it was only the last part of this message that smacked of the desperation Max must have felt as he and Minnie remained trapped in a country where all the exits had been barred.

Some months later, at the end of the summer of 1940, Max wrote his last surviving letter. It was a response to an aerogram that had been mailed on 27 March 1940 by friends who had fled to Buenos Aires, and which had taken almost four months to reach Munich. Max's letter is as conspicuous for what it omitted as what it imparted – probably because he feared that it would not survive the censors. It also contained faint notes of optimism, which, given Max's propensity for despondency and depression, read like an attempt at false bravado. Max did not reveal in his reply to his friend in Buenos Aires that in the spring of 1939, he and Minnie had been forced to hand over their valuables (jewellery, silverware and even a gold dental crown), or that they had been made to abandon their furniture and other possessions when they were ousted from their apartment on the Georgenstrasse.

Instead, he confined himself to a dry bulletin, explaining that the most recent news they had received from my father and Ernest was four months earlier (before the Netherlands, Belgium, Luxembourg, France and Norway had been overrun; before Winston Churchill became Britain's prime minister; before Dunkirk; and before the start of the Battle of Britain). Max and Minnie had read about Ernest's ambition to go to university and Max noted, 'Of course we do not know now what has become or will become of these plans. However, we do not believe that we need to be particularly concerned about their welfare.' At the time, his elder son was behind a barbed-wire fence on the Isle of Man, and his younger son was behind another in New Brunswick, Canada.

In his letter, Max also provided updates about his family, mutual friends and acquaintances who had succeeded in escaping, or remained in Munich, where one had found work as a gardener. He also noted the arrival of a new cantor at the synagogue. Max mentioned that his brother, Oskar, together with Oskar's wife Rosa and their son Freddy, were still in Miltenberg, where they were trying to secure passage and entry to the US. His sister, Zilla, had found refuge in Hartford, Connecticut, in April 1939 where she ran a boarding house while her son worked as a waiter, and where she had secured an affidavit for Max and Minnie attesting that they would be able to support themselves whenever their quota number – 35098 – was called. Max acknowledged that their number was not likely to be called for at least a year. Meanwhile, one of Minnie's sisters had reached Montevideo, Uruguay, after travelling via Russia, Japan and San Francisco, while another, Friedericke, remained stuck in Essen with Minnie's mother.

Max only hinted at the discomfort he and Minnie must have felt in the three-room apartment in which they been forced to live, and which housed five other occupants – part of a drive by the Nazis to herd the Jews into ever tighter surrounds. In 1941, Max and Minnie, now compelled to wear the yellow star bearing the word '*Jude*' on the left breast of their clothing, were forced to move about two miles into an apartment, which, including themselves, housed eleven. There, Minnie prepared

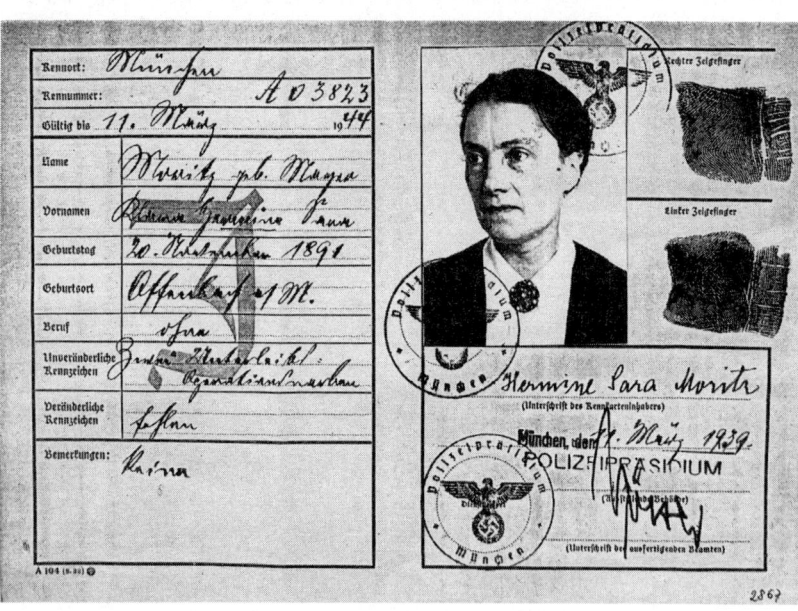

Max and Minnie's ID cards, spring 1939

meals on a table in the hallway and worked as a nurse, while Max, who was forced to move to another building, became a voluntary caretaker and was press-ganged into building wooden barracks in Milbertshofen, halfway between central Munich and Dachau.

One of the commentaries included in an edition of the diaries of Victor Klemperer, a German academic, who had become a Protestant in 1912 but whom the Nazis considered Jewish, gives a sharp sense for how the lives of people like Max and Minnie had been squeezed into thimbles:

> He must leave his beloved house for cold rooms in 'Jews' Houses' — but he must keep paying the old home's taxes and repairs. Under a rain of daily decrees he must surrender radio and telephone, also give up theater, movies, concerts, libraries; then no more magazines or newspapers; no more Jews on buses, no sitting on trams — except to distant forced labor; no more tobacco, flowers, milk; also no more haircuts; turn in the typewriter, also furs, blankets, fabrics; no more biking; now kill the cat and all other pets; no walking on such-and-such streets; no storing food at home; no eating at restaurants; no clothing card, no fish card; just one hour a day for shopping; turn in all appliances, keys, metals, lamps...

In early 1942, like millions of other Jews, Max and Minnie experienced the almost immediate effects of the plan made during the ninety-minute conference in the villa beside the Wannsee. In February of that year, Max was moved again, while Minnie was compelled to share a room with two other nurses in a Jewish retirement home.

Just weeks later, towards the end of March and about a week

before Passover, Max and Minnie received news about their deportation to the east – a journey which they and their fellow Jews had, inadvertently, made easier for the Nazis. The willingness of Munich's Jews – like their brethren throughout Germany – to comply with laws and edicts meant that copies of their addresses existed not just in the office of the Jewish community but were also on file at Munich's Aryanisation department and Gestapo headquarters. The community's natural disposition towards obedience, discipline and order ultimately worked against them. Max and Minnie were both moved to the barracks in Milbertshofen that Max had helped to build. Perhaps at this juncture they believed that, since they fell into one of the categories ordained by the Wannsee Conference (people over the age of sixty-five, war invalids, or those who had been decorated with the Iron Cross), they would be sent to the newly established 'old people's ghetto' – Theresienstadt – in Czechoslovakia, not Poland. The secrecy surrounding the concentration camps during this phase of the war meant that some deportees, despite everything they had experienced, were under the impression that Theresienstadt was a form of resort.

According to a letter my father and Ernest received from a family friend after the war, Max, on the day before he was transported to Milbertshofen, gave this man 1,000 Reichsmarks – perhaps for safekeeping or perhaps because he had a premonition of what lay ahead. I am inclined to believe the former because of the manner in which the Nazis managed to contain information about the capacity of their industrial-sized killing factories. Few knew that they had decided Zyklon B was a deadlier killing agent than carbon monoxide and that concrete gas chambers were far more efficient than shooting Jews alongside trenches dug in frozen ground or gassing them in the rear of converted army trucks. Why should Max and Minnie have thought they were irretrievably doomed? How could they possibly have imagined that 6 million Jews would perish and that they would be two of the victims? It must have been as hard for them as it is for me to grapple with the idea that if a calamity has not happened, it will not happen.

It is most likely that Max and Minnie, along with others, were picked up from their cramped apartments by the Gestapo during the night or in the early hours of the morning, thrust into large, closed removal vans before being taken to the barracks near one of the railway goods stations favoured by the Nazis. About the time Max and Minnie were being shoved into the Gestapo vans, seventy-five Munich Jews, who had been sequestered in a convent before also being moved to Milbertshofen, had attended a short communal service where they had recited Psalm 94, which includes a passage suggesting that the Almighty will eventually ensure justice is done:

> *Understand, ye brutish among the people: and ye fools, when will ye be wise?*
> *He that planted the ear, shall he not hear? he that formed the eye, shall he not see?*
> *He that chastiseth the heathen, shall not he correct? he that teacheth man knowledge, shall not he know?*

In the early hours of Passover, on 4 April 1942 – a Saturday – a total of 774 people, including Max and Minnie, were roused from the straw-strewn floors of the barracks at Knorrstrasse 148 and herded to Milbertshofen station. Max and Minnie had the misfortune of being forced onto the second, most densely packed, of the thirty-seven trains that shipped the Jews of Munich to their deaths between 1941 and 1945. As a result of the Wannsee Conference, most of the deportation trains were redirected from Minsk or Riga to ghettos and camps around Lublin – within distance of the new killing factories. The manifest of the Jews who boarded this transport is now part of the digital archives of Yad Vashem, the World Holocaust Remembrance Center in Jerusalem. Minnie is listed as 'B. 16'; Max is 'B. 102'. No Jew on this train saw the west again. Later, the Nazi authorities noted that Max and Minnie's bank balance was confiscated after the couple had 'moved away to an unknown place', since their assets had 'lapsed'.

If Max and Minnie survived the train journey and the subsequent arduous seven-mile slog by foot from Trawniki to Piaski, fifteen miles from Lublin, they must have felt as if they had been shipped back 250 years to a village of cramped wooden houses with unpaved streets, little electricity, no running water and only one usable well. Six thousand Jews were crammed into Piaski, from which its previous inhabitants – around 4,000 Yiddish-speaking Hasidic Jews, no doubt clinging to every word of their rabbis – had already been removed and killed.

I do not know if Max and Minnie survived the hunger and diseases that felled many who made it to Piaski, but if they did, then they may have been part of another brutal round-up on 22 June 1942, which would have sent them about fifty miles to Sobibor. On 5 July 1942, a woman in Munich who had escaped deportation wrote in her diary, 'For fourteen days there has been no news of our deportees from Piaski and we no longer entertain any hope of seeing them again after the war.' *Piaski*. It is where Max and Minnie vanish from existence, with a note in the record that says '*tod unbekannt*' – 'death unknown'. It was not until 1949 that the Munich authorities officially recorded the deaths of Max and Minnie Moritz. It was midnight on 8

May 1945 – the time at which the war in Europe came to an official close, and when those who could not be accounted for were formally declared dead.

I have never attempted to picture what happened to Max and Minnie once they disappeared from the official record. Their existence fades to black. They could have died on the train. They could have perished shortly after reaching Poland or in one of the nearby gas chambers. Instead, it is the little comforts that I wonder about. As the air was squeezed out of their days, did they ever pine for a time when they had clean pillowcases and could listen to the gramophone or settle in an armchair and read the newspaper; when they did not have to talk in whispers; when people greeted them on the street and they could stroll into a café and sit at an unoccupied table; when Max could go for a shave or Minnie could go to the hairdresser; when they did not have to worry if they would be permitted to swim in a nearby pool or sit on a park bench while Max smoked a cigar. Their lives had been extinguished long before they died.

Max's brother, Oskar, was also deported towards Lublin, to Izbica, a shtetl that lay twenty-five miles to the south of Piaski. (Like Max and Minnie, the application made by Oskar and his wife Rosa to enter the US had been denied.) The final meeting of the Jewish community of Miltenberg, the little town on the bend of the River Main, had taken place in 1938, and by the end of 1939, only eighteen Jews, including Oskar, remained.

The most damning images of Oskar's deportation come from a sheet of six photographs aligned in pairs that I found lodged deep in the Würzburg State Archives. This formed part of an album that had been prepared, despite orders to the contrary, by two German policemen in honour of Michael Völkl, a Gestapo officer who oversaw the deportation of the 850 Jews from eighty communities surrounding Würzburg.

The Gestapo album documents every step of their passage. The Jews are shown sorting and separating their possessions in the Würzburg municipal park amid handcarts and piles of suitcases and blankets. One of them, presumably a dentist or doctor, is examining someone's mouth. A subsequent image shows them dressed in winter coats and hats on a sunny day, carrying bags and bundles, guarded by German policemen as they are marched down the centre of a street towards the train station. On either side of the road the citizens of Würzburg watch the procession. The remaining photographs are of their train, Nazi guards and more possessions dumped on the railway platforms. The last photograph I found of Oskar was taken after he, like all the other deportees, had been forced to hand over the keys to his family's apartment and provide the Nazis with a list of all his remaining property. It was taken twenty-one days after Max and Minnie had been forced aboard the train at the Milbertshofen goods station. The image below is a cropped portion of the photograph that appears earlier showing Oskar standing near the rear door of the bus that had taken him, his wife, Rosa, and his cousin, Mira Marx, from Miltenberg. Here the yellow badge shaped like the Star of David with '*Jude*' sewn in black across the centre is more visible. But so too is the white armband that designated him as a steward, appointed by the Gestapo, who had been compelled to help organise and round up every last Jew of Miltenberg.

Another photograph, which must have been taken moments later, shows an anxious, hunched Mira dressed in a heavy coat (probably covering several layers of clothing) and felt hat,

Mira Marx before losing most of her last belongings, Würzburg, April 25th 1942

Oskar Moritz, with yellow star and white armband

scurrying past the front of the bus with her gaze averted. Her head barely reaches the hood of the vehicle, and she is weighed down by large bundles of clothing and bedding, which she holds in her right hand and clutches with her left arm. The parents of Oskar's young shop assistant, Leopold Halberstadt, who had managed to escape Germany for Palestine, were also on the same bus and destined for the same fate.

After the war, a court exonerated Völkl because it could not determine if he knew about the slaughterhouses in the east when he dispatched the Jews of Miltenberg. The photographs I unearthed were part of the heaps of evidence presented during the post-war trials of Nazi criminals. If Völkl did not know about the industrial killing centres – a claim that is as hard to believe as the thousands of similar claims of innocence made by others who also got off scot-free – I can almost hear him chortling at, or repeating, the scornful, handwritten captions of the photographs in the album that his colleagues presented, 'The Jewish Mischpoche arrives in herds at the evacuation point.'

'The Jewish scum is being loaded.'

'The later the hour, the more handsome the guests.'

These are the sort of taunts I can imagine emanating from the mouths of the white supremacists who marched in Charlottesville in 2017 bearing their flaming torches and chanting, 'Jews will not replace us.'

There is no record of how long Oskar, Rosa and Mira survived in Izbica, which is where the official documents recorded their death – if, indeed, they even made it there. Perhaps they understood when they arrived that most of the long-time inhabitants of Izbica had been murdered to make room for Jews like them; maybe they sensed that they would never see the River Main again. I wonder if they knew that the Izbica Gestapo chief, Kurt Engels, had ordered Jews to demolish the gravestones in the Jewish cemetery and use the fragments to build a wall around the fire station, which served as the Gestapo prison. This same man killed many Jews in the street or whipped them from his horse, while his deputy, Ludwig Klemm, shot Jews who did not doff their hats to him and had no qualms about murdering women and children on the spot.

Engels and Klemm survived the war. The former operated a Café Engels in Berlin until, after having been arrested for his war crimes and imprisoned, he ended his life by taking an overdose on New Year's Eve in 1958. Ludwig Klemm was more devious. In 1945, he changed his name, his place and date of birth, invented a past as a Luftwaffe pilot and became an accountant in Düsseldorf before retiring with his third wife to Allendorf, a picturesque town 125 miles to the east of the Ruhr. There he sanded and painted neighbours' fences, drove housewives to the supermarket, watched crime programmes on television and listened to Mozart, Bach and Chopin. On 17 January 1979, his past also came back to haunt him and he was finally arrested, handcuffed and driven to a nearby prison, where four months later he hanged himself with a bedsheet knotted to the bars of his cell window. The date of Klemm's arrest helps explain why World War II and these relatives I never knew were, and remain, so present in my life. I discovered that Klemm's arrest occurred two weeks after I showed up for my first day of work in my first full-time job, as a correspondent for *TIME* in Detroit. For me, January 1979 is yesterday.

Today, when I think of paying my respects to Max, Minnie, Oskar, Andreas and all those others, I am not drawn to Piaski or Izbica or one of the nearby extermination centres. Instead, I am tugged towards the train stations where they disappeared from the towns and cities they once considered home. Before I die, I have vowed to take some small pebbles from the beach near our home on the Pacific and travel to the municipal train station of Würzburg and the goods stations of Düsseldorf and Milbertshofen where I will place each – in the Jewish tradition – on one of the sleepers.

A CRIME WITHOUT A NAME

WHEN THE FIRST heavy storm of winter blew in from the Pacific on 13 December 2020, a Sunday, I built a fire in our house and sifted through more of the papers that were left by my mother after she was taken away by stretcher from her home in Wales and where she, for the last time, saw the painting of a train steaming alongside a lake that contained a diagonal scar in the canvas.

By coincidence I found a short, twelve-page printed service for a 'Day of Fasting Mourning and Prayer for the Victims of Mass Massacres of Jews in Nazi Lands'. The date was given in both the Jewish calendar – 5th Tebeth, 5703 – and the Roman calendar, which also happened to be 13 December, and a Sunday, although in this case the year was 1942. The service had been organised by the chief rabbi of Britain. The Sunday in 2020 when I found this leaflet was the day before the first vaccines were due to be administered in the US and Harriet and I had just put the finishing touches to a card greeting the imminent arrival of the new year: 'Here's hoping you will be kinder to everyone than your predecessor.' On 13 December 1942, when my parents had both attended the memorial services at their respective synagogues, there was little light on the horizon.

By 1942, the Nazis had slaughtered about 2.6 million Jews, or about half of the total number exterminated between 1941

בכי תמרורים

ביום צום ומספד

על אחינו חללי הרצח

בכל הארצות תחת ממשלת הזדון

יום א׳ פרשת ויגש

שנה. כה תברכנו לפ״ק

Order of Service

ON THE

Day of Fasting Mourning and Prayer

FOR THE

Victims of Mass Massacres of Jews in Nazi Lands

Sunday, 5th Tebeth, 5703—13th December, 1942

LONDON
OFFICE OF THE CHIEF RABBI
5703—1942

and 1945. Yet since even most of those transported to way stations like Piaski and Izbica failed to comprehend, prior to their deportations, that they would be gassed and burned and would disappear as smoke in one of the camps that formed a circle around Lublin, it was little wonder that in faraway places, their relatives could not fathom the consequences of the lethal combination of the concentration camp and the gas chamber.

For the refugees in Britain, the few words that – during the early stages of the war – had trickled out of Germany dried up. More Red Cross cards were returned undelivered. In 1941, rumours of the mass murders conducted by the Germans as they advanced east after launching Operation Barbarossa were spread via the Polish underground. In August 1941, Winston Churchill had declared, 'We are in the presence of a crime without a name.'

In June 1942, the Polish government in exile received word that the Germans were now murdering Jews throughout their country, and a headline in *The Times* of London read, 'Massacre of Jews – Over 1,000,000 Dead Since the War Began'.

On 13 December 1942, the 'Day of Fasting Mourning and Prayer for the Victims of Mass Massacres of Jews in Nazi Lands', the CBS radio network in the US reported, 'Millions of human beings, most of them Jews, are being gathered up with ruthless efficiency, and murdered. The phrase "concentration camps" is obsolete, as out-of-date as economic sanctions or non-recognition. It is now possible only to speak of extermination camps.' And, four days later, eleven Allied governments issued a declaration that included the following:

> The German authorities, not content with denying
> to persons of the Jewish race in all the territories over
> which their barbarous rule has been extended the
> most elementary human rights, are now carrying into
> effect Hitler's oft-repeated intention to exterminate the
> Jewish people of Europe… Jews are being transported
> in conditions of appalling horror and brutality to Eastern
> Europe. In Poland, which has been made the principal
> Nazi slaughterhouse, the ghettos established by the
> German invaders are being systematically emptied of all
> Jews except a few highly skilled workers required for
> war industries. None of those taken away are ever heard
> of again. The able-bodied are slowly worked to death
> in labor camps. The infirm are left to die of exposure
> and starvation or are deliberately massacred in mass
> executions. The number of victims of these bloody
> cruelties is reckoned in many hundreds of thousands
> of entirely innocent men, women, and children.

I never heard my parents speak of these months in 1942 or what they remembered of those days. I do not know when they first understood that Max and Minnie, and Oskar and Rosa, and Andreas and all the other relatives and friends they had thought they would see again, were dead. Maybe they nursed a faint hope that these people would survive until, years later, those wishes were extinguished. Perhaps, on that Sunday in December 1942, they already knew.

ANY JEWS HERE?

ONE OF THE PHOTOGRAPHS I took with my box camera in 1965 is of a building jutting out over a river embankment. The river is the Nederrijn, one of the many waterways on which barges course through the Netherlands and move deep into Germany. The building in the photo was a restaurant in Arnhem where we had lunch with Sara Rath, one of Salli's sisters.

Sara, for some reason, had chosen not to accept the offer to join Salli, Louise and their daughters in their move to New Zealand. Thus, when Salli and Louise sailed for England, Sara, who never married, stayed behind in Germany. Later, she fled to Winterswijk in Holland which, ironically, was closer to the German border than Kempen. (There she was later joined by a sister, Lea, and a brother-in-law, Hermann. Lea died in Holland. Hermann made it to the US.) Sara spent the entire war in hiding in and around Arnhem.

At the end of the war, aged sixty-three, Sara weighed seventy pounds. My mother had only seen her a few times since her own childhood and Sara was almost a stranger to my father. When we met her in 1965, she was small, severe, grey and shrivelled. The lunch conversation was conducted in German. Sara had a twin who died at birth. I knew nothing of her background, had not then heard of Anne Frank, and for me the

Sara Rath, 1950s

memorable aspect of the lunch was not meeting a great-aunt who, through a combination of fortune, fortitude and the Dutch resistance, had survived the fears and deprivations of years spent in isolation, but the large tank at the front of the restaurant, from which the waiter used a small net to scoop up the fish that later appeared on my father's plate. I knew nothing of Sara's background and of the fact that, tormented by her experiences in hiding, she spent most of the years between 1954 and her death in 1968 in the mental ward of the Arnhem community hospital.

There are not many differences between the farmland that lies on either side of the River Meuse as it winds through Holland close to the German border. The village names on either bank of the river could be German or Dutch. Since the mid-nineteenth century, plenty of Rhineland Jews – including many from my grandmother Louise's side – had moved to Holland for both marriage and jobs. They had settled in Amsterdam, Rotterdam and Haarlem, and had taken Dutch wives and husbands. Later the ranks of the Jewish population of Holland were swollen by refugees fleeing the Third Reich. The only difference between the treatment meted out to the Jews of Holland and that inflicted on the Jews of Germany, Austria and Czechoslovakia was that it came slightly later. Nearly three quarters of the Jewish population in the Netherlands – 104,000 – were murdered.

Nijmegen is about forty-five miles from Kempen and less than fifteen miles from Arnhem, and it was there that Sara had been in hiding while the Allies, in the disastrous Operation Market Garden of the late summer of 1944, had tried to outflank German defences by seizing bridges across Dutch rivers that would provide an easier route to the industrial Ruhr, some fifty miles east of Kempen.

Sara was but one of the victims of the German occupation of Holland which followed the pattern put in place by the Third Reich: establishment of military control of the government; swift suspension of the rule of law; brutal suppression of protests; and, for the Jews, segregation, seizure of assets, yellow stars on the breast pocket, and specially stamped passports. Because Holland was a small country and most of the Jews, many of them poor, lived in Amsterdam, the Nazis had an easy time corralling them in the principal transit centre, Westerbork. Around a dozen relatives of my mother's side of the family were funnelled through Westerbork, including one of Sara's sisters and two of my mother's first cousins. But there was also at least one relative from my father's side who got corralled in Westerbork – Alfred Cohn, who, like his cousin my father, also bore the name of the uncle killed during World War I. Having fled to Holland, Alfred managed to evade the Nazis for three years, before being consigned to Westerbork and thence to Auschwitz. He was on one of the last of the sixty-five train loads that took the Westerbork Jews to the killing centres. By contrast around two thirds of the 25,000 Jews who were secreted by the Dutch underground in attics, basements, warehouses and hamlets survived. (Alfred survived the marches and cattle-wagons that the Nazis used, near the end of the war, to shuttle the Auschwitz survivors to other concentration camps until he finally escaped from a train being strafed by the Royal Air Force in Czechoslovakia. In 1952 he emigrated to Israel where he worked for Tnuva, the largest Israeli dairy company, until his retirement.)

In the summer of 2019, I was telling the little I knew about Sara Rath's life in Holland during World War II to a guest at Borgo Pignano. The guest, Dolf Horneman, was a Dutchman who lived in Switzerland, and although he had a head of silvery hair and was in his late seventies, he had the outlook of a man with decades in front of him. We had talked several times during his stay but on this occasion, shortly before his departure, he gave me the potted story of his life.

Dolf had been born in the Netherlands in 1942 to Jewish parents. His father was shipped off to a concentration camp and killed. His mother, who survived the war, gave the newborn Dolf to the Dutch underground who smuggled him for safekeeping to the Ardennes, where he was given refuge by a Catholic family. In the summer of 1962, Dolf, then aged nineteen and living with his mother in the Netherlands, had just started his compulsory military service when, one morning, the platoon sergeant demanded a volunteer for garrison duty on a weekend when the recruits were due leave. After nobody volunteered, the sergeant, despite the history of the prior thirty years, asked, 'Are there any Jews here?' Dolf, being the only Jew, was confined to quarters and, as a result, took a train home by himself on a Sunday afternoon. The carriages were empty and the ticket conductor struck up a conversation with Dolf. He asked why Dolf, dressed in his recruit's uniform, was travelling by himself on a Sunday and hadn't taken the special military train that had departed on the Friday. Dolf explained how he had been selected and the conductor, appalled at the discriminatory nature of his selection, told Dolf that he and his wife, who at the time had been married for twelve years but were childless, had sheltered a Jewish baby from May 1943 until October 1944 in their home in Weert, in the south of Holland. When the Germans mounted their Ardennes offensive, the conductor and his wife passed their charge off to others and thereafter wondered what had become of the boy. They had kept a photograph of the baby on their staircase and had always referred to him as 'their missing child' since, after Dolf's arrival, they had two children of their own. Dolf told the conductor that his story struck home because he too had been sheltered during the war. He enquired whether the conductor knew the baby's name. 'Dolf Horneman', was the conductor's reply.

ENEMY ALIENS?

IT IS A DARK, WINTRY AFTERNOON in 1958, the windshield wipers are struggling to sweep the rain from the windshield, and my father is looking for road signs from behind the Bakelite steering wheel of his first car – a pre-owned 1953 Hillman Minx of which he proudly made photographs. It has no radio or seatbelts, the rear window is fogged up, the floor mats are damp, the orange flip-arm indicators are frozen shut. We are stuck behind a truck in a slow-moving traffic jam. It is my first memory of being in a car and I am sitting, legs folded beneath me, on the front bench seat. I am five. My father and I are making our way from Cardiff to Manchester, then an eight- or nine-hour journey, which required slowly threading through the town centres of Birmingham, Walsall and Stoke-on-Trent. We are on the road between Bromsgrove and Manchester, the two places – about a hundred miles apart – where, after being released from internment in 1941, the Moritz brothers, still deemed unsuitable for military duties, wound up working on factory floors.

My father, as was his wont, said little about how he lived in a series of rented rooms between the time he was released from the Isle of Man and before he resumed his interrupted studies at Oxford after the war. In 1941, a tutor had vouched for his loyalty to Britain and recommended him for service in the Royal Corps of Signals, but the appeal fell on deaf ears.

Alfred's first car – a pre-owned 1953 Hillman Minx

While at school in Wales, I remember the embarrassment of not being able to say that my father had fought in North Africa, or at Monte Cassino, or landed on the Normandy beaches; try explaining to other ten- or eleven-year-olds in Wales in the 1960s the consequences of being an Enemy Alien – particularly a German and Jewish one. My schoolmates viewed my explanation with almost as much suspicion as the authorities that had rounded up the Enemy Aliens. My father, after a short spell as a tractor driver, worked as a draughtsman and inspector of drop forgings at Deritend Stamping of Bromsgrove, a factory commandeered to make precision parts for aeroplanes and whose telegraph address referred to its manufacturing origins, 'horse-shoes'. Later, the works manager commended his contribution organising debates and brain-trust sessions as part of the 'indoor entertainment' for employees.

The only aspect of what must have been a bleak and lonely working life that my father recounted to me was that it had introduced him to the powers of the slide rule – a mechanical, analogue calculator that was the length of an ordinary ruler but a little wider. Even after my father became enamoured with pocket calculators and personal computers, he sometimes still made calculations on his World War II slide rule, which remained in his desk drawer until he died. When I was a teenager and struggling with mathematics, my father tried to explain to me the computational powers of the slide rule, but the logarithmic scales and quadratic equations that so fascinated him were mysteries to me.

Ernest, more expansive on the topic of his wartime experiences in Manchester after returning from Canada, had sharp recollections of what it felt like to be a young, Jewish, German refugee (although by then he spoke English with no trace of an accent) working among other lathe operators who, for the most part, had left school at fourteen, had never met a German and did not know another Jew. Yet they 'knew enough' to rub their betting slips against my uncle's waistcoat before going to see their bookie because it was considered good luck. In his 1990 memoir, completed, as he noted, on Simchat Torah, the day in the Jewish calendar that marks the end and beginning of the annual cycle of Torah readings, my uncle compiled two columns to illustrate the gap:

They	I
English	German
Christian	Jewish
Craftsmen	Semi-skilled at best
Daily Mirror	Manchester Guardian

Primary School	University
Northern	Southern
Manchester accent	Posh accent
Married with kids	Unmarried
Weekly perspective	Long term ambitions

The young man with the long-term ambitions, who aspired to enter university after the war, was working at the British Trailer Company, in the heart of Trafford Park, Britain's largest industrial estate – now a semi-gentrified collection of red-brick buildings and small warehouses but in those days wreathed in smoke and fumes and the refuse of heavy industry. The British Trailer Company built trailers for trucks – its most famous being the Map Caravan used by General Montgomery for the D-Day landings and the drive towards Berlin.

The war upended Ernest's plans to apply for a university place and interrupted my father's studies. As for my mother, I don't think university was ever contemplated. Despite the two semesters she spent at Berlin's Private Waldschule Kaliski, she did not possess the gymnasium-level grounding that my father and Ernest had received, and which stood them in good stead when they arrived in England. My mother and her sister also had to contend with the extra complication of Salli and Louise's arrival in Cambridge following their eleventh-hour escape from Germany.

The Rath sisters had been rescued from Liverpool Street station's cavernous waiting room by one of those unworshipped saints of the Kindertransport, Greta Burkill, the wife of a Cambridge mathematician who had organised the Cambridge Children's Refugee Committee. Burkill was one of the many from a potpourri of refugee organisations – some Jewish, some

Quaker and some, like the various children's aid committees, secular – who felt impelled to help. The modesty of those associated with the Kindertransport was epitomised by Sir Nicholas Winton, who led the effort to pluck almost 700 children from Czechoslovakia and whose quiet deeds (including placing photographs in *Picture Post* of children needing homes) went unheralded for almost half a century. The same went for families who took a child into their midst, including some, with large houses, who generously accommodated several.

Children who had not been assigned guardians and had watched as others, like the Rath sisters, left Liverpool Street station waiting room, were housed in holiday camps, where they waited for Saturdays and Sundays when grown-ups appeared to look them over as if selecting a pet from the pound. Like puppies and kittens, the younger children had an advantage over their elders. A few of the guardians treated the children as a convenient source of unpaid labour, using them as household maids. However, the vast majority were treated well, and those charged with their care attempted to bridge the chasm in cultures and accommodate themselves to the emotions of children who had been whipped up by vile winds and separated from all that was familiar.

The Rath sisters were assigned to Maria Rickard, a young woman and the only child of a wealthy businessman, with whom she lived along with his nurse and several cats. Their guardian was only about ten years older than her charges and oversaw a house – staffed by a housekeeper, cook and gardener – that was larger than any my mother had ever seen, complete with greenhouses and a tennis court. The prim young foster parent, whom my mother was instructed to call 'Auntie' (although her friends called her 'Queenie'), was a regular churchgoer and Girl Guide leader, never went to the dentist (the calamitous consequences of which were apparent in the days when I eventually knew her) and during the war kept chickens in her garden. After the war, the young woman continued to house children – in this case British orphans – but they were always outnumbered by the many cats, rabbits, guinea pigs, tortoises, canaries, budgerigars and fantail pigeons she ministered to for years.

One item my mother kept hold of from her two years in the keep of the woman she always referred to as 'Miss Rickard' was a heavy wooden tennis racquet which, thirty years later, together with its heavy wooden press fastened by four bolts and nuts, was bequeathed to me when my mother insisted that if it had been good enough for her, it was certainly good enough for me.

During my mother's last months in the nursing home in London, I attempted to learn how Salli and Louise gave up their plans to emigrate to New Zealand and had, instead, started to rebuild their lives in Cambridge, unable to speak even rudimentary English. How had Salli and Louise paid their rent, or even for a bus ticket? I asked my mother directly, but she was not forthcoming. She was lying on her bed, propped up by a pillow, when her voice dropped to a whisper and a guilty look crossed her face. 'My father knew what he was doing,' she murmured. I knew that Salli and Louise had crossed the border between Germany and Holland in a car at Venlo – thirteen miles from Kempen. But I did not know what my mother then whispered to me: 'He had money sewn into his overcoat.' It was only a few weeks before she died that I pried this nugget loose. I don't know how much money Salli was able to smuggle out, nor do I know how long the money stretched after he and Louise reached Cambridge. About the only other recollection of wartime my mother mentioned, beyond her annual observance of

Kristallnacht and her solemn devotion to acknowledging Hitler's birthday, was the orange glow in the sky from London that was visible sixty miles away in Cambridge during the height of the Blitz.

My mother, after spending two years on a scholarship at the Perse School in Cambridge (during which, according to her report cards, she was only absent twice), left two years before the end of high school. For her, as for the Moritz brothers, the sudden immersion in a British classroom had been full of surprises. One reminder of the difference between school in the little town in the Rhineland and the university town on the River Cam was the reaction of her classmates when she answered a teacher's question about her shoe size by announcing 'thirty-nine' – the European measurement, which, in England, would have been large enough for a stegosaurus. The embarrassment of that moment never left her.

My mother's first report card provides a picture of what it must have been like adjusting to a world where goods were bought with farthings, pennies, threepenny bits, sixpenny pieces, shillings, half-crowns, crowns, pounds and guineas; where weight was measured in ounces, pounds, stones, quarters and hundredweights; where distance was marked in feet, inches, yards, furlongs and miles; where the beds had sheets and blankets; and where the favoured drink was tea. A sympathetic English teacher noted, 'She must not despair when she cannot easily understand her work.'

The war, perhaps the lack of parental support, the fact she was female and the need to help Salli and Louise must have been the reasons my mother left school at sixteen. Her confidence cannot have been helped by the fact that Salli never hid his

Louise, Erika, Salli and Doris, Cambridge, 1940s

disappointment that he had not fathered a son. He had gone so far as to buy a bronze bust of a young man, which he nicknamed Walter and which, by the time I was old enough to learn of its existence, had been moved from the mantelpiece and tucked into a large breakfront, which also housed his stash of cigars and Louise's chocolates.

My mother took typing and shorthand lessons and, during the war, worked for a year in the office of a garden nursery that had turned its grounds over to food production, before joining the National Fire Service in a similar role. I suspect part of the reason she never proceeded towards university was because of a fear that she maintained all her life. She did not want to stand out, draw attention to herself, be seen as elbowing others aside or become the tallest poppy whose head got lopped off. The pamphlet handed to refugees after arrival in Britain had emphasised that 'The Home Office cannot allow anything which will be to the detriment of British employers and workpeople, or take work away from them.'

Towards the end of 1944, however, my mother did conceive a modest and seemly ambition for a young Jewish refugee: to become an elementary-school teacher. About a year after the war ended, she began her teacher training outside London, even though her father had made no secret of his belief that she should have followed him into the cattle business.

Salli and Louise spent the war years in Cambridge. They moved between several rented apartments, forever seeking to lower their living costs. Salli was a man dispossessed – of country, language, income and means of employment. He was no longer, as he had been in the late 1920s and early 1930s, a man about town – albeit a blind man in a small town – and a principal member of the local Jewish community. He had succeeded in acquiring and managing pastureland, and raising and trading cattle, and in the early 1930s had netted 10,000 deutschmarks a year (roughly equivalent to $130,000 of pre-tax income today) – a sum that dwindled in the latter part of that decade until it reached zero. In England, he was reduced to peeling potatoes and apples, learning to type and taking English lessons laid on for refugees by the British government. He was a minister without portfolio.

THERE IS NO MORE JOY

I NEVER TALKED to my parents or grandparents about what they had done on the day when the war in Europe had come to an end or when, after Hiroshima, the war in the Pacific was over. Svetlana Alexievich, the great Belarusian writer, tellingly observed that, in contrast to those who lived through it, birds soon forgot the war. But my parents did not have wings. My father once mentioned that, shortly after the signing of the surrender, he attended a performance of Verdi's 'Requiem' in Manchester, where he worked for a short time as a schoolteacher.

Almost nobody in Europe survived World War II unscathed. The dwindling days of the war were savage for the inhabitants of Kempen, the little town in the Rhineland surrounded by pastures. In early February 1945, almost six months after the failure of Operation Market Garden, which had been fought some sixty miles to the northwest, a squadron of American planes bombed Kempen, killing ninety people – including seventy-three civilians – and destroying the house where Salli and Louise had temporarily lived before escaping. A carpenter was felled while he scurried for safety, the widow of a man killed in Stalingrad lost her children, and in the bakery where Salli and Louise had once bought their bread, five of the owner's family died.

A couple of weeks after this bombing raid and when Kempen had fallen within artillery range of the advancing Allies, the town's mayor ordered an evacuation and a round-the-clock lookout from a water tower. By then, however, the only fighting force that remained was a ragtag collection of the Wehrmacht – along with hurriedly organised and untrained teenagers, a few elderly men and scarcely any ammunition. On the afternoon of 3 March 1945, Kempen was captured by the 333rd First Infantry Regiment of the US 84th Infantry Division and tanks of a company of the 771st Battalion. An account written afterwards noted that Kempen's capture was 'One of the strangest scenes in the campaign… As the column entered the town from the south, a few bursts of burp gun fire greeted the leading vehicles. The infantry and tanks immediately opened up. The column roared through the streets to the square in the heart of the town. In a church on that square, services were in progress. As the column passed by, everyone in the church came out, knelt on the steps of the church, and waved at our men with everything from white handkerchiefs to white sheets.'

The allied troops in Kempen, and indeed elsewhere, did not necessarily behave in the style portrayed by the newsreels – handing out cigarettes to adults and chocolate to children. Instead, according to some, the GIs stripped the German soldiers of their watches, smashed their rifles, tore their epaulettes from their shoulders, and, with kicks and blows, marched them out of town towards hastily established prisoner-of-war camps. A curfew was imposed for those who remained, and the 300 male citizens of Kempen were confined in a cellar. Women and children were ordered to stay in their houses, which were then scoured by the American troops for liquor and Nazi paraphernalia.

For my family, the interrupted narrative of the fate of the European Jews between the outbreak of war and the chaos that followed Germany's collapse was picked up in 1946 after the German postal service stuttered back to life. The most painful letter sent to the Moritz brothers was mailed in February 1946 and came not from Germany but from New York, where the rabbi of their synagogue had lived since 1940, following his escape from Munich. The letter, written in German, from the Washington Heights synagogue in New York, where the rabbi led a congregation consisting mostly of refugee Germans and Austrians, confirmed the news that Max and Minnie were dead, saying, 'It is very painful for us that we are not in a position to give more favorable information or to express optimism.'

After the war, there was no letter for the Moritz brothers from Miltenberg, where Max and Oskar had been born and the latter had operated his small shop on the town square. The four letters that did arrive carried messages of consolation from friends of Max and Minnie from Munich – where only sixty of the 10,000 Jews who had lived there in 1933 had survived. One writer, who lived in the apartment block in which my father had been raised, mentioned that he had heard the news of Max and Minnie's fate from the boys' former nanny, Anna. He apologised for not being able to return an encyclopaedia, a German–English dictionary and a book on English style that had belonged to Max. These had been lost when his apartment had been destroyed by three bombs in July 1944, while he and his wife took refuge in an air-raid shelter. In another letter, Ernest received word that a friend of his, who at the age of sixteen had refused to join the SS, had been transferred to the Russian front for engaging in anti-Nazi activities and was never heard from again. A friend of Max's wrote in October 1946, apologising for the delay in returning Max and Minnie's birth and marriage certificates, as well as records of Max's war service and his professional good standing in the Munich District Court – by explaining that the Deutsche Post had placed a limit on the weight of letters. He promised to send them as soon as heavier packages were permitted. Another, who had lived with Max and Minnie before they were deported, signed off with words of comfort: 'You dear Alfred and Ernest will not have a bad time in life. The blessings of parents build houses for children.'

Most of the post-war letters that I found among the boxes my sister had shipped from Britain were postmarked in Kempen and addressed to Salli and Louise in Cambridge. In these, fellow farmers and cattle grazers in the Rhineland tried to pick up from seven years earlier. The pages drew a portrait of a town that had become a nest of informers, in which friends had turned on neighbours, where some lost sight of any moral bearings while others clung to their sense of decency – although they did so in silence. The letters described the end of the war; of nearby bridges being blown up; of sons and brothers who had been killed or had returned home with missing limbs; of others who were missing and had not been heard from; of acquaintances who were prisoners of war in France and Yugoslavia; of friends who had died of natural causes during the intervening years.

The harshness of post-war life in Germany was aggravated by the extreme cold of the first winter, when there was little coal to go around, forcing schools to close and requiring people to don layers of clothing before going to bed. Even bread and potatoes were scarce. The canola, barley and winter-clover crops had all failed, fuel shortages and the absence of fertiliser meant that fields went untilled, and cattle were but a fraction of their pre-war weight. One writer informed Salli and Louise about a friend blown up by an unexploded grenade in a field he was tilling during the first peace-time harvest. He wrote too of Russians and Poles, foreign slave workers imported by the Nazis to work in the factories of the Ruhr and replace the agricultural machines of the Rhineland. After the war ended, these same men roamed the countryside taking watches and bicycles from people in broad daylight, hammering on farm doors demanding meat, butter, eggs and clothes and going on murder sprees with knives, hatchets and guns so that fearful farmers abandoned their isolated houses and barns to seek refuge at night with friends in Kempen. Another correspondent made a list of the people who had been stabbed to death in their beds by these marauders. Some wrote of being forced to billet soldiers – Germans during the war, and Allies in the aftermath – and named some of the townsfolk who regretted that they could no longer read *Der Stürmer*, the Nazis' weekly tabloid.

One friend wrote of the penalties of being caught selling goods on the black market – a woman had been sentenced to three months in prison for selling potatoes and a man had been imprisoned for a year for illicitly selling a pair of capons. Another correspondent, recognising that conditions were better in Cambridge than in Kempen, said, 'You asked if we needed anything' and responded with a plea for nutmeg, pepper, cloves, toilet soap and coffee, while imploring, 'Please only send things if they don't cost you much.' Two years after the end of the war, one letter writer plaintively asked whether it would be possible for Salli and Louise to send some cigarettes or tobacco, with the promise of repayment as soon as money transfers resumed. Occasionally there were glimpses of brief interludes of happiness, which were usually associated with a Church event – a first communion, an Easter Mass or a parish fair.

The startling contents of some of this correspondence further softened the prejudices against Germans that I had absorbed from my schoolmates in Cardiff and which was always stirred up by Britain's tabloid press whenever England played Germany in an international soccer game, with jingoistic headlines such as 'Herr We Go, Bring on the Krauts' and 'Let's Blitz Fritz'.

The letters of Salli, my blind grandfather, were models of tolerance. He and Louise reported to their friends in Kempen that the citizens of Cambridge had been sympathetic to their plight, and that they had received considerable help from refugee organisations. They had been introduced to English and a rudimentary grounding in British history and literature, and Cambridge had been spared destruction. But Salli's life as he knew it had been wrecked. He was a blind man in his late fifties and ruefully admitted that he had acquired English like a six-year-old – by listening and repeating phrases rather than by reading textbooks and newspapers or referring to a dictionary. He learned to touch-type but the sense of loss was evident in one of the letters he sent to a friend in Kempen: 'I once believed that the Rhone, the Moselle and the Alps belonged to me as they did to all other Germans.'

Unlike others who had escaped the horrors and turned their back on Germany for the remainder of their lives, Salli, Louise and my parents retained an ability to remember that all Germans were not created equal. They understood the nuances – in a manner that I as a boy (and also, I'm sad to admit, for much of my adult life) – did not. There were Germans who were Nazis but who were not members of the NSDAP (the official Nazi party) and there were members of the NSDAP who were either horrified or opposed to its policies but who, to maintain their livelihoods, had been compelled to join.

Despite my childhood trips to Bavaria, for decades I fell back on the prejudices of my schooldays. In the playground we were ready to issue blanket judgments against anyone from Switzerland, Austria or Germany. They were all German. They were all Nazis. They were all murderers. The plastic aeroplane kits dangling from the ceiling of my bedroom were Spitfires, Hurricanes and Lancasters – not Messerschmitts, Stukas or Heinkels.

For me, reading the correspondence between Salli and his former neighbours and associates was the finest of civics lessons. I still find it hard to understand how Salli could display such tolerance. Despite everything he had experienced in Germany, they brim with an arresting solicitude. In one letter, Salli typed, 'I love to hear from the old Heimat. It pleases me immensely if I can now help the decent people in my former Heimat.' Answering another old friend he said, 'How can you think I have forgotten Kempen, where I spent fifty-five years of my life and where our family has been so closely linked with the country and its people for 150 years?' In a letter to the County Savings Bank, in which Salli sought information about balances in his personal and business bank accounts, he added a postscript in which he conveyed his greetings to five pre-war bank employees and expressed the hope that they had survived the war and were still working. One, the supervisor of the savings department who had started work at the bank in 1907, replied, 'The years from 1914 until today's catastrophe have been increasingly less worth living. There is no more joy of living.' Another wanted to be put out of his misery: 'Most people just wish for an atomic bomb.'

The Allies, dealing with millions of Germans (many of them displaced from towns and cities into the countryside), foreign slave workers and prisoners of war, had a much greater challenge. Their task was complicated by the desire to root out the architects, principal perpetrators and all the collaborators who had torn the world to shreds, and a predisposition to view all who had survived the Third Reich in the same light. Unlike Salli, they did not have detailed knowledge of individuals – save for the most notorious. As a result, any number of perpetrators evaded arrest, while many others, particularly officials who were automatically assumed to have been Nazi sympathisers, were immediately prime suspects.

Salli did his best to help clear the names of those he knew were innocent and had been wrongly removed from their posts or arrested. He wrote a character reference for the town superintendent, Josef Bemelmans, whom he had known for twenty-five years, describing how his behaviour towards the Jews had been 'as correct and decent as it was towards other citizens'. There was another for the mayor, who had ordered the evacuation of the town and organised the twenty-four-hour lookout from the water tower as the Americans had advanced in March 1945, and who sought a reference he could use with the Allies to defend himself against the denunciation of a young priest who had singled him out as a Nazi. Salli had not forgotten how the mayor had helped him sell his land so he could pay the special Nazi taxes levied on emigrants and his support in extracting a relative from Dachau after Kristallnacht. He penned a similar letter for a district administrator who had been sequestered by the Americans. 'I would like to repeat what I said at my farewell visit when I came to thank you. You are a courageous character and a noble human being!' The sentiments were

returned. Friends reminisced fondly about the evenings they had spent in each other's homes, and one harboured the hope that 'when the time is right you and your family would take possession of your property and houses and live here again'. Another wrote, 'You still adhere to the principle you have often voiced: we have the law in our hearts, we don't need a court or lawyer for that.'

One of Salli's more protracted defences was on behalf of Ewald vom Rath, a Kempen judge who had stood by him in the 1930s but had the misfortune of having the same last name (including the preposition that once denoted the origin of a person) as the junior Nazi diplomat – Ernst vom Rath – whose assassination by a seventeen-year-old Polish-German Jew in Paris in November 1938 had been used as the pretext for the launch of Kristallnacht. The Allies, who had difficulty discerning the difference between an Ewald and an Ernst, imprisoned Salli's friend for over a year in prisoner-of-war camps in Holland after his army unit had surrendered. Salli leapt to his defence. Salli's vom Rath had resisted the formation of Nazi student movements while at university. In the late 1920s, he had taken a public stand against one of Hermann Göring's screeds and after 1933, when the Nazi party came to power and began passing anti-Jewish laws, including the boycotting of Jewish products, had continued to frequent Jewish shops. As a judge, he had clung to the idea of an independent judiciary. Later, he was one of the courageous individuals who copied and distributed pastoral letters of the few Catholic bishops prepared to stand up to the Nazis. These included the bishop of Münster, Clemens August Graf von Galen, who in 1941, at great personal risk, vilified the Nazis for the murder of 70,000 mentally or physically disabled

Germans considered an embarrassment to the Aryan myth. 'Woe to us German people', he wrote, 'if we not only license this heinous offence but allow it to be committed with impunity!' The only reason von Galen escaped death was because of the Nazis' fear of a popular backlash.

Equally, Salli did not forget those neighbours who had torched the synagogue, or the many who betrayed their Jewish friends and acquaintances, or the thugs who had smashed the contents of his house on Kristallnacht. He did not forgive the man who insisted the Jewish community pay for the repairs to the synagogue, or the mill owner who also forced the Jews to pay for the damage to his home adjoining the synagogue. The descendants of many of the people whom Salli did not forgive still live in the area, and among them are owners of a cosmetics shop, a Christmas-tree farm, a berry farm and a horse-carriage business.

Some of Salli's post-war correspondence dealt with his desire to sell his pastures after title had been restored in his name. In one letter he asked to be reminded of the differences between the Prussian morgen and Dutch morgen (the measure of a plot of land) and admitted that he no longer retained a sense of the value of his property while also knowing that the deutschmark was worthless and that any transaction would need to be in pounds or dollars. In another he conjured up the direction in which one of his lots lay: 'When you are standing in Kauertz Kullken and looking towards the path to the Waldschlösschen, you will see right in front of you and to your left the property of the von der Leyen.' I recognised the name and discovered that the land Salli was remembering had once been owned by the family of the husband of the current (as I write) head of the European Union.

PASS FREELY

MY FATHER'S FIRST BRITISH PASSPORT, issued in 1949, described its twenty-eight-year-old holder, who had become a British citizen in 1947, as a 'Research Worker' living in Oxford. He was no longer an Enemy Alien. On the paper inside the thin, oval cutout of the dark-blue passport cover of the United Kingdom of Great Britain and Northern Ireland, a Foreign Office official had written in neat turquoise ink, 'MR L. A. MORITZ'. The blind embossing of the royal coat of arms was heavily worn. My father, while waiting at border crossings, or sitting in a railway carriage, or standing in a queue, must have used his thumb to rub the crown, the quartered shield, the rampant English lion and chained Scottish unicorn – knowing that this document, the cover of which carried the motto '*Honi soit qui mal y pense*' ('shame on him who thinks evil of it') was a sober riposte to the passport that he would have been forced to carry in the Germany of 1939. That document would have been stamped with a large 'J' and his name would have been recorded as 'HERR LUDWIG ISRAEL MORITZ'. Inside the front cover of the British passport was a message of imperial laissez-passer from my father's new protectors:

We, Ernest Bevin, a Member of His Britannic Majesty's Most Honourable Privy Council, a Member of Parliament, etc, etc, etc. His Majesty's Principal Secretary of State for Foreign Affairs, Request and require in the Name of His Majesty and all those whom it may concern to allow the bearer to pass freely without let or hindrance, and to afford him every assistance and protection of which he may stand in need.

In the passport photograph, all traces of the youth evident in the pictures taken while my father was an internee have evaporated. The teenager has been replaced by a heavyset man with a receding hairline gazing gravely at the camera, wearing a donnish sweater and jacket with wide lapels. My father had generous lips and a dewlap that brushed his collar and thickly knotted tie. The top of a pen protruded from his breast pocket.

The passport was issued in the same year in which my parents got married. When I consider my father and mother meeting for the first time, the place I think about is a butterscotch-coloured Regency building in central London overlooking The Mall and St James's Park and which, since 1967, has housed the Royal Society, which honours individuals who have made significant contributions to science. My only visit was when I went there for a press conference to help announce the formation of the Crankstart scholarship scheme at the University of Oxford. On that occasion I had been shown the book containing the roll of members of the society, in which the carefully chosen fellows sign their names after their admission. The first name on the list is Isaac Newton, and he, over the centuries, was followed by, among others, Michael Faraday, Charles Darwin, Alan Turing, Stephen Hawking and several dozen Nobel laureates, including

Albert Einstein. Another signature belongs to Fritz Ursell, a cousin of the Moritz brothers, who, in 1972, and by then the much-revered Professor of Applied Mathematics at the University of Manchester, became entitled to put three letters after his name, FRS – Fellow of the Royal Society.

Fritz, after being plucked from Germany by the same woman who helped my father and uncle find schools in England, demonstrated his precocity as a mathematician by being accepted at Trinity College Cambridge, where one of the five students in his tutorial group was Freeman Dyson, the quantum physicist and Nobel laureate. Fritz's talent was recognised and, although excluded from intelligence work (because he too was an Enemy Alien), he was posted to the British Admiralty, where he helped devise forecasts of ocean waves – work used to predict the conditions for the Normandy landings and, later, for operations in the Pacific. This became his specialty: the 'Ursell number' is a long-established component of fluid dynamics. But, before becoming an FRS, Fritz had paid a previous visit to the very same butterscotch-coloured building on Carlton House Terrace. It had been in 1938, when it housed the embassy for the Third Reich – before it was seized as enemy property. At that time, it was home to Joachim Ribbentrop, Hitler's ambassador, who later became his foreign minister and helped orchestrate the Nazis' alliance with Stalin in the Molotov–Ribbentrop Pact. Then, Fritz had been forced to linger for an uncomfortable afternoon waiting for a visa to be issued to permit him to visit his parents in Düsseldorf, while SS guards were posted outside, and a swastika flew from the flagpole overhead.

In the immediate post-war years, Fritz and his mother, Leni, Minnie's sister, occupied a flat in Cambridge. Like Minnie, Leni had served as a nurse during World War I. In Germany, the two

Leni Ursell (Minnie's sister) and her son Fritz Ursell, Cambridge, 1940s

sisters had been very close. Later, as the only member of the previous generation of my father's family to have made it to Britain, she called herself my 'honorary grandmother', although our relationship was limited to the occasional afternoon visit in Cambridge, and birthday cards. Leni had an independent spirit – cycling about Cambridge until she was in her late seventies – and an impish sharpness. For my father, in the 1940s, Leni and Fritz were the two surviving members of his family who lived closest to Oxford.

On one of the weekends during which my father took a train from Oxford to Cambridge to see Leni and Fritz, he met my mother. I don't know the precise date, the circumstances of their meeting or the length of their courtship. Given the times, their penurious circumstances, their backgrounds, my father's shyness, my mother's insecurities and the fact that they had both attended single-sex schools, I doubt whether either of them had much experience with romance before they met. For their wedding in 1949 my mother, not wanting to waste money on a dress that she would wear only once, bought a practical two-piece suit. Beneath the column labelled 'Condition', the British marriage certificate describes my twenty-eight-year-old father as a 'Bachelor' and my twenty-five-year-old mother as a 'Spinster'. The photographs of the occasion are sparse – four shots of the two of them alone on the steps outside the synagogue. By contrast, at the 1921 wedding of Salli and Louise, thirty-two of their closest relatives spanning four generations had posed for the official photographer, with Louise at their centre, veiled in white with two bridesmaids at her feet. The men were clad in dinner jackets with starched collars and white ties. I find the difference between the two photographs wrenching. The generations had disappeared.

My parents travelled by train for their two-day honeymoon at a small, thatched seventeenth-century hotel on the River Exe near Exeter. In the photographs of the two of them beside the river, they look happy and relaxed. I hope they were. Because later, in the last decade of my father's life, that did not seem to be the case. I remember them posing after the lunch they arranged for their fiftieth wedding anniversary in 1999 at a hotel near Reading, in England. The two of them were standing side by side not touching and looking in the opposite direction. That scene had a joyless, forlorn air.

Who really knows what goes on between a couple unless you are one of them; what happens behind a curtain or a closed bedroom door or when the lights are out? My parents were so different – one bookish, introverted, sedentary and cautious; the other energetic, judgmental and pugnacious – that, apart from family, religion, ritual and, through no fault of their own, the emotional wreckage of being refugees, they had little in common.

Perhaps after they both retired in the 1980s, their proximity became a curse. The chief pursuits of life – survival, career, raising children – were over. However, freed from urgent daily necessities, instead of drawing closer, there seemed to be little to distract them from what they found grating about each other. The contentment, the vitality, the satisfaction of knowing there is another in your life, the miracle of having escaped the Shoah – all of which I detect in the honeymoon photographs – had been replaced by a brittle sourness, as if they had finally been defeated by one another.

Alfred and Doris, wedding day, 1949

Salli and Louise, wedding day, 1921

A few months after my parents' wedding, my father set off by train, and then ferry, for Germany. The third page of his passport is filled with stamps in English, French and German, giving the holder permission to enter the US, British and French zones of Germany, which were in the west and south of the country, while the Soviet Union controlled the east. The following pages were littered with small square, rectangular and triangular stamps. He had been permitted to leave for Germany with £50 in foreign currency – of which he returned with £16. The passport-control stamp for the young *Bundesrepublik* was dark blue and its triangular shape resembled the top half of the Star of David that the Jews of Germany had been forced to wear.

I don't know what drew my father back to Munich – a city which, in the perverted philology of the Third Reich, was known as '*Hauptstadt der deutschen Kunst*' and '*Hauptstadt der Bewegung*' ('Capital of German Art' in 1933 and 'Capital of the Movement' in 1935); definitions that excluded the artists the Nazis labelled as 'degenerates' and the writers whose books were tossed into the flames.

Why did he return – not just in 1949 but also in 1950, 1951 and 1952 – when other refugees refused to ever set foot in Germany, or speak German, again, or even admit that there were any good Germans? I could not fathom the impulse, the force or the ties that pulled him back. Was it curiosity? Was it an absurd delusion that nothing had changed? Or perhaps he sought confirmation that nothing remained of the serene times. He never volunteered any of the details of this visit (or subsequent ones) or, more importantly, the emotions they triggered. He never volunteered why he went. And for some reason, I never asked.

Sepp Volk and Alfred, Bühl-am-Alpsee, 1949

I doubt whether there was anyone to greet him at Munich train station in 1949 – or to accompany him through the heaps of rubble in the streets, past the empty lots where synagogues had once stood or through the bedraggled English Garden, the city's largest park. The mountains of Austria must have still seemed to throw a protective wall around the city. The waters of the Isar River continued to carry the spring and summer melts from the Tyrolean Alps. It was the Isar too which, just two years earlier, had borne the ashes of all the Nazi leaders who had been condemned to death at the Nuremberg trials and subsequently been cremated in Munich, including Hans Frank – the Butcher of Poland, Max's former boss and fellow alumnus of the Maximiliansgymnasium.

What did my father make of the citizens of Munich, like most Europeans still shabby and thin from a decade of food shortages and rationing? What did he think of all these unfamiliar men and women – some of whom had fought in Russia, or killed Americans or British or French soldiers, or worked in the concentration camps, or moved into the apartments once occupied by Jews, or bought Jewish businesses at artificially low prices, or arrested his family members, or escorted his mother and father to the trains? Did he stop to wonder which of them had tried to help Munich's Jews and had wept as they saw the Gestapo vans pull away from apartments; those who had raised their arms to Hitler, or stayed silent as their former neighbours and friends had lost their jobs, been forced to walk in the gutter and, on their hands and knees, clean the sidewalks? How could he tell the decent and innocent from those who had tossed books onto bonfires, or pulled the beards of elderly Jews, or just watched as groups of men, women and children with the yellow badges on the breasts of their coats, and blue-and-white armbands on their sleeves, clutching their bundles and bags, were marched through the city streets at the beginning of their journeys to Dachau or the east? How could he differentiate? Or did he start to understand that for some of these people, now living in abject poverty, what had at first seemed unimaginable had gradually become ordinary?

My father would have been unaware that among Munich's inhabitants, and living under his own name until he died in 1975, was Franz Josef Huber, who had joined the city's police department in 1922 where, during his early years, he had helped suppress the Nazis and other extremists. Huber had, however, switched allegiances and eventually become so senior in the Gestapo that much of Austria, including Vienna, was put under his control. After the war, he worked for German and US intelligence services. Hitler's goddaughter, Edda Göring, also called Munich home until her death in 2018, where she lived with her lover, the man who peddled Hitler's forged diaries in the early 1980s. The pair sometimes sailed on a motor yacht that had once been owned by the former Reichsmarschall. And it was Munich too that provided safe shelter to Cornelius Gurlitt, who lived in a fifth-floor apartment in a modern building, less than two miles from the apartment where my father had grown up and in which, until he was accidentally unmasked in 2010, he had kept and occasionally traded some of the 1,400 paintings that he had inherited from his father – about half of which were subsequently deemed to have been pillaged by the Nazis.

I imagine that the real motive of my father's return to Germany was to visit Bühl-am-Alpsee. There are photographs from this visit – my father posing with Anna and Sepp, in the field outside their home. There is no suggestion of tragedy – just of warmth, of people who cared deeply for each other, and of a house with a peaked roof where in previous summers, four people named Moritz had been treated with kindness and sympathy. For both my father and Ernest, Bühl, in the post-war years, became the link to a time that was out of reach. My father looks as happy and peaceful in these photographs as in any I possess. Or perhaps that is just what I want to believe.

I doubt whether my father was able to unravel the complicated emotions the trip must have stirred up in him, or that he delved into its visceral meaning when he relayed the account of his journey to my mother after his return to Oxford. Did he pause to wonder how the railway inspector who punched his tickets had, a few years earlier, perhaps dealt with Jews he had found sitting in areas they were not permitted to occupy? I am sure my father would not have known of a debate I read about between Göring and Goebbels, which took place three days after Kristallnacht, and which struck me as hideously ironic as I thought about him travelling on the German railway. The two Nazis had discussed how best to restrict Jews on German trains. Hitler's propagandist had posited, 'Let's suppose that there are not so many Jews travelling to Munich on an express train. Let's say two Jews sit in the train and the other compartments are overflowing. These two Jews would have a special section for themselves. Therefore, we must say, the Jews only have a right to a seat after all the Germans are seated.' My father might have just shaken his head in bemusement. But since the end of the war, things had changed. And my father knew then what I know now. The reason he could occupy a seat was because His Britannic Majesty had requested that L. A. Moritz, bearing a passport of the United Kingdom of Great Britain and Northern Ireland, be allowed 'to pass freely without let or hindrance'.

DO NOT MAKE YOURSELF CONSPICUOUS

NEITHER OF MY PARENTS EVER complained about their misfortunes beyond the refrains usually employed with children such as 'You don't know how lucky you are!' or 'Eat all your food. A lot of children are starving.' Instead, my father chuckled at the memory of how his natural left-handedness had been considered a stigma and how, like others of that generation, he had been trained to write with his right hand even though for the rest of his life he turned a screwdriver, sliced a loaf, picked up a magnifying glass, uncorked a bottle of wine and tamped his pipe with his left. He did not curse being a casualty of the worst conflagration in history, and he did not complain about his threadbare existence in London, Oxford or Bromsgrove, when money was so scarce, he was forced to extract his own troublesome teeth. He did not harbour jealousy for those whose parents had the means to pay the tuition fees of their children, nor did he question his internment or Ernest's crossings of the North Atlantic. He did not bear a grudge that, unlike some of his less talented peers, he did not have the means to sustain himself through the financially barren years required to become a barrister – the calling that, judging by the eagerness with which he later suggested I consider the same pursuit, was where his heart lay. There was no apparent self-pity. Instead, both he and my mother would acknowledge the good fortune that had allowed them to survive. Unlike other refugees who thought the Shoah was proof that God did not exist, my parents chose to believe that their escape meant the opposite.

It has taken me a long time to understand – since I was not forced to flee my homeland, exiled to a country whose tongue I did not speak, imperilled if I failed to secure a scholarship, or forced to extract my own teeth rather than visit a dentist – why it was that my family was so conscious of money. Each week, Louise, my grandmother, cut the *Radio Times* into sections so that the newsprint could be used for toilet paper; she also rolled the twine and smoothed out the paper from packages, stashing them away, while hanging every rubber band on her kitchen door handle. One of the last letters she wrote to me, in September 1976, after I had enrolled at the University of Pennsylvania, arrived in a gossamer-thin airmail envelope, which was part of her pre-war stock. My mother inherited Louise's frugal habits and, for years, ironed wrapping paper for reuse and collected milk-bottle tops to give to the local Institute for the Blind.

When my mother instructed me to buy a raincoat in my mid-teens, I scurried off to find a garment calculated to impress young ladies: a black, mid-length, mock-leather number. After I presented the bill to my father, he erupted, and I recall standing behind his left shoulder as, lips tightly pursed, he wrote out a cheque for £10. I was as surprised by the force of my father's reaction as I was baffled by his habit of filing away bank statements, bills from the telephone, gas and electric companies or, later, why, until his death, he performed an itemised check of every posting on his credit card statements. I completely failed to understand the reasons behind his concern about my bank overdrafts, my cavalier regard for saving and indifference to parking tickets. I was impatient when he asked whether I was sure I wanted to leave *TIME* – an employer who offered a pension scheme.

The concern about my irresponsible ways was a constant refrain. One week in 1980, I received a letter in Los Angeles from my mother, who wrote, 'I had an awful dream the other day. In fact I woke up as a result of that terrible sick feeling it gave me. You had invested all your surplus cash in shares of one company and that company had gone crash.' There was another within the same month after I had overdrawn my bank account in Britain: 'We are astonished that you cannot keep your finances straight and that you do not meet your outstanding bills. I seem to think that in my last letter I mentioned something about

One of Louise's pre-World War II airmail envelopes, used in 1976

credit cards not being good for you. It is a mug's game to pay high interest charges. Keep your spending WITHIN your income. Any spare cash you have can always go to good causes instead of higher profits for banks.' Then, some weeks later, there was yet another warning. 'I heard a commentary by one of the BBC fellows this week who talked about the Americans who spend every penny of what they earn and then have nothing in case of emergency. Don't follow that example!'

My parents' worries about money never evaporated. Once, after treating them to drinks at the Four Seasons near Central Park, my mother expressed her disapproval of my extravagance. In her last decades, she would frequently announce, 'You have more money than sense.' These sorts of outbursts, and the abiding memory of my father's anger on learning the cost of my mock-leather coat, may explain why I had so much trouble disclosing to Harriet the price I paid for a dark cashmere overcoat I bought well after I had passed my fiftieth birthday and many years after I had accumulated more than I could ever spend. Or why, after I bought my first Mercedes, it took me months to disclose as much to my parents. When I finally admitted the purchase, my mother greeted the news by thereafter spitting out the word 'Mercedes' in the German manner, replacing the 'c' with a curt 'tz'.

When, after Yahoo!, PayPal and Google became well known and a few references to me started appearing in the British press, my mother always insisted on responding to any reporter who tracked her down by informing them that I once had no money. Now I wonder whether my mother's anxiety stemmed from what had happened in the 1930s or whether it was commingled with one of the many instructions contained within the small,

Alfred's World War II Post Office Savings Bank book and post-war unemployment card

twenty-four-page manual she, my father and other refugees had received after arriving in Britain. One of its instructions read,

> Do not make yourself conspicuous by speaking loudly, nor by your manner or dress. The Englishman greatly dislikes ostentation, loudness of dress or manner, or unconventionality of dress or manner. The Englishman attaches very great importance to modesty, understatement in speech rather than overstatement, and quietness of dress and manner. He values good manners far more than he values the evidence of wealth. (You will find that he says 'Thank you' for the slightest service – even for a penny bus ticket for which he has paid.)

After carefully leafing through the yellowed correspondence of my father's job applications in the late 1940s, I now understand their anxieties, which stemmed from the fragility of their circumstances and the absence of any safety net. When he got married, my father – who immediately after the war had experienced a brief spell of unemployment, as well as a stint as a teacher at William Hulme's Grammar School in Manchester – was working on his doctoral thesis about milling and bread-making techniques in ancient times, supported by grants from the National Association of British and Irish Flour Millers and the Rank Foundation, founded by J. Arthur Rank who, though he started work in his father's flour and milling business, became known for his movie studios and the chain of cinemas he operated throughout the UK. My father had also patched together tutoring assignments at four different Oxford colleges, which provided between £70–100 to supplement his part-time job teaching women at Bedford College in London, for which he was paid £550 a year until 1953. He failed to win a fellowship at All Souls College, Oxford (for which a tutor's letter of recommendation had included the explanation 'He is a Jew with the good qualities of his race'), or to land a couple of lectureships (one of which was at the University of Glasgow, which would have resulted in me being Scottish not Welsh and a fan of Glasgow Rangers rather than Manchester United) until, in 1952, good fortune struck, and he was asked by his Oxford college to stand in for a tutor who had taken a year's leave of absence. This, together with his job in London, meant that for a year, on top of my mother's schoolteacher's £330 salary, and the free college lunches and dinners to which my father was temporarily entitled, the two of them could count on his £837 to see them through the year. The anxiety must have been great, for I stumbled across a reference to it – one of the few that my father made about the past – in a letter he sent me in 1976, relaying how precarious he felt in 1952 when 'There were only two jobs going and I had applied for both without even being shortlisted. Yet it turned out all right only a few months later.'

In the summer of 1953, after being reimbursed the cost of his third-class railway ticket and his hotel room, he landed a full-time lectureship in Latin at the University of Cardiff, which would pay £800 a year (about $35,000 as I write) and, along with a £50 bump for each child, would have annual rises of £50 increments until it topped out at £1,100. It was an easy decision. He immediately entered the pension scheme, to which he began contributing £40 a year, and the university £80 – an impulse I suspect was inherited from the faith that Max had placed in his pension. This was the first time my thirty-two-year-old father had experienced a glimmer of financial security since he was twelve years old, when his world began to crumple after the Nazis seized power. This new job left my parents, after taxes, with £400 on which to live for a year – at a time when four pounds of meat cost about £1 and a new four-door Morris Minor with a top speed of sixty-two miles per hour cost £631. So, having drained their savings by putting down a 10 per cent deposit of £265, they bought a house and began planting fresh roots.

My parents arrived in Cardiff in 1953, halfway between the Jewish New Year and Yom Kippur, the Day of Atonement, and joined the synagogue to which they would belong all their lives, and whose rabbi, born and educated in Berlin, had also escaped the Shoah. Except for one brief interlude, my father lived in the same neighbourhood for the rest of his days until he lay dead in their car, parked with its hazards blinking on a double-yellow line outside his doctor's office. My mother did likewise, save for her final year, when she was taken from her bedroom on a stretcher and, for the last time, saw the painting of the train with the diagonal scar across its canvas.

The only person they knew when they moved to Cardiff was Ilse Jones, a small, plump woman with a warm smile, who spoke English with both a German and a Welsh accent and who also happened to have settled in Cardiff where both she and her husband were nurses and bicycled to work until they retired. As a boy, long before I learned about Oskar, I knew Ilse as a cousin of my father and the mother of three girls. I did not know that Ilse had a brother named Freddy who, aged twenty, had been shipped to Riga and murdered, nor that her name had once been Ilse Moritz, nor that she had been born in that same little town on a bend in the River Main and raised in the house overlooking the town square that I had photographed on a hot summer day in 1963. I had not known that her mother was named Rosa, or that her father, Oskar, had, in 1933, been

Ilse Jones and her three daughters, Cardiff, 1950s

prisoner number 13 when his head had been covered in wax, his eye colour registered as 8, and the skin colour on his forehead deemed slightly lighter than 13. She was Ilse who spoke English with both a German and Welsh accent.

THE BEST GERMAN-ENGLISH

AN ONYX CLOCK SITS on a bookshelf in my office at our home in San Francisco. From a distance, it appears dark but when caught by sunlight, streaks of ochre and umber appear and the olive green turns the colour of absinthe. The stone has softly rounded edges and is about the size of three hardcover books. It is silent now, the key long lost. This clock, belonging to Salli and Louise, along with whatever furniture had survived or been repaired following Kristallnacht, had been spirited into a private warehouse in Copenhagen before war broke out, where it eluded the Nazis after their invasion of Denmark. In May 1946, the clock and the furniture were shipped to Cambridge. Possessions survived. Relatives and friends did not.

Throughout my childhood this clock sat on the mantelpiece in the front room of the house in Cambridge that Salli and Louise had bought in 1947, using money they had squirrelled out of Germany and sales of pastureland in the war's aftermath. The front room was where they passed much of the day and was one of the three they occupied in their narrow, four-storey house – the other two being the kitchen and their bedroom. They shared the one bathroom, where a coin-operated hot-water tank was mounted above the tub, with the tenants of the four other rooms. The onyx clock could well have been a wedding present and I like to think that, if I could find the

Lloyds Bank Limited

CAMBRIDGE.

Schedule of securities held on behalf of:-

Salli Rath and Luise Rath

on 12th September, 1972

250	Burmah Oil Co. Ltd. Ordy £1 s.u.
538	Dunlop Co, Ltd., Ord 50p shs. f.p.
300	Guest Keen and Nettlefold Ltd. Ordy £1 s.u.
900	Marks & Spencer Ltd. Ord 25p shs. f.p.
500	Ranks Hovis McDougall Ltd. Ord shs. 50p s.u.
800	British American Tobacco Co. Ltd. Ord shs. 50p s.u.
266	J. Lyons and Co. Ltd. "A" Non-Voting Ord shs. £1 s.u.
400	Unigate Ltd. Ord. shs. 25p f.p.
520	Coates Bros. and Co. Ltd. Ord shs. 25p f.p.
400	Spillers Ltd. Ord. 25p shs. f.p.
125	Premium Savings Bonds in n/o L. Rath
400	Schweppes Ltd. Ord. 25p shs. s.u.
900	Shell Transport & Trading Co. Ltd. Ord shs. 25p f.p.
1950	Great Universal Stores Ltd. "A" Ord shs. 25p stock units.
200	Bowater Paper Co. Ltd. Ord. £1 stock units.
200	Commercial Union Assce. Co. Ltd. Ord. 25p shs. f.p.
200	Kennedy Leigh Properties Ltd. Ord. 25p. shs. f.p.
200	Mitchell Construction Holdings Ltd. Ord. 25p. shs. f.p. *now 537 Thomas Tilling Ltd. (rec'd by Bank on 17/1/73)*
840	Vokes Group Ltd. Ord. 30p shs. f.p.
600	English Calico Ltd. Ord. shs. 25p f.p.
2812	Brooke Bond Liebig Ltd. "B" Ord shs. 25pf.p.
1600	General Electric and English Electric Co. Ltd. 25p. Ord. shs f.p..28
280	Coates Bros. & Co. Ltd. "A" Ord. Non-voting 25p
1710	Montagu Trust Ltd. Ord. 25pshs. f.p.

Salli's schedule of investments at death, 1972

key and wind it up, the round dial would become a small video screen which would allow me to rerun everything that happened in the room where Salli and Louise spent their final decades.

In this room, beneath the gaze of the clock, my maternal grandparents went about reassembling their lives. Here they ate their meals, entertained the occasional visitor and housed the infrequent overnight guest on the sofa. It was here that Salli smoked, stroked the face of his Braille pocket watch to make sure he did not miss a BBC news bulletin, and listened to Louise – once they could both cope with English – read from the *Daily Telegraph*, starting with the business news and stock prices.

By the time I became curious about the way Salli built his investment portfolio, my father, for whom the stock market seemed perilous territory, was long dead. I was astonished that Salli had developed the knowledge and judgment to build a portfolio of dividend-yielding British stocks that would be worth around $700,000 as I write and included British stalwarts such as Great Universal Stores, Spillers and British American Tobacco.

Some sixteen years after he had fled Germany, Salli was doing well enough to pay for a small wedding lunch for the marriage of Erika, my mother's younger sister, to Erwin Plaut, another refugee who later became a specialist in the chemistries associated with printing the colour magazines that started accompanying mass-circulation newspapers in the 1960s. The master of ceremonies was a refugee from Munich whose remarks had been carefully typed beforehand. In Munich, he had inherited a fifty-year-old kitchenware and dinnerware shop, which occupied its own ornate building and housed a pewter foundry and art studio. It was one of dozens of the small Bavarian companies that decorated beer steins, glasses, figurines and other pieces of china with elaborately painted rococo scenes of Munich. Until 1938, the bottoms of these pieces were marked 'Martin Pauson, München'. On 23 July 1938, an advertisement appeared in the local newspapers announcing that the firm was now German, and owned and operated by Fritz Haertle, without mentioning that the master of ceremonies at the wedding in Cambridge in 1955 had been forcibly dispossessed.

Embracing the spirit of the wedding, the dispossessed master of ceremonies did not open with a maudlin recitation of all the missing guests. Instead, he announced to this gathering of refugees that there would be an English pronunciation competition followed by twenty questions that would be judged by the two ladies who had organised housing in Cambridge for the children from the Kindertransport. The winner, he said, would receive a plaque engraved with the question 'Is your English really necessary?' He also advised that, should they feel the need to express themselves in both English and German, they should refer to a book available for one guinea and published by the Cambridge University Press that was titled *The Best German-English Mixture*, which had been compiled by 'S. Rath' – my grandfather. Salli entered the spirit of the occasion by announcing that the only time he gave speeches in English was when one of his daughters married.

The much-thinned ranks of relatives had been scattered to distant parts of the globe. My grandmother kept two registers of these people until the end of her life. One was tucked into a book containing dozens of recipes written in a neat, German script and the other in a carefully organised folder along with photographs. My parents did the same with the little address books they had brought from Germany. A handful of the

Salli at his daughter Erika's wedding, 1955

entries in their books were for contacts who could help them in the UK, and some were for relatives and friends who remained in Germany or Holland. For a time, or at least until they were married, they had added entries for new acquaintances or, in a rare instance, scratched out an address in Germany and replaced it with one far away.

The mail that was pushed through the letterbox of the rooming house in Cambridge came from places such as Paris, Venlo, Dunedin, Santiago, Montevideo, São Paulo, New York, Baltimore, Los Angeles, Eugene and San Francisco. The number

Clare, Salli, Louise, Doris and me, late 1950s

of cities suggests that many relatives and friends had escaped. But that wasn't the case. These were the lucky few – often just one or two members of families that, a few years earlier, had numbered in the dozens. The photographs accompanying the letters showed not just the passage of lives – a young couple, baby photos, children, awkward teenagers and, in time, grandchildren – but the progress of lives apart.

Occasionally one or two strangers would appear for tea at my grandparents' home. All of them had trodden a refugee's journey and all had stories of displacement and, most, tragedy – although I knew none of these at the time. A brother of Salli's, who, with his wife, had fled Germany via the Trans-Siberian railway, spent part of the war living in Shanghai. The couple arrived in San Francisco in 1946 where, before moving to Los Angeles, I discovered they had found lodging in a house sixteen blocks from our home.

One cousin of my mother's, Denise Gompertz, who always struck me as a gregarious, multilingual buxom force, which almost certainly cloaked an inner darkness, converted to Catholicism and finally chose to end her own life by assisted suicide. Ursula Gompertz, another cousin of my mother's, made occasional appearances in Cambridge with her husband, Ben Shaw (previously Schwartz). Ben's parents, desperate to leave Europe, had been sold forged visas by an official at the Uruguayan embassy in Paris, which were only discovered as they and Ben boarded their ship for Montevideo. A frantic quest followed and these three Berliners managed to obtain visas for Bolivia which is how they wound up 11,500 feet above sea level in La Paz. Ursula Gompertz's nightmares began five months before she was born when her father, Emil Gompertz, was killed during Germany's last attempt to break through the Allied lines of the Somme. (Morbid curiosity made me uncover thirty-four-year-old Emil's last address. It is: Grave 470, Block 2, German Military Cemetery, 80700 Andechy, France, where he lies among 2,251 other Germans.)

In the late 1930s, forced to leave Germany, Ursula found work as a seamstress in Cambridge, UK. She was followed by her mother Erna (Emil's widow), who scraped out a living as a housekeeper. Fearing for the life of her only son and Ursula's older brother, with whom contact had been lost after the outbreak of war, Erna, then aged fifty, ended her life by jumping from the bleakly named Underbarrow Scar, an exposed cliff in the English Lake District. She was buried in a remote graveyard, having made out a will leaving all her savings to her daughter, Ursula – £81, 1 shilling, and 5 pence.

Two members of this shrunken family were treated with special reverence when they visited Cambridge. They were another two cousins of my mother – Hilde Bruch and Dick Gompertz. Hilde (an abbreviation for Brunhilde) was matronly, had an air of authority and wore heavy spectacles. At the time I had no clue about the arc of her life or how she had defied the odds for any woman born in Germany in 1904. Unlike most girls of the era, she gained admission to university, where she studied medicine. After getting a whiff of Hitler, she bolted for the US, where she was employed in New York at Columbia University Medical School. (Two of Hilde's six siblings went on to be exterminated.) Thereafter, she rescued and supported her brother's son from Germany and moved to Houston, where she became a mainstay of Baylor University's medical faculty and from where her eminence as a psychiatrist spread around the world.

When I mention the name Hilde Bruch to someone acquainted with childhood anorexia, there is always a gasp. For it was she who, in 1973, published *Eating Disorders: Obesity, Anorexia Nervosa, and the Person Within*, the culmination of pioneering research she had conducted over the prior forty years into what was then a medical backwater – childhood eating disorders. Her case studies, drawn from patients who travelled to her Houston clinic from all over the world, have all the clarity that modern readers associate with the riveting *New Yorker* dispatches written by Oliver Sacks. Until weakened by Parkinson's, Hilde motored around Houston in a Rolls-Royce, her way of refusing to conform with most well-to-do Texan doctors, who preferred tooling about in Cadillacs.

But of all the ghosts who frequented Salli and Louise's front room, it is Dieter (Dick) Gompertz whose story captivated me. Dick had headed the NASA department that developed the first stage of the Saturn rockets, which eventually sent the Apollo astronauts to the moon. He was tall and lean, spoke with an American accent and radiated a confidence and assurance unlike any I associated with my family. I did not know that he had been born in Berlin in 1919, or that his father, Max, a chemical engineer, had committed suicide in 1935. I didn't know that Franz-Dieter Emil Gompertz had entered the US in Miami during the week that war broke out in Europe, or that in December 1941, when he filled out the form declaring his intention to seek permanent residency in the US, he had modified his name to Frank 'Dick' Gompertz, or that in seeking sanctuary he had renounced his ties to other nations, and, as required, attested, 'I am not an anarchist; I am not a polygamist nor a believer in the practice of polygamy.'

Dick had enlisted in the US Army and participated in the frenzied race by the Allies to seize Nazi rocketry knowledge before the Russians could do the same – hunting down the Nazi scientists, their documents, technical papers and the remaining V2 rockets, which had reigned terror over London and other European cities in the closing months of World War II. He was present when the Nazi scientists – including Wernher von Braun and Kurt Debus, both acolytes of Hitler and later pivotal leaders of the US space programme – demonstrated missile launches for the Allies. Dick became an expert in rocket propulsion and, in the early 1950s at Edwards Air Force Base, oversaw the Rocket Engine Test Laboratory, where the engine that propelled the Bell X-1 aeroplane, in which Chuck Yeager was the first man to break the sound barrier, was developed. Dick died in 1978 from leukaemia caused by radiation poisoning to which he had been exposed while working at NASA.

For Salli and Louise, the much-anticipated visits of these relatives provided a sense of what life might have looked like had their world remained intact – most of their relatives and friends having been, during the 1920s, within easy calling distance or not more than a couple of hundred miles away. After the war there were few shared evenings or morning coffees, and just a handful of birthday parties and anniversaries. Relatives and friends who once spoke German now lived in different hemispheres and conducted their lives in Portuguese, Spanish, French and Hebrew. News of deaths arrived by telegram, such as the one announcing the death of one of Louise's brothers, Paul Gompertz, whose Chilean death certificate gave his name as Pablo Gompertz.

Louise herself died in 1977 from a heart attack as she sat alone on a bench in the garden of a nursing home in London. By then I was in America and did not return for the funeral, where she was laid to rest next to Salli. He had also died from a heart attack, which struck as he sat on the edge of his bed tying his shoelaces, on 3 September 1972. It was a Sunday morning when the phone rang in Wales and my mother heard the news. She rushed, distraught, from the telephone. It is the only time I remember her in tears. Before hurtling into the living room and slamming the door, she berated me in advance for a sacrilege I would, for once, never have committed, by screaming, 'I expect you will find a way to make a joke out of this!' Salli died less than forty-eight hours before word came from Munich that eleven members of the Israeli delegation to the 1972 Olympic Games were being held hostage by Black September, a Palestinian terrorist group. Two were killed immediately and the other nine died in a botched shoot-out with German police the next day.

Now, my memories of Salli's death and the Munich Olympics blur together. Oddly, I always think of them through the gauze of Apple's famous Super Bowl commercial of 1984, which introduced the Macintosh computer and was supposed to celebrate the triumph of the individual – freeing consumers from the uniformity of the IBM personal computer and all its clones. That's not how I have ever interpreted the commercial. I have always thought that it could have been directed by Leni Riefenstahl, who made some of the Nazis' most powerful propaganda films. In Apple's advertisement, storm troopers march dozens of men, heads shaved, into a packed hall where the audience stares at a flickering black-and-white screen, on which a dictator delivers a speech. 'We are one people, with one will, one resolve, one cause,' the dictator says – in tones that to me have always sounded like '*Ein Volk, Ein Reich, Ein Führer*' – one of the Nazis' favourite slogans. Then a blond woman, dressed in a white singlet and red shorts, runs down the centre of the aisle wielding a sledgehammer and looking eerily like the female variant of the blond German athlete (in a white singlet but with white shorts) who bore the torch during the opening ceremony of the 1936 Olympic Games in Berlin. In the commercial, the athlete hurls the sledgehammer, and there is an explosion as it shatters the screen. A gust of wind washes over the ranks of grey, shaved figures – transforming them into ghosts, mouths agape, as in the moment of death. I have always associated these sixty seconds not with the introduction of the Macintosh but the Shoah. Fortunately for Apple, consumers did not make the same connection.

When the Olympics returned to Germany for the first time since the end of World War II, it was to a stadium and village built on land which had housed the airfield where Neville Chamberlain landed in 1938 to sign what he thought was a peace agreement with Hitler. But for me, there was a more intimate connection. The building in which the Israeli athletes were mutilated and murdered was just 1,000 yards away from the goods station where Max and Minnie Moritz had been forced to board the train that carried them to their deaths.

In 1972, Salli was trundled to his grave on a wooden cart pulled by two men dressed in black and wearing top hats, who waited while the Kaddish was recited and the nine mourners scattered earth on the coffin. Two days afterwards it was Rosh Hashanah – the Jewish New Year. Synagogues around the world had soldiers, policeman and guards standing at their entrances. The guards standing outside ours, the converted Salem Welsh Baptist Chapel, were all refugees.

PASSOVER REUNION

ALMOST A YEAR HAD PASSED since I had been walking with Harriet at twilight on California pastureland under a cornflower-blue spring sky traced with cloud and given myself a deadline for the completion of the first draft of this book. I only realised the date I had chosen was the eve of Passover 2022 after we started receiving marketing emails for Seder dinner plates from our favourite neighbourhood grocery store in San Francisco.

According to the Jewish calendar, the eve of Passover 2022 was precisely eighty years since the night Max and Minnie had been roused from the straw-strewn floors of the barracks at Knorrstrasse 148 and herded to Milbertshofen station where, according to the documents inside a folder with a light-blue cover compiled by the Gestapo, they had been given the numbers B. 102 and B. 16, before being forced to board a train in a goods yard a few blocks from where Israeli Olympic athletes were mutilated and murdered thirty years later.

For me, Passover has become an excuse to gather friends and family rather than to conduct any Jewish ceremony. In 2022 I had also been invited to join, via Zoom, a Seder in Manchester. As the morning sun streamed through my windows in California, I gazed at a little video tile in which Max and Minnie's youngest great-great-granddaughter sang in Hebrew the explanation of why the night of Passover is different from all others. Later, another participant read an excerpt from Ernest's memoir, in which he had recalled the Passovers of his youth.

Ernest had written about the thorough cleaning of the family apartment in Munich before the start of Passover. This ritual, conducted by observant Jews, is not done to impress visiting mothers-in-law but to purge the home of any trace of leavened bread – even a crumb, which might defile the premises and incur the wrath of God. Ernest remembered how his father, carrying a lit candle and goose feather, had performed a ceremonial inspection of each room for any remaining evidence of such. Ernest recalled the smell of beeswax; the dining-room table carefully set with the best linens, china and silverware and lengthened to its fullest extent; the light blazing from the ceiling lamp, which was only illuminated for special occasions; and the aroma of the matzo-ball soup. Ernest's memoir mentioned how just four of those Seder attendees had survived the Shoah and how he had come to derive great solace from one of the sayings invoked during this ritual: 'In every generation men rise up against us to destroy us, but the Holy One, blessed be He, delivers us from their hands.' It is the same sentiment that the Jews of Munich had expressed when they recited Psalm 94 on the day before they were shipped east.

Leafing through the Passovers of memory, I realise that, like birthdays and anniversaries, most have disappeared into the mists but, the further back I go, the more vivid they become. One which makes me cringe with shame took place nearly forty years ago. My parents were visiting California and meeting Harriet for the first time. My father had brought his yarmulka and Haggadah (the book containing the Seder service), my mother had assembled the Seder plate and the pair of them were ready to recreate the Passover of their youths.

I was too callow to understand how much this night signified to them and was rolling my eyes at the prospect of what lay ahead. I had never stopped to think of the memories it aroused or the emotions it stirred up for my parents. Harriet and I had made an improvised dinner from store-bought matzo-ball soup and barbecued lamb. Soon after my father began the ceremonies, a pair of friends whom we had also invited rose and announced that they needed to depart for a flight to Latin America. I had understood in the moment, judging by the look on my father's face, that he was crushed, but I stayed mute. If there was one message I wish I had relayed to my father and mother before they died, it would be to apologise for this Seder.

In California in 2022, we enjoyed the happiest, most riotous and meaningful Passover any of us could recall. We added a fifth question to the traditional four, by wondering whether in this particular year the Israelites would have chosen to flee Egypt by clambering over the containers piled on the ship that had wedged itself across the width of the Suez Canal, rather than counting on a miraculous parting of the Red Sea some miles to the south. Our tablecloth was embroidered with little red poppies and a vase containing an effervescent spray of lupins, daffodils, tulips, roses, freesias and sweet peas spoke of spring and hope.

Then, I began imagining ghosts seated around the table – not just the ghosts of childhood but also the ghosts I had come to know while writing this book, and who, when the Seder was over, having enjoyed one glass too many, I imagined answering the questions I had never thought to pose.

Sitting side by side, with their backs to the twilight, were a pair of men from the nineteenth century dressed in shirts with detachable collars – my great-grandfathers, Leopold Gompertz,

Louise's father, and Carl Nathan Mayer, Minnie's father, both baffled by the casual surrounds of a California evening and the unfamiliar faces of a couple of generations born long after their own deaths. There were Max and Minnie, one stout and solid, the other brushing a wisp of hair from her forehead, explaining to Leopold and Carl why they had not managed to leave Munich, and disputing my mother's claim that they would not have been prepared to sew glass eyes on teddy bears. There was Hilde Bruch, briskly describing what had made her purchase a Rolls-Royce so that she would not be driving a Cadillac like all the other eminent doctors in Houston, and struggling to converse with Sara Rath, the unsmiling pint-sized woman seated across from her, tight-lipped about how she had managed to stay hidden in Holland for five years. Here was Louise, quietly nudging Salli to recount how, after the end of the war, he had wanted to return to the little town in the Rhineland surrounded by pastures. Sitting next to me was Ludwig Alfred Mayer, the man after whom both my father and one of his cousins had been named, dressed in a German uniform had died, aged twenty, in 1915.

There was Fritz Ursell, wry and soft-spoken, patiently describing why he had required mathematics to unravel the pattern of waves that he had not deciphered while observing them on the beaches of southern England in 1943. A thirty-four-year-old Emil Gompertz – killed five months before the end of World War I – recounting to Louise, his sister, how he had kept the photographs of his two little children in his breast pocket, wondering what had happened to them during the life he never knew and learning how his wife, filled with despair, had killed herself in England in 1941. Then there was Oskar, alongside his wife Rosa, bowing his head in shame when recounting how he had been press-ganged by the Gestapo into helping organise the Jews of the little town on the bend of the River Main. And sitting next to Oskar, beaming with delight at his presence and with her arm linked through his, was his daughter, Ilse Jones, the nurse and mother of three girls who spoke English with a Welsh and German accent.

Sitting quietly in the place of honour between the ghosts of the two Moritz brothers – my father and Ernest – was their nanny, Anna Volk, with a small crucifix lying atop her grey dress and her neatly ironed white collar, gently stroking her lips with the top of her right knuckle, as she often did, and representing all that was good and courageous about people who said more by their actions than their words.

THE SINS OF THE PAST

FROM THE DAWN OF THE AGE of Trump to the consequences of 7 October 2023, I was reminded with increasing frequency that I was an Ashkenazi Jew – a member of an ethnic minority that was different and didn't count. In San Francisco, during the pandemic, there had been much commotion about the inequitable treatment of other minorities. A battle royal had erupted over murals in a public high school that depicted Black slaves in the background of a painting honouring George Washington. There was an equally heated debate over plans to change the names of forty-four San Francisco schools bearing the identities of, among others, a Scottish novelist, a woman mayor, an Irish-born mayor, a Spanish philosopher, a female Jewish philanthropist, the author of the American national anthem and a long list of American presidents. Everyone, it seemed, had a beef with the past. Removing paintings, changing names, tearing down statues, altering textbooks and demanding reparation payments were seen as ways to rectify the cruelties of history.

These debates were followed by a proposal from a city supervisor to issue $5 million to every San Francisco resident over the age of eighteen who identified as being Black and of African American heritage and who met a minimum of two out of eight criteria for eligibility, which included: being a descendant of a slave; being someone who had experienced lending discrimination; or someone who had been jailed as part of the war on drugs. The allegations of the wrongs perpetrated against Black people, both today and in the past, are indisputable. So is the silence regarding the injustices rendered to other marginalised long-time citizens of San Francisco: indigenous Americans who were descendants of people whose lands had been seized and who had been butchered by settlers; Latinx whose ancestors had once farmed territories that fell into American hands as part of the relentless thrust westwards; descendants of Chinese labourers who toiled in terrible conditions while building the nineteenth-century railroads and were subsequently shunted into their equivalent of the European ghetto, Chinatowns; those of Japanese descent whose forbears had been thrown into internment camps during World War II; those whose families hailed from Hawaii or Guam and whose livelihoods had been disrupted after the US pushed west across the Pacific; the Vietnamese people forced to seek refuge after the Vietnam War; the generations of women deprived of their proper place in society; members of the LGBTQ+ community who had long been forced to live their lives in fear of the law; the wrongfully incarcerated; the hundreds of thousands jailed because of the 'Three Strikes and Out' law; the list is endless. The sins of the past inexhaustible. The catalogue of cruelties visited upon man by his fellow man interminable.

As editorial columnists debated the virtues of the obligation one generation has for the deeds perpetrated by their ancestors, I could hear the sharp report of the keys of my father's typewriter as he spent Sunday afternoons corresponding with German officials concerning compensation for the murders of his father, his mother, his uncles, his aunts and his cousins.

Restitution, or reparation payments, had been the political wallpaper of my father's own childhood – but these were the financial settlements between nations, not between a nation and individuals. When Max returned from Verdun, it was to a country that soon groaned under the weight of the payments demanded by the victors in recompense for their war losses. The burden of these stipulations was one of the issues Hitler seized upon during his quest for power – particularly a revised agreement negotiated in the early 1920s extending the scheduled payments into the 1980s.

In contrast to the Moritz brothers, Salli had a strong grasp of his financial losses, which he itemised in legal filings in the late 1940s. These were settled by a local court in Kempen in 1954. His most substantial claim, for half of the value from the forced seizure of his business, Gebruder Rath, was rejected because the assets were insufficiently documented. Other claims, for the payment of the Nazi-inspired *Judenvermogensabgabe*, *Reichsfluchtsteuer* and *Golddiskontbank*, forced 'cultural contributions' and for damage to his home, were all rejected, while one for some confiscated silverware was delayed. Several claims, such as money deposited in savings accounts, were palmed off as the responsibility of the federal government. However, he was compensated for the sale – on distressed terms – of his pastureland and home, both of which fell under the purview of the local court.

One of the documents Salli submitted for the court's consideration reduces everything to a more human level. He sought compensation for possessions destroyed during Kristallnacht and, to support the claim, included a statement from a plumber who had been summoned to make repairs. The plumber testified that he had known Salli since 1902 and had been in his eight-room home on several occasions. He stated, 'When I entered the apartment, I saw a scene of indescribable chaos. Some people, whom I didn't know, were still in the apartment, smashing furniture. Most of the furnishings had either been completely destroyed or severely damaged.'

Salli was more precise and listed the belongings that had been vandalised in addition to the furniture, a radio, a typewriter, a laundry wringer, a piano, some paintings and several lamps (including a pair made of alabaster) as well as:

> 1 Fürstenberg coffee set for 12 people
> 1 Hutschenreuther dinnerware set for 18 people
> 7 dozen crystal glasses
> 5 crystal bowls
> 1 mocha set for 6 people
> 2 Meissen vases and 3 Meissen plates [which he labelled 'heirlooms']
> Daily dinnerware and coffee sets for 12 people

Given his nature, my father must have contemplated – as he composed his letters to the German authorities – the larger questions prompted by reparations and attempts to exorcise the past. How do you repair the damage caused by a current generation, let alone prior generations? How do you make up for the sins of the past? How do you demonstrate that barbaric behaviour won't be tolerated in the future? How do you assess damages, and who should be the judge?

I don't know what, beyond financial hardship, caused my father and Ernest to begin seeking restitution from the new German government in the late 1940s – a correspondence that continued, in fits and starts, for sixty years, even though in our family, no Rembrandts, Van Goghs, Vermeers or Monets had been stolen. Our heirlooms were china, dining tables and candlesticks. I doubt that the Moritz brothers hoped to be paid handsomely; perhaps they merely sought whatever was on offer, or maybe they were just hoping for formal recognition and a heartfelt apology for crimes of the past. I don't think they were seeking, in the deadly metaphor that Shakespeare applied to Shylock – the figure with whom my high school English teacher had also linked me – 'a pound of flesh'. It certainly would never have crossed their minds to file for the vast sums plaintiffs' lawyers demand in the US today, nor do I imagine that my father ever considered seeking reparations from Washington for refusing to grant immigration papers to Max and Minnie and, indirectly, consigning them to their fate.

The debate over who should determine these awards was especially loaded in Germany during the 1950s and 1960s, since a large proportion of the civil service had, at a minimum, carried Nazi-party cards and, in some cases, had been enthusiastic supporters of Hitler. Some of the respondents to my father's letters were almost certainly people who had received *Persilschein* – 'Persil notes' – which whitewashed them of blame for the crimes of the 1930s and 1940s and permitted them to return to their jobs and pensions. Many of these officials harboured no great desire to help and proved formidable barriers to those who sought some form of recompense. There was a widespread view in Germany, which lingered for a generation, that the real victims of the Nazi era were the German people themselves, who had to contend with the destruction of their country by the Allies, the loss of millions of men and the fracturing of their territory into East and West.

Over three quarters of the members of Germany's Federal Ministry of Justice of the 1950s with which Salli and the

Moritz brothers were corresponding had carried the card of the Nazi party. Hans Globke, for a decade the chief of staff and right-hand man of Germany's first post-war chancellor, Konrad Adenauer, had, in the 1930s, helped write the laws that stripped non-Aryans of their legal rights, forbade intercourse between Aryans and Jews (even if conducted outside the Third Reich), banned women below the age of forty-five from working in Jewish households, and ensured that when Max and Minnie went to their deaths, their official names were Israel and Sara. In 1951, Globke helped draft another law, which restored the pay and pensions of civil servants who had worked under the Third Reich, including his own. The argument supplied by Adenauer (a man who, like one of his successors, Willy Brandt, was much admired by my father for his abhorrence of the Third Reich and his post-war dedication to liberal democracy) was that Germany had to tolerate former Nazis throughout the layers of post-war government since: 'You don't throw out dirty water when you don't have any clean water.'

In 1949, after the Moritz brothers had received confirmation of the deaths of Max and Minnie, there was a flurry of correspondence between them, the courts in Munich and officials in Miltenberg, the little town on the bend of the River Main. In 1957, they filed claims for the deaths – or in the legal jargon of the time, 'the loss of freedom' – of Max and Minnie. In 1958, they received 1,500 deutschmarks, and, in 1959, a further 1,350 deutschmarks, which as I write, would be worth about $3,446. The Munich court determined the sum assuming that Max and Minnie had died, as their death certificates stated, when the clock struck midnight on 8 May 1945, the official end of the war, rather than 1942. When the Moritz brothers later pointed out this discrepancy, the court was unmoved.

In 1957, the Bavarian state compensation court was similarly unimpressed by my father's claim that his entry into the workforce had been delayed by six or seven years because of having to emigrate. The court in Munich pointed out that, had my father stayed in Germany, he would have been called up in June 1940 as a member of the 1921 birth cohort to fulfil his obligatory six months in the Reich Labour Service and subsequently would have continued as a soldier until the end of the war. It was a line of argument that Franz Kafka would have been pressed to concoct. My father appealed.

A decade later, in 1967, the Regional Court in Munich issued a 3,500-word judgment in my father's case that awarded him 10,700 deutschmarks – worth about $25,000 at the time of writing. It took into consideration the sums my father paid for the four hours of English lessons he received in each of the six weeks after his arrival in London in 1937, at a rate of 7s/6d (seven shillings and sixpence) per hour, and for the cost of schoolbooks and two years of boarding fees, which had amounted to £1 15s per week. Yet the court dismissed part of this claim, as my father's education had been covered by a scholarship and the cost of a comparable education in Munich, during the period when the Nazis had been rounding up the Jews, had been cheaper.

In Munich, a non-Jew, an academic who helped me by translating these documents, could not restrain himself when he came upon passages of obstructionism. He left withering comments in the margins, which read like apologies for actions in which he had not participated but for which he felt deep shame. His comments included remarks such as 'This is typical German understatement for persecution, expulsion, flight and rescue. It seems hard for them to say or write "murdered by the Nazis". He added other biting remarks, such as 'They are saying that despite the death certificate and the alleged date of death they would not compensate for the assumed length of incarceration because of a loophole in the law... It seems to have been impossible for non-Jewish Germans to think of Jews as Germans... It is clear they did not want to give "that Jewish professor" anything.'

Other non-sanctioned attempts to make up for the past were equally tone-deaf. My favourite is one offered to a former tutor of mine at Oxford – a refugee from Vienna, who devoted his life to the historical study of European Jewry. After retiring, he had become chairman of the Leo Baeck Institute, named after a revered Berlin rabbi who survived Theresienstadt, and it was in this capacity that he was offered the royalties from the sales of the English edition of *Mein Kampf*.

For my parents, the question of reparations dribbled on for decades as one or another aspect of life aspects of life in the Third Reich came to light. I was astonished to find among my mother's papers a letter she wrote in 2006 acknowledging the receipt of a pair of insurance policies taken out by Salli in the early 1930s and subsequently cancelled by the Nazis. At the age of eighty-two, thirty-four years after Salli had died, my mother received a cheque for the equivalent of what was worth, as I write, about $27,334, courtesy of the work of the International Commission on Holocaust Era Insurance Claims (ICHEIC). It was a tribute to persistence as, among Salli's papers, I found a document issued by the insurance company in 1952 stating that 'The insurance policies have expired due to relocation and have been registered as deleted.'

But my parents did have something that no reparation payment could buy – the education they had received as children and young adults. This was a gift given to them not by the civil servants of post-war Germany but by others. By Max and Minnie, and Salli and Louise, who summoned up the bravery to be separated from their sons and daughters; by the benefactors in Britain who helped underwrite their studies; by the schoolmasters and tutors who encouraged them and displayed admiration for their fortitude; and by their own wit and determination. It meant they could establish a footing in a foreign place, gradually scratch together enough money to buy a house, solidly lodge themselves in the middle class and provide the foundation on which my life and those of my sister and our children have been built. But in doing so, their own sense of belonging had been extinguished and the large family web would never be rebuilt. It was lost forever. No reparations can eradicate the sins of the past – not in Germany, nor in the US.

AUSLÄNDER

ONE DAY A YOUNG FRIEND in California asked whether I considered the US or the UK home. I answered 'neither'. Not San Francisco, where I met and married Harriet, and our two sons were born, raised and schooled; not Silicon Valley, where I have worked for so long; not California, the state in which I live; not the US, where I had become a citizen in a moving ceremony held in the auditorium of the Masonic Grand Lodge of California at the top of San Francisco's Nob Hill, surrounded by tearful immigrants from Latin America and Southeast Asia. Nor was my home Wales, where I had been born and raised and lived until I was nineteen, where my parents had moved to make new lives for themselves, where they had both worked until they could no longer do so and where my father had died, and my mother had been cremated. I have two passports – one British, one American – but neither is for a country I consider home. In one country strangers sometimes remark that I sound like a cowboy, in the other they occasionally ask if I am Australian.

The vastness, splendour and savagery of America still startle me. Its sunshine always seems brighter and its storms always seem heavier and wetter than they should be. The hurricanes, tornadoes, earthquakes and forest fires speak of an untamed land. I still find it difficult to believe that one country can contain deserts, mountains, tropical islands and a river whose width, at its widest point, is half the breadth of the sometimes violent sea that separates England from France. The idea that a California mountain lion will occasionally prowl the perimeter of campsites, or that 4 per cent of the world's population own 40 per cent of its guns and that more Americans have been killed by guns since 1975 than in all the country's wars (including the Revolution) seems absurd. But these facts are no more peculiar than the democratic distortions of the electoral college, the imperial nature of presidential pardons and the initiatives and propositions that litter California's ballots.

Even after all these years, small things still surprise me: the flags; the military uniforms; country mailboxes; grits at breakfast; cavernous college stadiums; class signet rings; large dinner plates; foot-long sandwiches; front doors with multiple deadbolts; snowploughs that keep airports and streets open; the rules of baseball, basketball and American football; Mexican cuisine; the ease of obtaining an MRI or PET scan; or the inconceivable practice of moving houses or beloved sports teams from one spot to another.

Despite having lived in America for almost half a century, the images, stories and posts that I see from Oklahoma, Montana, Texas, Louisiana, Mississippi, Alabama, West Virginia and plenty of other places seem more foreign to me than the histories of Poland or the Czech Republic or France, or a Europe where I can predict the coldness of the winters and understand the roots of hatred, cruelty and strife. It has taken me a long time to understand that the Civil War is still being fought in America. This battle is unlike anything I had experienced as a boy growing up on the edge of Europe. America sometimes seems as distant as it did when, in 1971 in a Welsh movie theatre, I first saw the opening shot of *The Last Picture Show* – a hot, arid wind blowing gusts of dust down a deserted street in a small Texas town in the early 1950s. Nothing could have seemed farther away.

Now, having been an immigrant, albeit of the most fortunate kind, I know that I should not confuse my father's fondness for visits to his former nanny in Bavaria or for bratwurst, sauerkraut, pretzels or a glass of Alsterwasser for anything beyond pining for a time when he felt safe – when the little world that he knew was secure, and his father went swimming in a one-piece suit and rode a bicycle with a lamp to work. It was not that he felt at home in a little village in the Allgäu or indeed in Germany. His home, and my mother's, had been lost forever. It cannot be replaced. When you arrive in a new country, a language is learned, an accent develops, signs, habits and customs become familiar, a life is established and, eventually, a grave is dug. But this does not mean it becomes home. It is just as the writer Jean Améry (whose last name was an anagram for his birth name, Mayer) had described, 'Home is the land of one's childhood and youth. Whoever has lost it remains lost himself, even if he had learned not to stumble about in the foreign country as if he were drunk, but rather to tread the ground with some fearlessness.' We were all strangers, we were all different – my father, my mother, my grandparents and I – just as a person who has lost a leg is defined by the absence of a limb or someone who has suffered a stroke is defined by the frozen portion of their being.

One of my vices during the pandemic was *A French Village*, a seven-season, seventy-two-episode television drama about a small town occupied by the Nazis in 1940, sixty miles from the Swiss border. It is a subtle portrayal of the choices people make, the nuances of human nature, the consequences of indifference and how rumours of barbarity are easy to sweep aside until evil is on the doorstep. The inhabitants of the French village in question – schoolteachers, contractors, nurses, postal workers, doctors, judges, civil servants – faced the dilemma of citizens in any country invaded by soldiers both charming and cruel. Do they curry favour with the oppressor? Should they betray old friends to save their own skins? Do they shelter the hunted? Do they seek sanctuary elsewhere? Should they just look the other way?

The characters in *A French Village* fall into three categories: 'Resisters', 'the Silent' and, as they were labelled in the show, '*Collabos*'. On Zoom calls I started sorting all the faces in the video thumbnails into these same three categories. The smallest group was always the Resisters. This diversion made me ponder my own safety – maybe just because apocalyptic times tend to produce paranoia. During the summer of 2020 when forest fires in California had turned morning into night, burned more than 4 million acres and destroyed 10,000 homes, I thought about the congresswoman from Georgia who had linked previous conflagrations to 'Rothschild Inc'. When other conspiracists began echoing this modern version of an ancient libel, my fears hardened, as they do every time I read that 'George Soros', who had come to replace 'Rothschild' as shorthand for 'Jewish interests', was the invisible hand that controlled everything. I was rattled further by ostensibly cultivated people who believed the assault by the mob on the Capitol in January 2021 had been blown out of proportion by the media. The pictures of the mob and the way people refused to believe what they had seen on television alarmed me as did the response to Trump's criminal conviction. Then came 7 October 2023 and the sense that, for many in the West, the conflict in Gaza only began when Israel started its counter-offensive twenty days after Hamas fighters raped Israeli women so savagely that they broke their pelvises, shot them in their vaginas or through their breasts, branded their child hostages with the burn marks from motorcycle exhaust pipes and beheaded soldiers with shovels.

And then, to top it all off, came 5 November 2024 when more than 77 million Americans, almost 15 million more than had voted for him in 2015, returned Donald Trump to the Oval Office. I was distraught but not surprised. Some months earlier, after the televised presidential debate in which Joe Biden appeared comatose, a *New York Times* reporter enquired as to whether I still supported him. I replied to the reporter, 'Sadly, President Biden has a choice – vanity or virtue. He can either condemn the country to dark and cruel times or heed the voice of Father Time. The clock has run out.' I said this because there had been nothing in the years which had passed since Donald Trump had made his 2015 presidential campaign entrance down the tawdry, fake-gold escalator in the atrium of Trump Tower, that had dampened my fears about the man. They had only sharpened.

I had never doubted that if enough Americans ignored Trump's criminal record, his incompetence as a businessman, his propensity to ignite chaos, his assaults on women, his long history of racist remarks, his suggestion of using household bleach as a solution for Covid, his effort to overturn the 2020 election, his encouragement of the attack on the Capitol on 6 January 2021 and his willingness to demonise and vilify those who obstructed his path, then his second term would unleash his worst impulses. But I had forgotten the exhaustion that trails in the wake of his extraordinary energy and his need to be in the limelight every hour of the day. I knew that evil doesn't suddenly appear, it creeps up step by step. And so, because of what happened to my family a handful of decades ago, ever since Trump was inaugurated for the second time, I have stood a morbid vigil watching this hoodlum on the loose.

The American people, or at least enough of them, decided that they would return to office a Queens wide boy – fast of lip, loose with the truth, short with the dollar – a tiny man in a large body. So, he was restored to office – still, at heart, his father's rent collector. A mean, callous, vindictive, selfish and humourless man – the most woeful figure to head the state since, take your pick, Warren Harding, Franklin Pierce, Andrew Johnson or James Buchanan. It was as if Trump embodied all the failings of his predecessors – harbouring no desire to heal the country of its rifts, utterly devoid of magnanimity or an ounce of compassion – while taking every opportunity to line his own pocket. Even Richard Nixon, insecure crook that he was, could not top Trump.

This is a man who probably has the most expansive view of presidential power of any American president and has said 'I have the right to do anything I want to do.' His definition is boundless – broader than that of Andrew Jackson, who forcibly relocated Native Americans, or Abraham Lincoln, who suspended habeas corpus during the Civil War, or Franklin Roosevelt, who erected a social safety net and who also tried hard to rejigger the Supreme Court. Almost every day there is something that Trump does which makes me think of the past.

Trump, like other nativist authoritarians, has always had a knack for inflaming a sore – an ability on which he has built his political career. He can scent blood. Many of Trump's claims, as with other autocrats, have contained a kernel of truth. Few could argue with his assertions that millions of blue-collar jobs have moved overseas; that, for many, the standard of living has not improved in years; that the drugs fuelling crime in the inner cities come over the southern border; that many of the intolerant, politically correct commissars who poisoned workplaces and university campuses with their cant had overstepped their bounds; that the government is hopelessly bloated; that petty rules and reams of regulation have impeded progress; that international aid is often siphoned off by crooks; that services like Voice of America have failed to adapt to the times; that China has ignored the rules of international trade; that the Europeans have not spent enough on their own defence; that Iran is the suppurating ulcer of the Middle East; and that the United Nations is a toothless entity. Somehow, he was also able to convince the religious right with their uncompromising stand on abortion that he shared their religious beliefs even though, as a thrice-married man and philanderer, his greatest public act of religious devotion was to hold a Bible upside down. In the meantime, his principal political advisor was ready to tell anyone who would listen that 'The Democrat Party is not a political party. It is a domestic extremist organization.' No wonder that the only people who might feel safe and comfortable under Trump are gun-owning Christians wearing white skins.

I knew that Trump would have little to lose in a second term. His selection of cabinet members and advisors telegraphed his disdain for the accomplished and experienced. It seemed as if the picks had been made during a bull session of late-night joke writers: a nominee for Attorney General who had been accused of child sex trafficking and statutory rape; a talk show personality to head the Defense Department who faced allegations of sexual misconduct, financial mismanagement and alcohol issues; a Secretary of Health and Human Services whose most significant qualifications for office were the voters he brought Trump's way and his last name, and who himself admitted that he had so many skeletons in his closet he wished they could vote; an FBI director determined to reverse the sentences of the January 6 rioters; and a former governor as head of the Department of Homeland Security whose memoir contained just one interesting anecdote – a description of how she shot her fourteen-month-old wirehaired pointer. This multiweek spectacle wasn't so much a series of nominations as it was a television casting call for a goon squad. It didn't take a great flight of fancy for me to think about another cabinet composed of a former wine salesman, an occult worshiper, a notorious womaniser, a failed writer and a convicted murderer.

The Trump administration's control and domination of messaging, albeit via "Truth Social", other social media channels, podcasters and friendly television outlets uses the old playbook – repeat lies often and loudly enough, and people will believe them. The entire spectacle of Trump's messy second term has been built around ratings – whether measured by the old-fangled metrics of television, or views on X, Tik-Tok, YouTube and Instagram. It is an administration wired for ratings, not accomplishments, programming not governing.

Hence the devotion to sets and props. (The period uniforms worn by soldiers during Trump's rain-soaked 2025 birthday parade were costumes furnished by Hollywood prop houses.) The Oval Office, which is now decked out like an anteroom to a bordello, and Cabinet Room are no longer forums where serious policy matters are debated. They are TV studios where distinguished guests such as the leaders of Ukraine and South Africa can be ambushed and humiliated and where viewers can bear witness to cabinet members spending hours paying fealty to their leader. As I write, towards the end of the first year of

Trump's second term, I am half expecting an announcement that he has issued himself a licence to turn his new 650-seat ballroom into a casino and convert Richard Nixon's one-lane bowling alley into a pistol range.

It requires many bedfellows for evil to creep up step by step. Trump has signalled his own proclivities by the associations he relishes – to instinctively gravitating towards men like Vladimir Putin, Viktor Orbán and Jair Bolsonaro. (His mutterings about Greenland and Canada contain echoes – albeit weak ones – of Putin's expansionist ambitions.) But Trump has many other accomplices – his cabinet, his coterie of advisors and, worst of all, Republican politicians, those sycophants and lickspittles, who, concealing their true feelings, do his bidding for fear of incurring his wrath and jeopardising their futures. Then there are the lapdogs like the Governor of Texas who decided to carve up the electoral districts in his state to try and maintain Republican control of the House of Representatives.

For me one of the sorriest sights of this administration was the spectacle of several leaders of large technology companies serving as a backdrop at the inauguration and, subsequently, responding to his every whistle. I know that most would have preferred to be elsewhere but were responding to an invitation that they could not refuse lest Trump turn the power of the state on their companies. It is why they make frequent cameo appearances in the Oval Office where the revolving cast of characters reminds me of the improvised meetings Tony Soprano once convened on the sidewalk outside Satriale's Pork Store. I'm sure they, despite their babysitting services, do not think, unlike the heads of German companies almost one hundred years ago, that they can keep this man, with all his brutish impulses, under their thumbs. The actions of others, with less at stake, is harder for me to understand. But I sensed I was now not just living in a land of '*Collabos*'. I was surrounded by millions of them.

There are the prominent businesspeople who had quickly repudiated Trump in the wake of the Capitol riots but who just as rapidly returned to the fold. There are religious types, who, although they would have never hired a man with his commercial record, quickly forgave his transgressions and argued that Trump – despite his lifetime association with profligacy and familiarity with bankruptcies – would trim the federal deficit. Instead, predictably, he has done the opposite. And then there are the Silicon Valley characters who fashioned themselves after Trump and who, with their vitriolic social media posts, have temporarily ingratiated themselves with a man whose loyalty is only to himself.

Most of all there are those who stay silent and don't realise that silence is the foundation on which cruelty grows. I feared that apartment dwellers would just turn up the volume of their televisions if they heard the sound of boots racing up a stairwell; or that drivers, at best, would engage in rubber-necking while federal agents hauled someone out of a car, and that pedestrians would meekly gaze or snap photos on the phones if they witnessed handcuffed people being marched down a street. Every day, life under Trump contained some echo of a past with which I was too well acquainted. I knew that, were he left unshackled, anyone who stood in his way or voiced dissent, no matter how insignificant, could feel his wrath. It was no time to stay silent.

The nominations of cabinet members were but preludes to the torrent of executive decrees and social media posts that rain down on the country every hour of the day. I kept thinking about what had happened during the first one hundred days after the establishment of other regimes elsewhere when hoods became officers of state, new laws were declared, institutions attacked or dismantled, and people rounded up. Great countries can be brought to their knees in one hundred days, and Trump and his acolytes seemed determined to do so.

No federal institution, no national agency, no state government, no business, no university, no arts organisation, museum or library was out of bounds. They all have been made to twitch while the brutes who vandalised the Capitol have been sprung free. And there, goading Trump along, is his closet kapo, Stephen Miller, his Deputy Chief of Staff – the descendant of Jewish immigrants who fled persecution and found refuge in the United States.

Trump's attacks on Harvard, and other universities, within weeks of his inauguration showed the Queens rent collector at work.[2] It was just a hold-up – as it was when, in a different context, he decided that the US government should seize 10 per cent ownership of Intel; or that every foreign country need pay a tariff to import goods into the United States; or that law firms should work for free for the government; or that media and technology companies settle his personal lawsuits if they were to expect his blessing for legislation or a merger; or the imposition of $100,000 levies on work visas; or that George Soros is a racketeer.

Trump's assault on truth and facts has taken many guises. The most serious have been the systematic attack on scientific research conducted at leading universities and within the agencies tasked with keeping Americans healthy and protecting the country against a changing climate. It is the approach of people who prefer to seek answers in the entrails of animals. Inconvenient facts, promulgated by scientists or statisticians labouring in government bureaus, have become unfashionable as have reports from intelligence agencies disputing Trump's claim that Iran's nuclear facilities were obliterated by the daring June 2025 raids.

Trump's vilification of cultural and creative types, though not as grotesque, reminded me of the impulses that led to the book burnings that had taken place in Germany or the destruction of so many ancient monuments by fanatics in Afghanistan, Iraq and Syria. There was his immediate impulse, following the frightful murder of the young conservative Charlie Kirk, to make him a martyr and use his death as an excuse to pursue and silence those he admitted to hating. Thus, pressure was exerted on broadcasters whose airtime was sometimes employed by critics – or silenced critics – of Trump.

Then there was the takeover of the Kennedy Center; the slashing of funding for the Public Broadcasting Service; the firing of the head of the National Portrait Gallery; and statements about politically acceptable museum exhibits, and the architectural styles suitable for federal buildings. In the meantime, the White House has been shorn of art or music – unless you include the sound of 'Let It Be' blaring from the loudspeakers over the newly paved Rose Garden.

Trump has run the country as he ran his company – living for the moment with scant regard for future jeopardy. He always embraced debts as the fuel for his misbegotten business forays and he has done the same with the US – expanding the budget (rightly characterised by Elon Musk as 'an abomination'). He is doing precisely the same with the U.S. economy by allowing debt to balloon and running to the bank to renegotiate. The difference is that this time the bank is The Federal Reserve whose governors he is pressuring to lower interest rates and thus lower debt payments.

During the time that Trump failed as a businessman in New York, some of his real estate competitors flourished. Something similar has occurred in the past year – although on a global, rather than civic, scale. Trump negotiates by using the rules of roulette while Xi Jinping plays chess. So, it is no surprise that China, the first global competitor ever faced by the United States, has been strengthened, not weakened, by Trump. Trump's policies have prompted other countries to coalesce around Beijing; his tariffs have forced Chinese companies to become even more efficient; and his bans on exports leave China with no choice but to become self-reliant and, in an increasing number of fields, surpass the United States. Cutting off much foreign aid, halting shipments of vaccines to African countries and dickering with a constantly changing menu of tariffs, are not the way to create friends. The United States before Trump, with all its weaknesses, was great. All Trump has done is to make America seem smaller to the rest of the world.

While he was running roughshod over America and any country that stood in his way, Trump, rather than place his financial interests on hold, has – like every self-respecting dictator – been busily feathering his nest everywhere except for New York where a judge had prohibited his company from conducting business. Membership fees for his various clubs have been raised. New hotel deals have been signed in choice spots around the world, crypto coins have been issued by the family to lure the suckers, and any halfwit can order his Victory 45–47 perfume and cologne set. Nothing topped this display of brazen venality more than the purported gift from the government of Qatar of a used Boeing 747-8 which purportedly will eventually be housed in Trump's presidential library. The White House had little to say about the $1 billion earmarked in the

Pentagon budget to equip the jet with the necessary security and communication systems.

We are witnessing the sorry spectacle of a rampaging bully: a president who renames the Department of Defense the Department of War; who has formed a virtual paramilitary – using immigration and customs enforcement officials to stage raids around the country; seizing and repatriating children; sending the US Marines to police the streets of Los Angeles over the objection of local officials and the National Guard to police the streets of other cities. This strongman is the same character who evaded the Vietnam draft by claiming he had bone spurs in his heels. It sometimes seemed, especially after his swing through Israel and Egypt after the hostages were released, that his goal was to secure peace overseas while inciting war at home.

During the time since Trump resumed office, I have travelled widely and talked to well-placed friends in many countries – Britain, Brazil, Italy, China, Israel, Singapore, India, Turkey. They all had the same questions and observations. All were quick to observe that they once considered the United States the leader of the world, as a source of stability, as a reliable partner. But they too have borne witness to the damage Trump has wrought. They also have seen the savagery and the unpredictability. Unfortunately, I was right in my response to the *New York Times*: the failings of Joe Biden and his supporters have condemned the United States to dark and cruel times.

For those who feel vulnerable, no place feels safe. When I started to think about a sanctuary, most of the world seemed hostile. In a flight of fancy, I considered using Louise and Salli's unused steamship tickets to New Zealand but thought that would mean I had concluded there was little, if any, hope for humanity in the northern hemisphere. So, I decided to take a step that would previously have been inconceivable: I applied for German citizenship. I did so, in part, because the ready freedom of residence within the countries of the European Union that I had previously enjoyed thanks to my British passport had been stripped by Brexit. I was also well aware of the huge surge in anti-semitism in the UK, which was put on full display with the killings on Yom Kippur 2025 at the Heaton Park synagogue in Manchester. Unlike all the murdered members of my family I decided to make sure no matter how remote the prospect, I had a safety line. Did I want to flee America and San Francisco? Did I sense there would soon be a knock on the door, and that men in uniforms would slash our paintings and herd me into a cattle car? Was I stirred to sign the forms because I knew, come what may, that I would never have to sew glass eyes onto teddy bears? No. I filled out the forms because 74 million people – 7 million more than the population of Germany in 1933 – had, in 2020, voted for a man who terrified me. I also believed that of those 74 million, the *Collabos* and the Silent would leave the number of Resisters in a tiny minority. There was also the consolation of knowing that I even had family living in Germany. My sister's daughter, Sophie, was drawn by the excitement of Berlin more than a decade ago and is now a German citizen. And both my sons had also obtained citizenship. There is the possibility – albeit faint – that eventually there will be three Moritz men, all Jews, living once more in the land of our ancestors.

    I chose Germany despite its own resurgence of fascist cabals, the heavy security outside its synagogues and its shift towards the political right. My choice reflected the fact that younger Germans, according to polls, have absorbed the lessons of history, are alert to the danger of repeating it and that, ironically, the popular constitutional government that was fashioned in Germany in the post-war years with the help of the Allies seemed more inured to extremists than that of the US. I chose to fill out the forms because after the Berlin Wall fell, West German leaders integrated millions of their countrymen in the East into a vibrant democracy. I chose it because Germany seemed vigilant to the threats of those with hate in their hearts.

I knew, even as I signed the forms, that Germany could never mean home. But part of me yearned to live in a country where I sensed reason had an upper hand, where, for most, extremism was considered a mortal danger, where science mattered, and where the leaders seemed competent and decent. There was something else at work – a subliminal undertow. It was drawing me back to a country I associated with darkness and light: to a place where the bones of my ancestors lie beneath the soil; to the railway stations from where so many relatives were shipped to be slaughtered; and to the source of the long shadows cast over my life. But it was also pulling me towards warmth and tenderness, to that village in Bavaria, and to the memory of walking up a road in the early morning holding on to my father with one hand and carrying a churn of milk in the other, while listening to the sound of cowbells and smelling freshly cut hay.

THANK YOU

CONTRIBUTORS, EDITORS AND READERS

Peter Blackstock
Mark Damazer
Niall Ferguson
Harriet Heyman
Courtney Hodell
Jon Meier
Ernest Moritz
Arthur Rock
Hannah Rothschild
Judith Thurman
Gaby Wood

RESEARCHERS

Jewish History Association of South Wales
Klavdija Erzen
Clemens-Maier-Wolthausen
Katja Wüstenbecker